Palgrave Studies in Economic History

Series Editor
Kent Deng, London School of Economics, London, UK

Palgrave Studies in Economic History is designed to illuminate and enrich our understanding of economies and economic phenomena of the past. The series covers a vast range of topics including financial history, labour history, development economics, commercialisation, urbanisation, industrialisation, modernisation, globalisation, and changes in world economic orders.

More information about this series at
https://link.springer.com/bookseries/14632

Karin Pallaver
Editor

Monetary Transitions

Currencies, Colonialism and African Societies

palgrave
macmillan

Editor
Karin Pallaver
Department of History and Cultures
University of Bologna
Bologna, Italy

ISSN 2662-6497 ISSN 2662-6500 (electronic)
Palgrave Studies in Economic History
ISBN 978-3-030-83460-9 ISBN 978-3-030-83461-6 (eBook)
https://doi.org/10.1007/978-3-030-83461-6

Cover illustration: Cloth traders in Bolgatanga (1940 ca.) Courtesy of Photothèque, Archives of the White Fathers, Rome

This Palgrave Macmillan imprint is published by the registered company Springer Nature Switzerland AG
The registered company address is: Gewerbestrasse 11, 6330 Cham, Switzerland

Contents

Notes on Contributors

Domenico Cristofaro (Ph.D., Bologna 2020) is currently working on the urban and economic history of Ghana. His Ph.D. research focused on the way mobility and transportation, currency introduction, trade development, and colonialism affected the growth of Bolgatanga, the capital of the Upper East Region in Ghana, during the early twentieth century. He worked with sources from colonial archives in Ghana and UK, catholic missionary records in Italy, complemented by a collection of several oral interviews and ethnographic data gathered in northern Ghana.

Alessandro De Cola is a Postdoctoral fellow of the International Studies Group (ISG), at the University of the Free State, South Africa. He earned his PhD in Global Histories, Cultures and Politics from the Department of History and Culture, at the University of Bologna, Italy. His thesis titled "Transitions in the monetary history of Eritrea. Colonial policies, military labour, and the Maria Theresa thaler (1885–1921)" focuses on the Italian failed attempts to build a colonial monetary system in Eritrea, the resilience of local regimes of value and the embeddedness of the Italian colony in broader regional monetary networks. He holds a Master's degree in Cultural Anthropology and his research fields are African economic and social history, with a special focus on pre-colonial and colonial money.

Catherine Eagleton (Ph.D.) is Director of Libraries and Museums at the University of St Andrews, Scotland, and she has previously worked at the

Smithsonian Institution, the British Library, and the British Museum. Her research on the history of currencies in Africa and the Indian Ocean was in part supported by a research project grant from the Leverhulme Trust, as well as by funding from the Arts and Humanities Research Council.

Gerold Krozewski is a professor of history at Osaka University, Japan. His research focuses on topics of Europe's imperial and colonial relationships in the nineteenth and twentieth centuries, with particular attention to Africa.

Akinobu Kuroda is a professor at the University of Tokyo. His research covers comparative studies of monetary history in East Asia, India, Africa, and Europe, as well as specific studies of China's monetary history. The concept of complementarity among monies, which he developed, has had some influence across monetary studies, economic history, and anthropology. His publications include, "What is the Complementarity among Monies? An Introductory Note," *Financial History Review* 15-1, 2008; "Anonymous Currencies or Named Debts?: Comparison of Currencies, Local Credits and Units of Account between China, Japan and England in the Pre-industrial Era," *Socio Economic Review* 11-1, 2013 and *A Global History of Money*, Routledge, 2020.

Toyomu Masaki is a professor in the Faculty of Economics and Management at Kanazawa University (Japan), where she has taught World Political Economy since 2004. Dr. Masaki holds a DEA from the University of Bordeaux IV in France and M.A. and Ph.D. degrees in Economics from Kobe University in Japan. Her research interests are monetary issues in French West Africa, including the historical development path of the monetary system and a transition to the new regime from the post-colonial system. Particularly, her work focuses on the cotton cloth used as money in western Sahel known as *guinée* and the CFA franc issue.

Admire Mseba is an assistant professor of African History in the Department of Black Studies and the Department of History at the University of Missouri-Columbia.

Tinashe Nyamunda is an Associate Professor in the Department of Historical and Heritage Studies at the University of Pretoria. His main research interests are in the twentieth and twenty-first-century Economic History of Southern Africa. He has particularly published on the monetary history of colonial and post-colonial Zimbabwe as well as on issues of informal economies, for example, artisanal diamond mining or illicit remittance networks. Nyamunda is also increasingly looking at the history of economics and its influence on policy and state and economy making on the African continent.

Karin Pallaver is an Associate Professor of African History at the Department of History and Cultures, University of Bologna, where she teaches African History and Indian Ocean History. Her main research interest is the history of money and currency in East Africa. On this topic she has coordinated two research projects (2017–2021) and published several articles and book chapters.

Luca Puddu is a Senior Research Fellow in the "Global History and Governance" program at the Scuola Superiore Meridionale, University Federico II, Naples, and lecturer of Modern and Contemporary African history at the Department of History and Cultures, University of Bologna. His research interests are mainly focused on the social, political, and economic history of Ethiopia and Eritrea. He has published on these subjects in *The Journal of African History*, the *Journal of Eastern African Studies*, and *Africa*.

Steven Serels is a Research Fellow at the Leibniz-Zentrum Moderner Orient. He holds a Master's (2007) and a Ph.D. in History (2012), both from McGill University, and a Bachelor of Fine Arts from The Cooper Union (2005). He previously was a fellow at Harvard University's Center for Middle Eastern Studies and Martin Luther Universität Halle-Wittenberg's *Zentrum für Interdisziplinäre Regionalstudien*. He is the author of *Starvation and the State: Famine, Slavery and Power in Sudan 1883–1956* (Palgrave Macmillan, 2013) and *The Impoverishment of the African Red Sea Littoral, c1640–1945* (Palgrave Macmillan, 2018).

List of Figures

List of Tables

CHAPTER 1

Introduction: Money, Colonialism and African Societies

Karin Pallaver

The object at the heart of this volume is money or, more specifically, currency. There is no doubt that money as a thing/object is among the most important in many people's ordinary lives: it has not only economic but also cultural and political value, an understanding of which can tell us a lot about the societies using it (Guyer 1995, p. 5). During the years of colonialism, one of the most pervasive ways in which exchange relationships were managed was the imposition of a single, government-issued currency. The analysis of the introduction, circulation and enforcement of currency in the colonial context is therefore crucial to studying how the colonial state and its authority was built as well as the transition from conquest to control. Colonialism had a "monetary dimension" stemming from the colonial state's need to simplify procedures for administering the colonies and promote intercolonial trade (Helleiner 2003, pp. 164–185).

K. Pallaver (✉)
Department of History and Cultures, University of Bologna, Bologna, Italy
e-mail: karin.pallaver@unibo.it

K. Pallaver (ed.), *Monetary Transitions*,
Palgrave Studies in Economic History,
https://doi.org/10.1007/978-3-030-83461-6_1

Discussions of colonial state formation in Africa, however, very rarely dedicate attention to currency or recognize its relevance for a broader understanding of the financial and economic dimension of the entire process. Currency is generally only mentioned in short sections with titles along the lines of "Notes on Currency and Measures" inserted at the beginning of volumes to define the symbols and abbreviations used in the text to refer to payments such as taxes and wages. Too often money in itself seems to be taken for granted as something that was a natural part of colonial rule and, therefore, arising spontaneously from it. However, as the chapters in this volume contend, the monetization of the colonial period did not take place through a sudden switch from certain commodities customarily used as currency to the coins and notes introduced by the colonial power.

Currency reforms in the colonies were driven by common forces and motivated by diverse goals. Colonial currencies helped to reduce the transaction costs of commercial exchanges between the metropole and the colonies as well as those involved in intercolonial trade. Inside each colony, they allowed the colonial power to control macroeconomic conditions and to reduce domestic transaction costs. In addition, currency reforms increased seigniorage profits for the metropole (Helleiner 2003, pp. 164–185). A new currency also served as an instrument for circumscribing the spatial reach of the colonial state, delimited by colonial borders but also defined by the circulation of a single legal tender (Mwangi 2001, p. 766). Bearing the symbols of the colonizing nation-states—such as the effigy of the ruling monarch—colonial coins and banknotes were also highly symbolic, and using them implied recognizing the legitimacy of the institutions that had issued them (Mwangi 2002). Their introduction thus served as a means to create and later reinforce an entirely new identity shaped by imperial ideologies (Helleiner 2003, p. 183). The move to introduce new coins and banknotes was also part of the European powers' supposed "civilising mission". Colonial money was considered an "evolutionary step" beyond those "primitive" African currencies such as cowrie shells, glass beads or cloth that proved so difficult for the colonial state to store, count and control (Hogendorn and Johnson 1986, p. 50).

The keywords of the colonial monetization process were standardization and homogenization. Replacing regional, locally circulating African currencies with a single currency built on the model of the state-based currencies in use in the European metropoles was a tool for rationalizing and simplifying colonial administration. Few signs of the extension of the colonial state's reach were as profound as a centrally issued metal currency and its acceptance in the rural areas of the colony (Herbst 2000, p. 202). Yet, a historical examination of this process reveals it to be less totalizing and homogenous than is often assumed. Processes of currency standardization and formalization were extended in the colonies in a piecemeal rather than uniform manner, and these efforts came up against the different values that colonized societies attached to different forms of currency, including colonial ones. The general assumption of a single, general-purpose currency is therefore "unsuitably narrow" (Zelizer 1989, p. 351) for understanding the relationship between money, colonialism and African societies.

The history of the introduction of colonial currencies in the African continent showcases a series of failures that shed light on the problematic nature of colonial control. Accepting or rejecting colonial money can be interpreted both as a conflict over the nature of colonial prerogatives and as the result of diverse geographies of currency circulation intersecting with the conceptual unity of the colonial state, space and rule (Mwangi 2001). Several studies have focussed on the relationship between money, empire and the construction of the colonial state. Eric Helleiner's research has been seminal in providing a historical understanding of money's diverse roles in the economies and societies of newly created nation-states, including colonies (Helleiner 2002, 2003). Jeffrey Herbst has highlighted the relationship between West African currencies and colonial state consolidation (Herbst 2000, pp. 201–226). The recent volume edited by Federico Neiburg and Nigel Dodd offers a view onto the cultural history of money in the age of empire, stressing the tension between the unifying tendencies of nations and empires and the on the ground multiplicity produced by the multiplication, invention and re-invention of currencies (Neiburg and Dodd 2021).

Colonial conquest imposed territorial borders that cut across long-distance trading networks in Africa as well as monopolies over growing spheres of external trade. In so doing, it transformed, damaged or destroyed more articulated trading systems running through wide regions, such as the Western Indian Ocean and Sahara Desert (Cooper 2001, p. 205), but also fostering new ones (see Eagleton, this volume). African traders continued to trade across colonial borders and currency zones so as to secure "marginal gains" above the rates of return that would have prevailed in a single market with a single scale of value (Guyer 2004). The increased variety and mobility of currencies generated by the imposition of colonial rule did not result in local peoples' swift adoption of outside notions of wealth; rather, these multiple and dynamic currencies became a critical instrument with which to negotiate values and create new forms of wealth in a period of change (Pallaver 2015, p. 499). African monetary exchanges had been characterized by asymmetrical transactions as a permanent and culturally marked feature, and colonial currency reforms could not replace the acts of negotiation underpinning these exchanges with an "unambiguously measured standard of value" (Guyer 2004, p. 27). Studying how colonial currencies were incorporated into economic practices in the framework of a long-term change process highlights the dynamism of African monetary practices as well as the limits of the colonial state's reach and ability to enforce currency reforms from the top down. Money, as Viviana Zelizer points out, belongs to the market but not exclusively so (Zelizer 1989, p. 344). The market is just one side of the coin: the other side, as Keith Hart has stressed, is the state. The state side is regulated by the enforcement of political authority, the market side by exchanges among groups and individuals. Money is therefore embedded in relations between people but, at the same time, is detached from people (Hart 1986, pp. 638–639). Alongside the money of the state and that of the market, Jane Guyer adds the "money of people's experience", using the latter to read the first two differently as part of an attempt to reconfigure them around the concerns of anthropology and history (Guyer 1995, p. 6). The existence of diverse attitudes towards colonial currencies as well as different forms of money reveals the dichotomous relationship between power and society (Dodd 2017, p. 237). African societies did not view the new colonial monetary order as a "radical leveler" producing standardization (Zelizer 1989, p. 346). Rather, colonial money was perceived in many ways, including, as Amy Kaler has argued in relation to colonial Malawi, as a source of "irrationality" (Kaler 2006). To respond to state-imposed conditions, different groups of people have generated various strategies for exchanging, converting, and saving money that necessarily involves a certain degree of choice (James and Hull 2012, p. 9). Understanding these strategies and putting them in a historical perspective helps to uncover "the positive power of indigenous agency" in shaping institutions (Austin 2008, p. 1020).

Studies on the transition from precolonial to colonial money have shown that the currencies early ethnographic studies deemed "primitive" (Einzig 1949; Quiggin 1949) were, ironically, more *modern* than colonial ones as they more effectively met the needs of African trade and African currency users. The reasons were varied, from the nature of local markets and their interregional and global connections to the suitability of specific currencies for local incomes and prices or the symbolical and ritual values attributed to different forms of money (Hogendorn and Johnson 1986; Naanen 1993; Ofonagoro 1979; Pallaver 2015; Swanepoel 2015). Compared to currencies of the precolonial period, colonial money was often inadequate and scarce, especially in the early years of colonial rule. As a consequence, Africans working for Europeans often refused to be paid in colonial currencies (Comaroff and Comaroff 2005; Pallaver 2019b). Currency shortages, especially of small-denominations—often connected to the seasonal circulation of coins as well as the colonial state's inability to supply sufficient coins—created voids that currency users on the ground filled by either creating and transforming currencies (Kuroda, this volume) or continuing to use precolonial ones (Pallaver 2015). Therefore, it was a matter of practical necessity for the colonial state to allow existing precolonial currencies to circulate, especially in the early colonial period when taxes could be paid in the same commodity currencies also used to pay African staff (Masaki, this volume).

Case studies from Africa provide significant contributions to the study of the history of money more broadly, and colonies in particular constitute illuminating points of observation for thinking about accounts of *modern* monies (Balachandran 2021, p. 54). Before the establishment of colonial rule, monetary multiplicity was a common characteristic of African currency systems. Inside self-governing societies, in trade networks over time and space, and in interactions with neighbouring peoples and outsiders bringing goods from other continents with an eye to purchasing African commodities, Africans employed multiple currencies (Guyer and Pallaver 2018). When transactions based on multiplicity were subjected to colonial rule, people continued to use precolonial currencies and often combined them with colonial ones. Multiplicity thus represents a crucial element in the study of the history of money in Africa during the period of colonial rule.

A Renaissance of African Monetary History

Research on the ways African societies were affected by the introduction of colonial currencies first developed in the field of ethnography, specifically the substantivist school. Paul Bohannan analyzed relations among what he called the "spheres of exchange" of the Tiv economy in Nigeria and argued that introducing British money led to the dissolution of the currency systems already in use and the transformation of the local, multicentric economy into a unicentric system (Bohannan 1959, p. 501). He defined this process as a "currency revolution" through which European colonial currencies replaced African ones. The history of money attracted considerable attention in the field of African economic history when it began to gain momentum in the 1960s. Scholarly attention was largely, if not solely, devoted to precolonial currencies. In the 1960s, the study of African currencies was informed by the canons of the newly-born discipline of African history, according to which studying an authentically African history meant investigating the period before colonialism, famously defined by Jacob Ajayi as an "episode in African history" (Ajayi [1969] 2000; Denoon and Kuper 1970). Of the publications in this period, Marion Johnson's pioneering studies on different types of African commodity currencies—including cloth strips and cowrie shells—rejected the definition of "primitive" currencies introduced by early ethnographies of African money. She showed that, far from being primitive, these currencies were actually "sophisticated" in their capability to adapt to the needs of West African trade (Johnson 1970, p. 17). Antony Hopkins studied the process of colonial monetization in South-West Nigeria and the establishment of the West African Currency Board (Hopkins 1966, 1970). Later, he also contributed by discussing the role of African precolonial currencies in the framework of the substantivist debate on the difference between general-purpose and special-purpose currencies.[1] His conclusion was that they were general-purpose currencies and functional to the expansion of trade, being "adequate for the needs of the time" (Hopkins 1973, pp. 66–70). The 1970s were a decade in which economic history "colonized" the continent (Hopkins 2009, p. 155) but for the study of money and

[1] According to Karl Polanyi, an object is called money when used in any one of the following ways: for payment, as a means of indirect exchange, or as a standard. Money can be all-purpose, lending itself to all of these uses, or special-purpose when its different uses are separated from one another (see Dalton 1971).

currency, this colonization remained limited almost exclusively to West Africa.[2] In this period, the study of money and currency became even more central to African history scholarship when "dependency theory" was formulated as a theoretical frame of reference to explain the long-term roots of African underdevelopment. Paul Lovejoy, for instance, studied the circulation of cowries in Nigeria as a way of evaluating the extent of interregional African trade and market development processes. His underlying aim was to ground the understanding of African underdevelopment in the economic history of the precolonial period (Lovejoy 1974). Philip Curtin moved beyond the substantivist debate, asserting that "[n]o currency is absolutely all-purpose in any society, simply because no society makes payments for all the purposes payments can be made" (Curtin 1975, p. 233). He made the highly important point that the key object of investigation should be processes of economic change, also in relation to currency circulation and use. According to Curtin, the prevailing representation of African precolonial currency systems in most twentieth-century ethnographies was misleading in that it misrepresented highly dynamic African currency systems as essentially unchanging (Curtin 1975, p. 234). Studies from this period also considered the transformative impact of colonialism on African precolonial currency systems. Kwame Arhin analyzed the "cash pressure" produced by British colonial monetization in Asante, finding that it had simplified trade and removed political constraints on money-making (Arhin 1976 p. 457). Walter Ofonagoro defined his study of colonial Nigeria an "analysis of a currency revolution" (Ofonagoro 1979). The term "revolution", understood as the forced overthrow of a system or order in favour of a new one, does not lend itself very well to explaining the process he describes, however, as it took more than fifty years for colonial coins and banknotes to replace African commodity currencies in Nigeria. With a few exceptions, among which Jan Hogendorn and Marion Johnson's noteworthy book on cowries that also briefly considered the impact of colonialism on the circulation of these shells, interest in the history of money diminished in the 1980s and 1990s, largely following the trajectory of the field of African economic history (Hopkins 2009).

Interest in the impact of colonial money introduction on African societies did not decline in the field of anthropology, however. In the late

[2] A limited number of studies were published in this period regarding other parts of the continent, such as Pankhurst (1962) on the "primitive money" of Ethiopia.

1980s, several anthropological works began to critique the "currency revolution" paradigm initially developed by Bohannan and subsequently adopted by economic historians interested in studying colonial money. The essays collected in the seminal volume edited by Jonathan Perry and Maurice Bloch called into doubt the underlying premise that money supposedly has an *intrinsic* power to revolutionize society and culture. Transformations did take place, they argued, but they were not as radical as many scholars had assumed them to be (Parry and Bloch 1989, p. 13). Later, Jane Guyer edited a volume that remains the most important reference for research on the impact of colonial currency reforms in Africa. In the introduction, she emphasizes that the term "revolution" (erroneously) suggests one state of being was quite abruptly supplanted by a new one. According to her, viewing the change process as revolutionary fails to capture the complexity of African currency changes over the *longue durée* (Guyer 1995, pp. 1–2). In his study of the French Upper Volta, Mahir Şaul shows that cowrie shells and colonial coins circulated side by side in the colonial period and stresses the need to engage more thoroughly with the analysis of competing currencies and their different implications for social relations and economic life in the colonial context (Şaul 2004, p. 71). Along these lines, Jean and John Comaroff have shown that the imposition of colonial currencies was challenged by African conceptions of value as connected to different types of currency (Comaroff and Comaroff 2005). Together, these studies call into question the "comforting plotline" of the impact of "modern" money on "traditional societies" and show that colonial period monetization was far from revolutionary, instead unfolding over long periods of time during which people continued to use multiple currencies (Maurer 2006, p. 17). As Nathalie Swanepoel has recently argued, it is more accurate to "talk about a currency transition rather than a currency revolution" (Swanepoel 2015, p. 45). In combination with studies stressing the changing nature of African precolonial currency systems, the analytical approach considering the introduction of colonial money as a gradual *transition* shows that the change resulting from the establishment of colonial rule was just one of many changes characterizing the continent's monetary history in the long term.

In the last decade, scholarly interest in the history of money in Africa and its analytical value for understanding broader processes of economic and social change during the colonial period has given rise to new collaborative and interdisciplinary research that represents a true "renaissance of African monetary history". The earliest development in this vein was a conference organized by Catherine Eagleton at the British Museum in 2007 bringing together anthropologists, historians of Africa, economic historians, material culture experts, archaeologists and linguists; the outcome was the publication of the volume *Money in Africa* (Eagleton et al. 2009). Eagleton later directed the "Money in Africa project" funded by the Leverhulme Trust (2010–2013) in which a team of researchers with different disciplinary backgrounds (economic history, history, material culture and anthropology) studied a range of cases relating to the history of currency in Africa as well as contemporary experiences. The two research projects Akinobu Kuroda conducted on complementarity among monies likewise included numerous case studies focussed on Africa.[3] Through multiple meetings and workshops, one of the most enduring outcomes of these projects has been to create an international network of scholars interested in investigating the multiplicity of and complementarity among money in different parts of the world. More recently, two research projects have started to delve into new aspects of the history of money in Africa. The project "Money in West Africa: The economic and social history of the transitions from commodity to colonial currencies" (Kanazawa University and Cambridge University), directed by Toyomu Masaki with the collaboration of Gareth Austin, is currently studying the transitional phase from commodity to colonial money in West Africa. The project revisits the scholarly tradition of 1960s–1970s studies on the monetary history of West Africa and reconstructs the historical origins of currency zones in this region as a way to explain how African monetary spheres and circuits were altered by the establishment of colonial rule and, at the same time, contribute to current debates about unified monetary areas in the region. The project at the University of Osaka co-directed by Gerold Krozewski and Tinashe Nyamunda, "Transnational Money and the Formation of Economies and States in Africa, 1870s–1960s", builds on studies investigating the relationship between money, empire and colonial state construction with the

[3] The two projects both based at the University of Tokyo—were: "Money as social circuit: interdisciplinary research on the complementarity between anonymous currency and named credit", Institute of Advanced Studies on Asia, University of Tokyo, funded by the Toyota Foundation (2010–2013), and the "International cooperative research on the complementarity among monies caused by temporality, seasonality, and locality in making transactions" funded by the Japanese Society for the Promotion of Science (2007–2012). See Kuroda (2020).

ultimate aim of positioning Africa within an imperial, global and transnational network of money relations. Finally, the projects I have coordinated at the University of Bologna, "Monetary Transitions: The introduction of colonial currencies in East Africa and their impact on indigenous societies and economies" funded by the Gerda Henkel Foundation and the Italian Ministry of Education, University and Research (2016–2021), investigated the impact of introducing colonial currencies in East Africa, an area that has been almost wholly neglected by historians and anthropologists studying money. The University of Bologna projects have focussed on monetary transitions in Kenya, Tanzania, Eritrea and Somalia (Pallaver and Podestà 2021).

Many of the participants in these diverse projects took part in a workshop I organized at the University of Bologna Department of History and Cultures with the financial support of the Gerda Henkel Foundation, which served as an initial venue for presenting many of the papers comprising this volume. *Monetary Transitions. Currencies, Colonialism and African Societies* joins a growing body of scholarship and research that has proposed new and more nuanced definitions and understandings of African money and its history in recent years. To do so, it adopts a broad definition of money, examining it not only as an economic phenomenon but also in terms of its geographical, political, social and cultural dynamics (Gilbert and Helleiner 1999). Focussing on different case studies, the chapters in the volume show that colonial period monetary transitions were not only driven by imperial monetary policies but were also shaped by actions and initiatives on the part of African societies as well as competing regional interests and politics. The volume considers the multiple nature and circulation of currencies in Africa and the ways in which African societies accepted, transformed, or rejected colonial currencies. It looks at the impact of colonial money introduction on wages, taxes and social payments, exploring changes and points of continuity in access to goods and wealth as well as the long-term impact of the introduction of colonial currencies on poverty and instability in certain African regions. It adopts a regional perspective to shed light on the way territorial currencies and the creation of colonial borders affected African trade networks and monetary practices. It situates currency reforms in the colonies within larger frameworks of colonial visions of economic development and transimperial connections. Finally, it addresses the relevance of the study of African monetary history for global monetary history.

Changes in monetary conditions have also been caused by local dynamics, and indeed African societies and history have long been distinguished by their assimilation of change in general, well before the establishment of colonial rule (Hopkins 1973, p. 206). The ultimate aim of this volume is to reassert the concept of historical change at the heart of African monetary history by combining perspectives from history, economics, anthropology, economic history and material culture in the framework of an in-depth understanding of the social, cultural and economic history of the areas analyzed.

Multifaceted Monetary Transitions: Concepts, Themes and Perspectives

This volume uses money as a lens through which to analyze certain aspects of the social and economic impact of colonialism on African societies and institutions. One of its contributions is to cast light on the divergence between the specificities of African monetary systems and the European intention of building a single currency in the colonies. Colonial rule was negotiated as well as imposed, and institutional change was "the product of African initiatives as well as of exogenous causes" (Hopkins 2009, p. 170). Yet, studies of the impact of currency reforms are hampered by the limited information available on how Africans experienced changing monetary conditions during colonial times, especially in the early colonial period. Data are generally patchy and scattered across different institutions and archives. Moreover, official documentary sources often have little to say about currency matters and especially the way African societies experienced currency changes. Unsurprisingly, finding an "African voice" in documents discussing financial matters or currency exchange rates is highly problematic. Even so, reading these administrative sources along and against the grain can allow us to recover fragments of the "voices" of African currency users, voices that can become more audible if combined with other sources. As Catherine Eagleton points out, the study of the monetary history of a place or region must look beyond the material held in the archives of the colonial power. In her chapter on Zanzibar, she not only uses documents from British archives but also mobilizes archival materials from the United States, France and India. Oral sources can also be employed to recover a memory of currency transitions in the colonial period. Through interviews with the elders of Bolgatanga in the Upper East Region of Ghana, Domenico Cristofaro has recovered information about the naming of precolonial and colonial currencies as well as the accounting units employed in market negotiations. In his chapter, he combines colonial, oral and missionary sources to understand how colonial coins were incorporated into existing monetary practices. As he shows, missionary sources often provide a more on the ground perspective than administrative ones do. Research on Uganda, for example, has shown that missionaries meticulously recorded the wages paid to their labourers, church offerings and prices on the local markets as well as bridewealth payments (Pallaver 2015). This kind of evidence is important for reconstructing changes in the ways people saved money as well as for providing an understanding of the types of currencies to which they attributed value. Missionaries were also actors who often "spoke in the name" of Africans in the public arena in which currency matters were discussed and from which African currency users were excluded (Pallaver 2019a). Other groups of currency users were able to make their voices heard quite well in this arena, especially to manifest their dissent towards the colonial state's currency policies, as in the case of the white settlers in Southern Rhodesia (Mseba; Nyamunda, this volume) or Italian banks in British-occupied Eritrea (Puddu, this volume). Indeed, colonial reforms were often shaped more by the outside interests of the imperial power than by the interests of officers or business groups viewing the situation on the ground (Helleiner 2003, p. 183; Puddu, this volume). In sum, as many chapters in this volume show, currency reforms had divergent impacts on different groups of currency users.

As mentioned above, the study of colonial currency introduction in the African continent reveals the gaps in and obstacles to colonial control. Documents reporting on the failures of colonial monetary policies themselves provide an important source of information about how African societies reacted to or resisted colonial monetary policies. One shape such opposition took was open acts of resistance. For example, Bamidele Aly discusses the case of several "Mohammedan boys" who rolled banknotes into cigarette-shaped cylinders and smoked them as a way of protesting the introduction of paper banknotes in Nigeria (Aly 2020). Attitudes towards colonial money were clearly ambivalent and time- and culture-specific, but as many of the chapters in this volume show they were the manifestation of complex strategies adopted to cope with changing monetary conditions. Individual or collective acts of *resistance* enacted by African societies in the face of colonial monetary reforms ranged from formal protests to selective acts of appropriation, or the refusal to accept certain colonial monetary forms. Looking at the ways in which colonial currencies were rejected, accepted, transformed and combined is a means of focussing on the "precise ways" in which colonial power was "engaged, contested, deflected, and appropriated" (Cooper 1994, pp. 1517, 1528). Collective and individual reactions to currency reforms were often not connected and came in many shapes and forms. Considered together, however, they engaged and contested the colonial regime and partly altered the boundaries of subordination imposed by the colonial state (Pallaver 2019a, p. 558).

When currency changes were introduced, the state was obliged to use propaganda to convince people that new forms of money were actually trustworthy (Pallaver 2019a, p. 555). And yet the acceptance of colonial money—or some of its forms—did not depend solely on the guarantee provided by the government or the colonial subjects' degree of trust (or distrust) in it. Currency acceptance was also a result of the uses that were made of diversified currencies in individual transactions, transactions that took place outside governmental control. Various works by anthropologists have shown that the complexity of money's operation in the colonial context was determined by the overlapping of colonial money with other means of payment and wealth storing, such as cattle (Comaroff and Comaroff 2005; Hutchinson 1992). Precolonial African currencies had multiple uses and values that extended beyond mere monetary use: they were vital for the acquisition of status and prestige and had ritual and religious values as well as aesthetic and practical uses. Other, "non-productive" values could therefore be considered more important than or as important as monetary ones, as Toby Green has recently discussed (Green 2019). In her contribution in this volume, Toyomu Masaki shows how French and African traders in nineteenth-century Senegal used both banknotes and different forms of commodity money, including *guinée* cloth and iron bars. Monetary spheres were not clearly discrete in this period, and differences in people's use of currency were not based on their being African or European. Rather, both Europeans and Africans chose to use the money that best suited their purposes, regardless of type. For example, the French colonial government resorted to the use of *guinée* cloth in areas of the colony of Senegal in which coins and notes were not adequately available, and even kept their accounts in cloth. Cristofaro investigates the rejection of British coins in Northern Ghana and contends that the introduction of taxes did not suffice to foster the use of colonial money. Rather, as he shows, colonial coins were integrated into existing systems of wealth accumulation. Cattle, he argues, remained the main basis for the accumulation of wealth throughout the colonial period. As Sharon Hutchinson has argued in her study of the Nuer in Sudan, money and cattle were slowly incorporated into a single system of wealth categories as a result of gradual social and economic shifts connected to the establishment of colonial rule and the spread of capitalist relations of production (Hutchinson 1992, p. 295). In some contexts, commodity currencies could prove more convenient than colonial ones. In West Africa, for example, while the price of palm oil changed, that of *manillas* remained stable, making it more expedient for people to use them than other currencies (Kuroda, this volume).

Projects to introduce a government-issued currency in the colonies were therefore protracted and complex, and generated processes of adaptation involving different sections of the colonial society, including European settlers. In Southern Rhodesia, for example, white settlers had to resort to a combination of various types of currencies, including stamps that were used to compensate for the scarcity of small-denomination coins (Nyamunda, this volume).

Especially in the early colonial period, the colonial state had only limited knowledge about currency matters, and so stereotypes and assumptions about how African systems of exchange worked were used in an effort to explain a sphere colonial authorities understood only in part. For example, in early colonial Uganda the British introduced coins with holes as a way to encourage people to use them instead of cowrie shells, as in precolonial Buganda the shells were threaded on strings called *kiasa* composed of 100 shells each. These strings facilitated the transport and counting of cowries and served to create larger "currency denominations". A *kiasa* could be easily divided into halves of fifty cowries each, and again into five parts of ten shells each, the smallest unit being five shells (Pallaver 2015, p. 477). The British issued their new coins in denominations of 1, 5, 10, 25 and 50 cents; hence, there was no need to put them on a string to create larger currency denominations. There is no evidence available that holed coins were strung, except to make necklaces and girdles.[4] It thus seems that the move to put holes in the coins only facilitated the work of craftsmen and jewellers rather than promoting

[4] See for example this Pokomo girdle included in the collection of the British Museum https://www.britishmuseum.org/collection/object/E_Af1914-0417-69. Accessed on 27 April 2021.

the use of British coins. Currency reform programmes were conceived by European treasuries and colonial officers, but when money actually enters into circulation "there isn't much that rulers and kings can do to determine how it is used" (Dodd 2017, p. 237).

One of the points that emerge from a combined reading of the chapters in this volume is the need to calibrate the historical study of currency circulation to its spatial and scalar dimensions (Gilbert 2005, p. 380). Colonial currencies served to differentiate between the spaces controlled by competing colonial powers (Mwangi 2001, p. 766). Nonetheless, the territorial spaces of African colonies were carved out of areas previously connected by regional and interregional trade flows in which multiple complementary currencies circulated. Colonial borders were fixed on maps, but on the ground they remained porous and were continually crossed by people, goods *and* currencies. It was thus extremely difficult to exert effective control over currency circulation and the acceptance of colonial money (see De Cola; Serels, this volume). Colonial currencies spilled over the borders of individual colonies, and studying their circulation thus necessarily requires the adoption of a regional perspective, as in several chapters of this volume. For example, by looking at Eritrea in the framework of the Red Sea Region (De Cola; Serels), at Zanzibar as part of the Western Indian Ocean (Eagleton), or at West Africa as a region in which British and French currency zones overlapped (Cristofaro; Masaki). In his chapter, Admire Mseba examines Southern Africa as a region including South Africa, Lesotho, Eswatini, Botswana, Zimbabwe and, to some extent, Mozambique. Through the adoption of this broad regional perspective, he effectively shows that the acceptance and use of certain currencies were dictated by both local conditions and the contingent interests of multiple actors: colonial governments, white settlers and an increasingly mobile African workforce that carried currencies across borders. These currencies were thus embedded in social transactions, including the payment of bridewealth, as part of a regional monetary system that had come about with the emergence of a regional capitalist economy. In the Horn of Africa, the Italian government's monetary policies in Eritrea met with very little success. Adopting a regional perspective as Alessandro De Cola does in his chapter clearly shows that the reason lies in the widespread acceptance of the Maria Theresa thaler, a coin that was trusted by traders in the entire Red Sea region and could not be replaced by a territorial currency such as the *tallero eritreo* or *tallero d'Italia* introduced by the Italians. This finding is further confirmed by the Emperor of Ethiopia's failed attempt to replace the Maria Theresa thaler in Ethiopia. In 1893, in response to the Italian introduction of the *tallero eritreo* in neighbouring Eritrea, he introduced his own thaler (known as the Menelik thaler) to replace the Maria Theresa one. Despite the Emperor's political and religious authority, the new thaler did not meet with the favour of traders and instead they continued to deal in Maria Theresa thalers (Pankhurst 1963, pp. 78–85). The regional success enjoyed by the Austrian coin is yet another example that sheds light on the complex nature of the relationship between currencies, the state power and transregional trade.

As several contributions to this volume show, the acceptability of currencies depended on a variety of factors, including the nature of local markets and their interregional and global connections as well as the complementary relationship of the currencies circulating across African regions. On the island of Zanzibar, for instance, a variety of international coins were in use. It was this multiplicity that colonial authorities came up against when they attempted to establish a new currency system (Eagleton, this volume). Various types of currency and their denominations circulated in a complementary way, eluding the control of the colonial state. As a matter of fact, the coexistence of different types of money was functional rather than incidental. As Akinobu Kuroda has shown for the Red Sea region, an assortment of monies could do what no single money was able to, and analyzing the circulation of complementary currencies—international, colonial, and local—can enrich our understanding of the specificities of African monetary systems (Kuroda 2007, 2008). In his contribution to this volume, Kuroda stresses that it was the shared recognition among dealers along a trade circuit that a given item constituted money, rather than any enforcement by the authorities and/or the intrinsic value of the item, which sustained that item's acceptability as money in long-distance exchange. And African traders and currency users were indeed very skilled in manipulating and negotiating different currencies, as shown by both Cristofaro and De Cola in their respective chapters. Multiple currencies were also accepted as part of the circulation of different colonial currencies within a single colony. As Luca Puddu highlights in his chapter, after the occupation of Eritrea during the Second World War, the British accepted the circulation of Italian currencies and introduced East African shillings, Indian rupees, Egyptian piastres and (again) Maria Theresa thalers. After the 1942 monetary proclamation establishing the East African shilling as the currency of

Eritrea, officials still allowed the circulation of the small-denomination lira coins that served the needs of African currency users and circulated in a complementary relationship with the shilling.

On-the-ground and regional approaches to the study of money must be combined with an exploration of the political, economic and financial motivations that led European colonial powers to introduce specific currencies in their colonies. As Krozewski shows in his chapter, a focus on the relationship between currency policies and economy-building across empires produces insights into the mutually constitutive characteristics of European currency policies. By adopting transnational and transimperial perspectives, researchers are able to unravel the way the colonial powers were or were not influenced by each other and uncover processes of collaboration, emulation or reciprocal influence (Subrahmanyam 2005). In this vein, it is quite telling that the Italians decided not to introduce the lira in Somalia in the early colonial period and instead usher in an Italian silver rupee in emulation of what the British had done in Kenya and Uganda and the Germans in German East Africa (Krozewski, this volume; Pallaver 2019a; Sessa 2020). Colonial monetary systems are often analyzed in isolation from each other or from a "national" point of view, and this perspective entails various limitations. European colonial states were managing and promoting their national economies at the same time as they were attempting to standardize currencies in their colonies. Policies for issuing a specific currency, as Krozewski argues in his chapter, reflected particular visions of economic development. In contrast to the British who compartmentalized the colonies and regulated currency via currency boards, the Germans in East Africa designed a monetary system meant to support the construction of a "global German economy". Both on-site monetary practices and the design of currency reforms were responsive to international and global monetary developments. Changes in the international monetary system influenced African economies as well as currency systems in the colonies, as Leigh Gardner has shown with her study of the Gambia (Gardner 2015). In his chapter, Kuroda contends that currency transitions in Africa in the early twentieth century were part of a global tide of monetary transformation penetrating to the ground level in which commodities, colonial and international currencies competed and complemented each other. As Eagleton demonstrates in her chapter, adopting a global perspective on monetary transitions can also help to counter the commonly-accepted argument that the Indian rupee was gradually and naturally accepted in Zanzibar and the East African coast thanks to the presence of Indian traders and Britain's political power in the Western Indian Ocean. Rather, as she convincingly argues, it was the American civil war, a conflict taking place "thousands of miles away", that precipitated the monetary transition in Zanzibar.

The volume also shows that some historical periods or events, such as the First World War, are crucial to the study of African monetary transitions. When the conflict erupted, colonial coins and banknotes had been already introduced all over the continent. However, the outbreak of war caused shortages in currency circulation in the continent due both to the decline in trade flows and the reduction in coins produced by European mints. The nickel and bronze generally employed to produce small-denomination coins were needed to produce arms and munitions (Osuntokun 1979; Pallaver 2019b; Wrangham 2013). During periods of crisis, administrative sources tend to mention *mundane* elements more frequently and, in the case of problems of currency circulation, these records provide unexpected insights into monetary practices on the ground (Maxon 1989; Mwangi 2001; Pallaver 2019a). As discussed in the chapter by De Cola, currency shortages in Eritrea roused the concern of Italian authorities in a period in which the Eritrean population was being pressured more and more intensely to contribute to the Italian war effort. These currency problems had disparate impacts on different groups of African currency users depending on the channels through which they gained access to money. As De Cola argues, caravan traders were able to exploit interregional trade networks and profit from different currency exchange rates across colonial borders while the *ascari* (colonial soldiers) suffered the most, as they received their wages from the colonial state.

One of the ways to address the problem of currency shortages during the war period was to issue banknotes. To pay labourers and soldiers, paper notes were issued in the Gold Coast (Killingray 1978, p. 45), Somalia (Caroselli 1922, p. 373) and the East Africa Protectorate (Pallaver 2019b). There is very little information available about the history of paper money in the African colonies. Colonial banknotes were an important tool for the colonial state to convey a precise image of itself and its "civilizing mission" (Mwangi 2002). African societies were particularly distrustful of paper money, and labourers often refused to be paid in banknotes as discussed by Nyamunda and Masaki in their chapters.[5] Accepting a piece of paper with no intrinsic value implied trust in a government that had yet to be built, especially in the first decades of colonial rule. Banknotes also presented practical problems, as they were prone to damage from water or insects (Comaroff and Comaroff 2005, p. 145). This volume demonstrates the importance of considering money's materiality and role in the construction of regimes of value in colonial contexts (Maurer 2006, p. 27; Miller 2005). To be accepted as means of payment and exchange, colonial currencies needed to have certain material characteristics—including durability and transportability—that colonial government did not take into due consideration when designing their currency policies. As the chapter by Masaki points out, considering the materiality of the currencies in use can provide significant insights into actions and events at all levels of the society in which they were introduced (Comaroff and Comaroff 2005; Haselgrove and Krmnicek 2012, p. 245). Coins for use in the colonies had to be "produced" and this required setting up a "commodity chain" (Gereffi and Korzeniewicz 1994, pp. 2–3) encompassing the design of coins and banknotes, their manufacturing, transportation to the colonies, and promotion by colonial authorities before entering circulation. The development of new materials and technologies for manufacturing coins and banknotes allowed colonial authorities to cut costs and augment the number of coins—especially small-denomination ones—that could be produced. At the same time, it reduced opportunities for counterfeiting (Feingold 2017; Olukoju 2000). Still, currency introduction was a complex process often based on misinterpretations or scarce knowledge that doomed new currencies to failure. For example, aluminium coins were introduced throughout the British colonies in the first decade of the twentieth century before it was discovered that they were unsuitable because they quickly corroded in tropical climates (Ofonagoro 1979, p. 649; Pallaver 2018, p. 299).

Credit and debt relationships are also key to the understanding of how African monetary systems operated on the ground. When credit was obtainable at the local level, it was not as important that large- and small-denomination currencies be available (Kuroda, this volume). The topic of banking is addressed by several authors in this volume. Formal banking took an extremely long time to become established in

[5] There were some exceptions, however. In her chapter, Masaki discusses a very early African use of banknotes in Senegal.

the colonies (Guyer 2004, p. 157) and Africans had only limited access to banks (Austin and Uche 2007; Uche 1999). Nonetheless, forms of indigenous banking developed in some colonies, as discussed by Tinashe Nyamunda in his chapter. He speaks to the tradition of studies of indigenous banking in Africa, in relation to processes of capital formation as well as the impact of colonial monetization on the development of social classes (see also Adebayo 1994). Africans also used European banking institutions, however. As Masaki shows in her chapter, African traders in nineteenth-century Senegal used the services of the Bank of Senegal, and banks also played an important role in the negotiations leading to currency reforms (Puddu, this volume).

One of the points this volume makes is the importance of considering the long-term consequences of colonial period currency reforms. As discussed above, this concern dominated historical studies on currency in the 1970s, especially those focussed on precolonial currencies. Of these, Walter Rodney pointed out that the introduction of imported currencies in West Africa during the Atlantic slave trade era was one of the elements that contributed to rendering Africa dependent on Europe and the Western world (Rodney [1972] 1982, pp. 110–111). Atlantic Africa was intensely shaped by its relations with Western currencies and the limits Europeans imposed on their convertibility. Yet, African trade grew and expanded on the basis of indigenous transactional conventions derived from the appropriation of these currencies (Guyer 2004, pp. 4–5). Nonetheless, as Green has recently underlined, African currencies depreciated in the long term, losing some of their relative global value as compared to silver and gold. Africans exported "hard currencies" that retained their value, whereas the currencies imported during the era of the Atlantic slave trade lost value over time and this had an effect on future economic trajectories (Green 2019, p. 14).

The relationship between colonial currency reforms and the consolidation of structural poverty in African countries is a topic that deserves further investigation. In his chapter, Steven Serels contends that the impoverishment of Eritrea formed the backdrop for the country's monetary transition in the colonial period. According to Serels, the spread of imperial currencies, transformation of traditional livelihoods, solidification of structural poverty and migration from the countryside to cities were intertwined. By investigating the lengthy monetary transition resulting from the lira's introduction in colonial Eritrea, Serels shows that imperial currencies were weak institutions. The limited reach of the Italian colonial state, led Eritreans to engage with imperial currencies selectively and to continue using existing ones. Over time, however, the impact of colonial rule on economic activities and food insecurity led Eritreans to look for additional cash income and so hire their labour out to the colonial state. At the end of the interwar period, the lira, the currency used to pay for this labour, suffered from instability and Eritreans ended up trapped in a "cycle of poverty" (Serels 2019, p. 156). The volume therefore also engages with the debate over the impact of colonialism on African societies in light of the recent literature on the "historical roots of African poverty" that has reinvigorated research on Africa's economic past in the last decade (Akyeampong et al. 2014). Starting from the insights of the "New Economic History of Africa" (Hopkins 2009) but avoiding that "compression of history" (Austin 2008) that derives from a limited understanding of African local and regional historical specificities in the long term, *Monetary Transitions* engages in new ways with the study of the African economic past, reinserting African societies and their uses of money into debates about the impact of colonialism on African economies and institutions as well as the development of the colonial state.

Conclusion and Paths Forward

Alternative currencies are growing rapidly nowadays, but monetary pluralism is not new; rather, it seems to represent "a return to the past" (Dodd 2017, p. 234). The specific contribution that African sources and narratives can make to the field of monetary history consists of an expanded understanding of the empirical intricacy of monetary multiplicity, especially in the precolonial period (Guyer and Pallaver 2018). By showing that this multiplicity characterized the colonial period as well, one of the main contributions of this volume is to conceptualize the colonial era as an extremely fruitful period for studying multiple forms of money and their historical genealogies.

This volume focuses on areas of the continent that previously have been largely neglected by scholars of African money. The analysis of case studies from East and Southern Africa as well as understudied areas of West Africa such as Senegal contributes to filling some of the geographical gaps in our knowledge about the history of money in colonial Africa. However, the history of the introduction of European currencies in some parts of the continent still remains poorly understood, for example in the Belgian, German and Portuguese colonies in the early twentieth century.

This volume focuses on sub-Saharan Africa, but there is still much to be done to further our understanding of the impact of colonialism on currency exchanges between North Africa and other African regions, for example along trans-Saharan trails.[6]

This volume shows that colonial currencies' replacement of African ones was a protracted transition involving the decades-long coexistence of multiple currencies. And yet, a full transition to metal coins and banknotes did occur at some point, as all African independent states introduced a new currency on becoming independent. Investigating the social acceptance of the currencies of newly independent states, including their design and symbolism, as well as the ways in which colonial currencies were demonetized or circulated alongside postcolonial ones would be an interesting way to complement the studies collected in this volume.[7]

There is still much more to be learned about African currencies, credit systems and other means of exchange and the ways colonial rule impacted them. A thorough quantitative analysis of the impact of colonial money introduction on commodity price levels, wages and tax rates, as well as trade flows, would contribute immensely to understanding what colonial period currency reforms meant for African living standards and existing social and economic institutions. The complexities of precolonial African monetary systems still need to be fully explored, especially for certain areas of the continent. The extension of currency areas and how they were formed is a topic that requires further investigation, especially for the precolonial period. Current literature provides some idea of currency circuits, but rarely a complete one. Nevertheless, "[w]e know enough to be able to imagine the complexity" (Guyer 1995, p. 86). Comparing this complexity to other world regions, as Kuroda does in his chapter, not only produces new understandings of African monetary history in its own terms—as James Webb put it in a famous article from the 1980s (Webb 1982)—it simultaneously clarifies "the distinctiveness and the universality of African societies in explicit connection and comparison with other regions" (Manning 2013, p. 330).

The trend to create supranational currencies and the increasing use of foreign currencies within national borders are clear indications that

[6] Regarding currency circulation along nineteenth-century trans-Saharan trails, see Lydon (2009, pp. 248, 257).

[7] Regarding post-independence currency design in Kenya, Tanzania and Uganda, see Eagleton (2016).

national currencies are facing a growing number of challenges in the current era. Most of the literature addressing monetary transformations and transitions has been written by economists and considers money primarily as an economic phenomenon. These studies often lack a historical perspective, and sometimes assume that the national currency is a sort of *natural* way of organizing money. A historical analysis of the currency reforms implemented in the colonial period shows that currencies might not be as totalizing or homogenous as is often assumed, and this insight has the potential to help us understand the challenges monetary structures are facing today as well as the significance of national money for nation-states.

Acknowledgements Many of the papers collected in this volume were presented during a workshop organized at the University of Bologna in January 2020. I wish to thank all the participants for the lively discussions and valuable insights. I also thank the Gerda Henkel Foundation (Project AZ/37/F/16) for their generous support, as well as the Department of History and Cultures for hosting us. Finally, I thank Alessandro De Cola for his invaluable help and support in the preparation of the volume.

References

Adebayo, Akanmu G. 1994. "Money, Credit, and Banking in Precolonial Africa. The Yoruba Experience." *Anthropos* 89: 379–400.

Ajayi, Jacob F. A. [1969] 2000. "Colonialism: An Episode in African History." In *Tradition and Change in Africa. The essays of J.F. Ade Ajayi*, edited by Toyin Falola, 165–174. Trenton; Asmara: Africa World Press.

Akyeampong, Emmanuel, Robert H. Bates, Nathan Nunn, and James Robinson, eds. 2014. *Africa's Development in Historical Perspective*. New York: Cambridge University Press.

Aly, Bamidele. 2020. "The Creation and the Issue of West African Sterling Notes in British West Africa (1915–1949)." Paper presented at the workshop "Monetary Transitions in Colonial Africa", University of Bologna, 15–16 January.

Arhin, Kwame. 1976. "The Pressure of Cash and Its Political Consequences in Asante in the Colonial Period, 1900–1940." *Journal of African Studies* 3 (4): 453–468.

Austin, Gareth. 2008. "The Reversal of Fortune Thesis and the Compression of History: Perspectives from African and Comparative Economic History." *Journal of International Development* 20: 996–1027.

Austin, Gareth, and Chibuike Uche. 2007. "Collusion and Competition in Colonial Economies: Banking in British West Africa, 1916–1960." *The Business History Review* 81 (1): 1–26.

Balachandran, Gopalan. 2021. "Money and Its Ideas. Colonial Currencies, Money Illusions." In *A Cultural History of Money in the Age of Empire*, edited by Federico Neiburg and Nigel Dodd, 35–55. London: Bloomsbury Publishing.

Bohannan, Paul. 1959. "The Impact of Money on an African Subsistence Economy." *The Journal of Economic History* 19 (4): 491–503.

Caroselli, Francesco. 1922. "Il sistema monetario in rupie nella economia e nella finanza della Somalia italiana." *Giornale degli economisti e rivista di statistica* 62: 364–380.

Comaroff, Jean, and John L. Comaroff. 2005. "Beasts, Banknotes and the Colour of Money in Colonial South Africa." *Archaeological Dialogues* 12 (2): 107–132.

Cooper, Frederick. 1994. "Conflict and Connection: Rethinking Colonial African History." *The American Historical Review* 99 (5): 1516–1545.

———. 2001. "What Is the Concept of Globalization Good For? An African Historian's Perspective." *African Affairs* 100 (399): 189–213.

Curtin, Philip. 1975. *Economic Change in Precolonial Africa. Senegambia in the Era of the Slave Trade*. Madison: University of Wisconsin Press.

Dalton, George, ed. 1971. *Primitive, Archaic and Modern Economies: Essays of Karl Polanyi*. Boston, MA: Beacon Press.

Denoon, Donald, and Adam Kuper. 1970. "Nationalist Historians in Search of a Nation: The 'New Historiography' in Dar es Salaam." *African Affairs* 69 (277): 329–349.

Dodd, Nigel. 2017. "Utopian Monies: Complementary Currencies, Bitcoin and the Social Life of Money." In *Money Talks. Explaining How Money Really Works* edited by Nina Bandelj, Frederick F. Wherry and Viviana A. Zelizer, 230–247. Princeton; Oxford: Princeton University Press.

Eagleton, Catherine, Harcourt Fuller, John Perkins, eds. 2009. *Money in Africa*. London: British Museum.

Eagleton, Catherine. 2016. "Designing Change: Coins and the Creation of the New National Identities." In *Cultures of Decolonisation. Transnational Productions and Practices, 1945–70*, edited by Ruth Craggs and Claire Wintle, 222–244. Manchester, New York: Manchester University Press.

Einzig, Paul. 1949. *Primitive Money: In Its Anthropological, Historical and Economic Aspects*. London: Eyre & Spottiswoode.

Feingold, Ellen. 2017. "International Currency Counterfeiting Schemes in Interwar West Africa." *Journal of West African History* 3 (1): 77–102.

Gardner, Leigh. 2015. "The Curious Incident of the Franc in the Gambia: Exchange Rate Instability and Imperial Monetary Systems in the 1920s." *Financial History Review* 22: 291–314.

Gereffi, Gary, and Miguel Korzeniewicz, eds. 1994. *Commodity Chains and Global Capitalism*. Westport, CT: Greenwood Press.

Gilbert, Emily. 2005. "Common Cents: Situating Money in Time and Place." *Economy and Society* 34 (3): 357–388.

Gilbert, Emily, and Eric Helleiner. 1999. "Introduction—Nation States and Money. Historical Contexts, Interdisciplinary Perspectives." In *Nation-States and Money. The Past, Present and Future of National Currencies*, edited by Eric Helleiner and Emily Gilbert, 1–22. Abingdon, New York: Routledge.

Green, Toby. 2019. *A Fistful of Shells: West Africa from the Rise of the Slave Trade to the Age of Revolution*. Chicago, IL: University of Chicago Press.

Guyer, Jane I., ed. 1995. *Money Matters. Instability, Values and Social Payments in the Modern History of West African Communities*. Portsmouth, NH: Heinemann.

———. 2004. *Marginal Gains: Monetary Transactions in Atlantic Africa*. Chicago, IL: University of Chicago Press.

Guyer, Jane I., and Karin Pallaver. 2018. "Money and Currency in African History." In *Oxford Research Encyclopedia of African History*, 1–29. Oxford: Oxford University Press.

Hart, Keith. 1986. "Heads or Tails? Two Sides of the Coin." *Man* 21 (4): 637–656.

Haselgrove, Colin, and Stefan Krmnicek. 2012. "The Archaeology of Money." *Annual Review of Anthropology* 41: 235–250.

Helleiner, Eric. 2002. "The Monetary Dimensions of Colonialism: Why Did Imperial Powers Create Currency Blocks?" *Geopolitics* 7 (1): 5–30.

———. 2003. *The Making of National Money: Territorial Currencies in Historical Perspective*. Ithaca, NY: Cornell University Press.

Herbst, Jeffrey. 2000. *States and Power in Africa. Comparative Lessons in Authority and* Control. Princeton, NJ: Princeton University Press.

Hogendorn, Jan, and Marion Johnson. 1986. *The Shell Money of the Slave Trade*. Cambridge: Cambridge University Press.

Hopkins, Antony G. 1966. "The Currency Revolution in South-West Nigeria in the Late Nineteenth Century." *Journal of the Historical Society of Nigeria* 3 (3): 471–483.

———. 1970. "The Creation of a Colonial Monetary System: The Origins of the West African Currency Board." *African Historical Studies* 3 (1): 101–132.

———. 1973. *An Economic History of West Africa*. London: Longman.

———. 2009. "The New Economic History of Africa." *The Journal of African History* 50 (2): 155–177.

Hutchinson, Sharon. 1992. "The Cattle of Money and the Cattle of Girls among the Nuer, 1930–83." *American Ethnologist* 19 (2): 294–316.
James, Deborah, and Elizabeth Hull, 2012. "Introduction: Popular Economies in South Africa." *Africa* 82 (1): 1–19.
Johnson, Marion. 1970. "The Cowrie Currencies of West Africa Part I." *The Journal of African History* 11 (1): 17–49.
Kaler, Amy. 2006. "When They See Money, They Think It's Life: Money, Modernity and Morality in Two Sites in Rural Malawi." *Journal of Southern African Studies* 32 (2): 335–349.
Killingray, David 1978. "Repercussions of World War I in the Gold Coast." *The Journal of African History*, 19 (1): 39–59.
Kuroda, Akinobu. 2007. "The Maria Theresa Dollar in the Early Twentieth-Century Red Sea Region: A Complementary Interface between Multiple Markets." *Financial History Review* 14 (1): 89–110.
———. 2008. "What Is the Complementarity among Monies? An Introductory Note." *Financial History Review* 15 (1): 7–15.
———. 2020. *A Global History of Money*. Abingdon, New York: Routledge.
Lovejoy, Paul E. 1974. "Interregional Monetary Flows in the Precolonial Trade of Nigeria." *The Journal of African History* 15 (4): 563–585.
Lydon, Ghislaine. 2009. *On Trans-Saharan Trails: Islamic Law, Trade Networks, and Cross-Cultural Exchange in Nineteenth-Century Western Africa*. New York: Cambridge University Press.
Manning, Patrick. 2013. "African and World Historiography." *The Journal of African History* 54: 319–330.
Maurer, Bill. 2006. "The Anthropology of Money." *Annual Review of Anthropology* 35: 15–36.
Maxon, Robert. 1989. "The Kenya Currency Crisis, 1919–21 and the Imperial Dilemma." *The Journal of Imperial and Commonwealth History* 17 (3): 323–348.
Miller, Daniel, ed. 2005. *Materiality*. Durham, NC: Duke University Press.
Mwangi, Wambui. 2001. "Of Coins and Conquest: The East African Currency Board, the Rupee Crisis, and the Problem of Colonialism and the East African Protectorate." *Comparative Studies in Society and History* 43 (4): 763–787.
———. 2002. "The Lion, the Native and the Coffee Plant: Political Imagery and the Ambiguous Art of Currency Design in Colonial Kenya." *Geopolitics* 7 (1): 31–62.
Naanen, Ben. 1993. "Economy Within an Economy: The Manilla Currency, Exchange Rate Instability, and Social Conditions in South-Eastern Nigeria, 1900–48." *The Journal of African History* 34 (3): 425–446.
Neiburg, Federico and Nigel Dodd. 2021. *A Cultural History of Money in the Age of Empire*. London: Bloomsbury Publishing.

Ofonagoro, Walter I. 1979. "From Traditional to British Currency in Southern Nigeria: Analysis of a Currency Revolution, 1880–1948." *The Journal of Economic History* 39 (3): 623–654.

Olukoju, Ayodeji. 2000. "Self-Help Criminality as Resistance? Currency Counterfeiting in Colonial Nigeria." *International Review of Social History* 45: 385–407.

Osuntokun, Akinjide. 1979. *Nigeria in the First World War*. London: Longman.

Pallaver, Karin. 2015. "'The African Native Has No Pocket': Monetary Practices and Currency Transitions in Early Colonial Uganda." *International Journal of African Historical Studies* 48 (3): 471–499.

———. 2018. "Paying in Cents, Paying in Rupees: Colonial Currencies, Labour Relations and the Payment of Wages in Kenya (1890–1920)." In *Colonialism, Institutional Change and Shifts in Global Labour Relations*, edited by Karin Hofmeester and Pim de Zwart, 295–325. Amsterdam: University of Amsterdam Press.

———. 2019a. "A Currency Muddle: Resistance, Materialities and the Local Use of Money during the East African Rupee Crisis (1919–1923)." *Journal of Eastern African Studies* 13 (3): 546–564.

———. 2019b. "Pockets Full of Rupees, But Bodies Very Weak: The Carrier Corps and Their Demobilization at the End of WWI in East Africa." *Afriche e Orienti* 3: 79–96.

Pallaver, Karin, and Gian Luca Podestà. 2021. *Una moneta per l'impero. Pratiche monetarie, economia e società nell'Africa Orientale Italiana*. Milan: FrancoAngeli.

Pankhurst, Richard. 1962. "Primitive Money in Ethiopia." *Journal de la Societé des Africanistes* 32 (2): 213–248.

———. 1963. "Ethiopian Monetary and Banking Innovations in the Nineteenth and Early Twentieth Centuries." *Journal of Ethiopian Studies* 1 (2): 64–120.

Parry, Jonathan, and Maurice Bloch, eds. 1989. *Money and the Morality of Exchange*. Cambridge: Cambridge University Press.

Quiggin, Alison. 1949. *A Survey of Primitive Money. The Beginnings of Currency*. London: Methuen & Co.

Rodney, Walter. [1972] 1982. *How Europe Underdeveloped Africa*. Washington, DC: Howard University Press.

Şaul, Mahir. 2004. "Money in Colonial Transition: Cowries and Francs in West Africa." *American Anthropologist* 106 (1): 71–84.

Serels, Steven. 2019. "The Circulation of Modern Currencies and the Impoverishment of the Red Sea World 1882–2010." In *Currencies of the Indian Ocean World*, edited by Steven Serels and Gwyn Campbell, 141–64. London: Palgrave Macmillan.

Sessa, Claudio. 2020. "Colonialismo monetario. L'esperienza italiana in Somalia e la difficile transizione (1905–1950)." PhD diss., University of Genoa.

Subrahmanyam, Sanjay. 2005. *Explorations in Connected History: Mughals and Franks*. Oxford: Oxford University Press.

Swanepoel, Natalie. 2015. "Small Change. Cowries, Coins and the Currency Transition in the Northern Territories of Colonial Ghana." In *Materializing Colonial Encounters. Archaeologies of African Experience*, edited by Francois Richard, 41–69. New York: Springer.

Uche, Chibuike. 1999. "Foreign Banks, Africans, and Credit in Colonial Nigeria, c. 1890–1912." *The Economic History Review* 52 (4): 669–691.

Webb, James L. A., Jr. 1982. "Toward the Comparative Study of Money: A Reconsideration of West African Currencies and Neoclassical Monetary Concepts." *International Journal of African Historical Studies* 15 (3): 455–466.

Wrangham, Elizabeth. 2013. *Ghana during the First World War: The Colonial Administration of Sir Hugh Clifford*. Durham: Carolina Academic Press.

Zelizer, Viviana. 1989. "The Social Meaning of Money: "Special Monies." *American Journal of Sociology* 95 (2): 342–377.

PART I

Early Colonial Transitions: Commodity, International and Colonial Currencies

CHAPTER 2

"Here There Is No Gold Standard. Cows Are the Standard". Multiple Currencies, Colonial Taxation and Monetary Transition in Upper Ghana (1896–1936)

Domenico Cristofaro

Introduction[1]

In 1919 Alan Wolsey Cardinall, the District Commissioner residing in Zuarungu, in present-day upper Ghana, wrote in his diary:

[1] The sources for this article come from the ethnographic fieldwork I conducted in Ghana between 2013 and 2019 and from colonial records I consulted in the National Archives in London (hereafter TNA), in the Bodleian Library in Oxford, and in the National Archives of Ghana, branches of Accra (hereafter NAG), and Tamale (hereafter NAG-T). Other sources consulted are the White Fathers' diaries and reports collected in their headquarters in Rome (hereafter A.G.M.Afr.).

D. Cristofaro (✉)
Department of Cultures, Politics and Society, University of Turin, Turin, Italy

K. Pallaver (ed.), *Monetary Transitions*, Palgrave Studies in Economic History, https://doi.org/10.1007/978-3-030-83461-6_2

> The shortage of money is very great here. Particularly is this so of nickel. Apparently it is valued locally as the material for rings and bracelets. ... Here of course there is no gold standard. Cows are the standard.[2]

The officer was worried about the circulation of colonial currency in the markets of the district. What concerned him most was his assumption that British coins were not used as such but melted to make jewellery. He also anticipated what Melville Herskovits would define some years later as the "cattle complex", or the colonial bias that centred African economic thought and practices on the ownership of cattle (Herskovits 1926).[3] On the same page of his diary, Cardinall wondered if punitive measures should be enacted to end the loss of coins. After almost 20 years of efforts to impose British currency in the region, colonial officers were still struggling with a social and economic context that rejected their coins. This chapter intends to shed light on this rejection. It will analyse the introduction of colonial currencies in the Gurensi[4] region in upper Ghana to investigate the reasons for their acceptance, circulation, and refusal in the first four decades of colonial occupation. The chapter will show that the acceptance of colonial coins depended on several factors, including African monetary practices, the circulation of multiple and often complementary currencies, and colonial policies in terms of labour recruitment and taxation.

The problems connected to the introduction and circulation of colonial coins were indeed the results of the existence of a monetary system formed by a plurality of currencies and its persistence in upper Ghana after the establishment of British colonial rule (Swanepoel 2015). This monetary system was not incidental but functional, as it has been in other places and times in history (Helleiner 2003; Kuroda 2008). When colonial officers introduced their coins in the Gurensi region, there was no "currency revolution" (Bohannan 1959; Hopkins 1966; Ofonagoro 1979). Multiple currencies continued to characterize the economic landscape of the region

[2] Navarro–Zouaragu Informal diary, entry for 17 August 1919, NAG-T, NRG 8/4/3.

[3] This "complex" was thoroughly discussed and deprived of his "mystical" *aura* only in 1978, by the work of R. M. G. Mtetwa (1978). On the relation between wealth and cattle see also Hutchinson (1992).

[4] The Gurensi region is the area today encircled by the municipalities of Bolgatanga and Bongo in the Upper East Region of Ghana. Gurensi is the name of the main ethnic group that inhabits the area, also known as Frafra or Nankanni.

for years, coexisting with colonial coins. The diachronic processes of introduction and circulation of colonial currencies are better defined by the term "transition", as has been aptly demonstrated for other parts of the African continent (Gardner 2018; Guyer 1995; Guyer and Pallaver 2018). The currency transition in the region was enhanced by colonial policies such as the creation of currency boards, the demonetization of indigenous currencies, the introduction of taxes to be paid in cash, and wage labour (Clauson 1944; Helleiner 2002; Hopkins 1973).

Focusing on the inefficacy of the early taxation policies and revealing the actual use of British coins in everyday commercial transactions, this case study demonstrates that Africans could limit colonial interference in matters of monetary practices and trade. Taxation, believed by the officers to spread coins and foster their acceptance, did not bring the expected results in the Gurensi region. As the chapter will show, Africans were able to adapt to colonial coinage and insert it in their economic life, circumventing colonial fiscal obligations. While taxation policies determined colonial practices of currency imposition, Africans' adoption or refusal of colonial coins depended on the contextual plurality, meaning, and practices associated with pre-existent currencies (Eagleton et al. 2009). Consequently, colonial coins remained for a long time just one currency among others.

The chapter is structured to follow the transition in the monetary system of the Gurensi region in the first four decades of colonial rule. The first part of the chapter will introduce the nineteenth-century economic context of the region and analyse the broad commercial networks that crossed the area. These networks fostered the use of different currencies and exchange systems, and therefore the coexistence of multiple currencies. In the Gurensi region, the main store of wealth was livestock, and it remained the basis for wealth accumulation processes also in the colonial period. The second part deals specifically with the British efforts to impose their currency after their occupation of the region. It starts by discussing the flaws in the implementation of the early taxation policy and shows the ways African traders reacted to tax collection. Then, it presents the introduction of silver, copper, and nickel coinage in the region.

Similarly to the North-western area, also in North-eastern Ghana the lack of a "positive network effect", or the increasing benefits derived from the adoption of a specific good or service (as currencies could be) from a growing number of its users, prevented the diffusion of colonial coins (Swanepoel 2015, p. 52). To demonstrate this, the third part of the chapter will provide some examples of the role of colonial coinage in everyday economic practices and the reasons behind their refusal. Firstly, British coins were not a convenient currency for most people, chiefly because of their too high value. Secondly, many traders specialized in currency smuggling and arbitrage,[5] which made British coins even less appealing for the typical buyer due to the disadvantageous exchange rates. The last part of the chapter will discuss the ways people inserted colonial coinage into their value system, linking coins denomination to a certain number of cowries. Coins and cowries were indeed regarded as similar, even though the latter were more popular and widespread. People did not ignore the function, value and use of colonial coins, but they deliberately did not regard them as a significant attribute of wealth, affecting in this way their popularity.

Interregional Commercial Networks, Livestock and Multiple Currencies in North-Eastern Ghana

At the end of the nineteenth century, the Gurensi region was in the middle of the caravan network that connected the northern savannah trade centres with the coastal ones (Arhin 1979; Lovejoy 1973, 1982), along which goods were traded using multiple currencies such as cowries, gold and cloth (Arhin 1974; Johnson 1968, 1970). In these territories, the slave trade was still thriving, and it gave a significant stimulus to this international commercial network (Der 1998; Johnson 1986; Kankpeyeng 2009). Cowries were the most common currency found along these routes.[6] Colonial reports document throughout the first

[5] Travelling merchants bought the coins at convenient prices in the northern markets, taking advantage of their limited diffusion and people's limited familiarity with exchange rates, and resold them in the southern ones with an increased gain. For more details see further.

[6] In the Gurensi region, archaeological excavations brought to light few shells of the *Cypraea moneta* species (Insoll et al. 2013, p. 167), while in the western part of upper Ghana both *Cypraea moneta* and *annulus* (dated between the fifteenth and seventeenth century) were found in greater quantity (Anquandah 1987, p. 179). After colonial occupation cowries continued to be preferred to coins (Evans 1985; Johnson 1970; Swanepoel 2015). In some areas of upper Ghana still in 2004 they were regarded as "legal tender" for specific transactions. See for example https://www.ghanaweb.com/GhanaHomePage/NewsArchive/Cowries-still-legal-tender-in-Upper-West-Region-62655. Accessed on 8 April 2021.

half of the twentieth century a widespread diffusion of cowries in upper Ghana, where they were ubiquitous in most transactions, especially in trading close to the Northern border (Evans 1985; Goody 1998, p. 239; Swanepoel 2015). Although some sources state that cowries were not the main currency in the Gurensi area (Insoll et al. 2013, pp. 167–168, 218; Tauxier 1912, p. 251), they were nonetheless used. Leaving the Gurensi region in 1888, Louis Binger paid the toll in cowries and met Mossi merchants on the other bank of the Volta river ready to cross, loaded with kola and cowries (Binger 1892, p. 40). Forty years later, cowries were still used as currency in the Gurensi markets or as payment for "medicine men" or musicians (Rattray 1932, pp. 154, 168, 173).

Like many other groups in this savannah belt, the Gurensi were a peasant non-centralized society that centred their subsistence on agriculture between the nineteenth and twentieth centuries. The wealth of a man derived from the number of cattle, wives, and children he had and his position in the "lineage-based gerontocracy" that regulated social life (Hart 1978, p. 191). Trade and raiding were among the few other opportunities for a man to become wealthier.

Along the caravan paths and in the markets, the Gurensi exchanged brass rods, iron hoes and salt for agricultural produce, cattle, and sometimes slaves, using the first as the main currencies (Hart 1978, p. 189). Cattle were a high-value currency and one of the most important stores of wealth, and therefore the basis of the accumulation process throughout the colonial period. The first colonial officers who visited the region explained the relationship between wealth and cattle, anticipating the "cattle complex". In the first medical report on Zuarungu, the first colonial station in the region, the Medical Officer Lundie noted indeed that cattle were "used as a convenient kind of large coinage", without being eaten or milked.[7]

Livestock was also one of the primary and most valuable goods traded along the caravan routes, one that did not require porterage and maintained its high value almost everywhere (Northcott 1899, pp. 46, 50–51).

[7] Since the first military raids, seizure of cattle was indeed considered a serious sanction against Gurensi settlements. On the importance of livestock as a wealth indicator for colonial officers see Duplicate Letter Book, NEPC to AgCCNT, 18 September 1910, enc.: Medical Report on the New Station at Zouaragu by Doctor A. Lundie W.A.M.S., 12 September 1910, NAG, ADM 56/1/7. See also Essays by Assistant District Commissioners on tribal history, Navarro District, p.16, NAG, ADM 11/1/824; "Agriculture in North Mamprusi", Pamphlet by C. W. Lynn, TNA, CO 96/751/14.

These qualities meant that it could easily be exchanged for food in times of scarcity. Some of my oldest informants still remember the exchange rates between cattle and millet in the 1930s, a transaction that they defined as "barter trade".[8] When famine struck in that period, some people resorted to selling off part of their family herds:

> Those days, you know the barter trade? Food for food, animal for animal…that's what they were doing when you have your animal to sell, normally they exchange… one cow is to six sheep, and then when you will run out of food, even though you haven't anything at all to eat and the hunger is aching you, you take one cow, for…they call that one *peu* [a basket], we use this millet stocks, that's what we use to weave that *peu*. So, a cow is to that *peu* full of millet, when you are hungry, and you can't get anything there else to take. That's why you send your animal if you have your animals, and then you can't even kill the animals and say "Oh, you have to go and exchange it for that *peu* of millet even to live." And then, maybe, if you don't have cows, then you have some sheep, you exchange it for a goat, or you want to take a goat to exchange with sheep. A sheep, one sheep, is two goats.[9]

However, as already mentioned, livestock was neither the only currency nor the only way of storing value. The exchange system operating in the region was based on a multiplicity of currency objects, including cowries, cloth, hoes and brass rods.[10]

[8] On the "myth" of barter, its ubiquity and historical inaccuracy see Graeber (2011, p. 21).

[9] Interview with Akapaŋa Amoah, 17 March 2015, Bukere; ellipsis in the original. Another unit of account used in the markets was the personal calabash. Buyers visited market stalls and sampled or measured goods for sale using a calabash they carried with them. In the case of cloth, people measured it "by using the tip of their fingers to the middle of the chest. There were [also] other ways of measuring objects and liquids. One of these was to measure from the elbow to the tip of the fingers and another was to measure with the foot of the leg" (Christopher Anabila Azaare. "Life in Bolga", unpublished).

[10] "Before the advent of the European [sic],… cowries were used as money, but owing to the limited amount obtainable, could only be used to buy small quantities of food, &c. In other cases, exchange was resorted to and is still largely used in preference to English money" Essays by Assistant District Commissioners on tribal history, Navarro District, NAG, ADM 11/1/824. For the use of brass and copper rods as currency see Annual Report 1904, Northern Territories of the Gold Coast, p. 8, TNA, CO 98/14. For hoes see Rattray (1932, pp. 170, 184) and Garrard (1986, p. 124).

In this area, as in the western part of upper Ghana, there was indeed "a fluid economic landscape characterized by a variety of currencies, overlapping currency zones and multiple regimes of value" (Swanepoel 2015, pp. 44–45). One of the first reports on military raids carried out in the region documents that a caravan passing through the region tried to exchange "country cloth for sheep".[11] Another document written ten years later reveals that what the officers defined as "exchange" or "barter" was still the primary method of purchasing goods.[12] It was in this context of currency multiplicity that the British, after the occupation of the area, attempted to introduce their coins and promote their circulation with the introduction of taxes, even though with meagre results.

Collecting Taxes and Introducing Coins: The Flaws in the Execution of Colonial Policies

Colonial officers introduced silver pence soon after the military occupation of the region they renamed the Northern Territories of the Gold Coast. In the southern part of the colony, silver coins were already in circulation by the end of the nineteenth century (Arhin 1976; Hill 1963, p. 165). Nevertheless, in the Northern Territories, they were a rarity. In the first instructions to administrators sent to the north, the introduction of coins was regarded as "one of the most important of the duties falling on Officers".[13] Officers tried to spread coinage as government wages, rewards for chiefs displaying their support and as the only medium accepted for paying taxes and buying European goods sold in government stores.[14] Tax collection and the introduction of coins were

[11] Further Correspondence relative to Boundary question in the Bend of the Niger, Maxwell to Chamberlain, 5 May 1897, enc. Stewart to Colonial Secretary, 27 March 1897, TNA, CO 879/48.

[12] Essays by Assistant District Commissioners on tribal history, Navarro District, NAG, ADM 11/1/824.

[13] Instructions to Officers in charge of Districts, Re. Administration of the Northern Territories, NAG, ADM 56/1/35. In the unsettled region of Tong, officers even pointed out the role of colonial currency as a "civilising medium", Duplicate Letter Book, Ag. CCNT to Lt. Tarrant, n.d, NAG, ADM 56/1/8.

[14] See for example the "present of 10 s" given to the chief of Bolgatanga for his supportive conduct in 1898 in Further Correspondence relating to the Northern Territories, Hodgson to Chamberlain, 25 June 1898, enc. Northcott to Colonial Secretary, 1 May 1898, TNA, CO 879/54.

part of a bigger plan devised to rule the newly acquired Protectorate, a large region that officials intended to administer at the lowest possible cost. The British programme relied on developing a basic structure of state control. The plan involved counting on chiefs to serve as gatherers of forced labour, making and policing roads, encouraging trade, and improving marketplaces.[15]

Simultaneously, taxation, considered proof of sovereignty, was implemented in 1899 through the so-called "maintenance tax", a tax levied directly on population,[16] and the "caravan tax", a tax imposed on traders. The "maintenance tax" did not last long. In 1901, the Commissioner and Commandant Lt.-Col. A. Morris argued that, while some sort of tribute was already customary among the Dagomba and Mamprusi, in the areas without a centralized form of government, such as the Gurensi region, this form of taxation was a complete novelty. In the period in which the tax was raised (1900–1901), according to the commissioner, it did more harm than good by fostering extortion on the part of the tax collectors, i.e. the chiefs.[17] He, therefore, abolished it.[18] The "caravan tax" lasted longer, until September 1908. From this date to the mid-1930s, the administration decided not to levy any poll or trade tax. However, in order to collect revenues, the British administration founded new headquarters close to the main known and attended trade routes to control better the flow of caravans passing through these trade centres. New posts were established in Wa, Gambaga, Salaga, Kintampo in 1902 and Navrongo in 1906 (Bening 1975).

In this initial stage, the flaws and ambivalences in the implementation of the taxing policy could be connected to the weak colonial presence and

[15] Further Correspondence relating to the Northern Territories, Northcott to Colonial Office, 9 July 1899, TNA, CO 879/58. See also Instructions to Officers in charge of Districts, Re. Administration of the Northern Territories, NAG, ADM 56/1/35.

[16] The definition and purposes of this tax were not clearly defined by the administrators themselves (Maasole 2017, pp. 272–274).

[17] Correspondence relating to the Administration of Ashanti and the Northern Territories, Governor to Chamberlain, enc.: Morris to Governor, 30 September 1901, TNA CO 879/67.

[18] With the elimination of the "maintenance tax", Morris proposed that a much better arrangement would be to ask for more forced labour, a suggestion that was readily accepted and implemented until 1936 (Grischow 2006, p. 48; Kunkel 2018, 2019; Maasole 2017).

control. Even though caravans were accustomed to paying tolls and tributes in those territories in precolonial time (Binger 1892, p. 40; Skinner 1962, p. 246), this did not naturally imply their intention to abide by colonial taxation. Archival sources reveal that tax evasion and bypassing of British collection centres were quite frequent indeed.[19] In the first decades of the twentieth century, colonial interference in African trade flows was limited to the immediate vicinity of the few British outposts in the region, small centres of control in a vast, uncontrolled territory (Cristofaro 2020a). Even though the colonial stations were strategically placed, direct colonial control over the trade routes was weak, and it was relatively easy for traders who knew the country well to avoid collection centres (Bening 1977, p. 70). The abolition of the "caravan tax" led to an even weaker control over trade, as the officers stopped to collect it from the passing caravans. In 1912, administrators admitted that only half of the passing traders in the Navrongo District were registered.[20] The process of collecting the tax and selecting the exaction centres started to modify the geography of commerce in the Protectorate.

The limited use of currency in the area represented a problem for passing merchants that needed to pay taxes to get southward. The introduction of colonial currency and the collection of taxes through this medium led to a slowdown in caravan flows, at least near the collection centres, the places where this control on trade was enacted. Some traders were able to easily exchange cloth for coins to pay revenues.[21] However, others did not. A clear example of this is the incident that took place in 1907 near the border with the French territories. A caravan of Mossi traders was observed stationing for days in Navrongo, close to the tax collection point, unable to continue its travel southwards. The traders were looking for someone able to exchange their products for British coins to pay the tolls. Eventually, the only ones who had enough colonial currency to act as money changers were the soldiers, one of the few categories of wage workers, who "not unnaturally, refused to purchase excepting at quite inadequate prices".[22]

[19] Northern Territories Annual Report 1899, TNA, CO 96/364; Departmental Reports 1902, TNA, CO 98/13; Despatches 1907, Caravan Tolls, TNA, CO 96/469.

[20] Trade and trade routes, AgCNEP to DC, 19 July 1912, NAG, ADM 56/1/147.

[21] Monthly Report Navarro District, NAG, ADM 56/1/429.

[22] Despatches, Caravan Tolls, Governor to the Earl of Elgin, 3 August 1907, TNA, CO 96/469.

During the first decade of colonial occupation, the Gurensi continued to exchange goods as they were doing in the previous years, sometimes adding British coins to the multiple currencies already in use. The situation led the Chief Commissioner of the Northern Territories to state "it will take years... before money will form the principal medium of exchange in the remote districts of the Protectorate".[23] Four years later, the District Commissioner of the Gurensi region wrote.

> Exchange is still the most customary method of effecting purchases. ... A certain amount of English money, gold and silver, is in circulation, but the quantities are far too small and at present the coins are not favoured by the natives, nor in fact, accepted everywhere by them.[24]

These statements clashed with many of the district reports on colonial coinage. In the following years, a certain optimism continued to be expressed in these reports on the spreading of coins.[25] At the same time, these records were characterized by a lack of emphasis on the connection between resistance to colonial domination and coinage acceptance. However, both optimism and the lack of emphasis on political resistance can be easily classified as literary stratagems to conceal officers' failures (Kuklick 1979, p. 160).

There was undoubtedly a political motivation behind coin refusal, as shown by Şaul in relation to French West Africa (Şaul 2004). In this regard, an African chief's voice stood out in a brief note written in the 1916 District Commissioner's diary. The Kunaab, a local chief whose paramountcy in the region was established by British officers (Anafu 1973), made a much-telling comment after the turmoil and confusion of the so-called Bongo "riots".[26] In expressing to the colonial officer his congratulations on the success of the British retaliation, he added that.

[23] Departmental Reports 1902, TNA, CO 98/13.

[24] Essays by Assistant District Commissioners on tribal history, Navarro District, NAG, ADM 11/1/824.

[25] See for example AgCCNT to Treasurer, 14 February 1910, NAG, ADM 56/1/9 and Annual Reports, Annual report on the Zouaragu District, 1911, NAG, ADM 56/1/463.

[26] People expressed resentment against some local chiefs who supported British domination, resulting in colonial retaliation and a bloodbath (Thomas 1983).

> now their crops were spoiled, the people would want the Whiteman's money. These people have always refused to take silver or copper in the markets and preferred to exchange sheep &c. for produce or use cowries.[27]

Breaking the silence of the officers' diaries on the use of coins, this comment reveals the practice of rejecting colonial currency for political motivations, what James Scott would call a "hidden transcript" of resistance, an act of resistance and critique beyond the powerholders' gaze (Scott 1990). However, coins were refused in the markets not only for political reasons or tax collection issues.

Silver was often reported to have too high a value that did not fit in the everyday exchanges and therefore did not insert appropriately into the local economic life.[28] The introduction of a new and smaller coinage was discussed since 1901,[29] but it was only in 1908 that the first samples of copper coins were introduced in the district. Cpt. Nash held palavers in the main settlements, displaying specimens and explaining to the chiefs how they should be used.[30] Most of the issued copper almost immediately found its way back to the government treasury through fines and fees.[31] When the officers opened the post in Zuarungu in 1910, they ascertained that "there is little else than the barter of livestock and foodstuffs" and "little exchange of either for cash or cloth though money is perfectly understood".[32]

Later, in 1912, nickel pence and shillings, lighter and less costly to mint, were introduced in response to the limited diffusion of copper.[33] Nickel coins had a bright colour, similar to silver, and for this reason could

[27] Zouaragu Station Official Diary, entry for 18 July 1916, NAG, ADM 68/5/1.

[28] Departmental Reports 1901, Annual Report for the Northern Territories for the year 1901, TNA, CO 98/10; Departmental Reports 1902, Report on the Northern Territories for the year 1902, TNA, CO 98/13.

[29] Further correspondence relating to the Currency of the West African Colonies, Nathan to Chamberlain, 11 January 1901; Chamberlain to Nathan, 30 April 1901; Nathan to Chamberlain, 13 January 1902, enc. CCNT to Colonial Secretary 7 June 1901, TNA, CO 879/66.

[30] District Record Book Navrongo, p.179, NAG, ADM 63/5/2.

[31] Annual Report N.E. Province for 1913, NAG, ADM 56/1/471.

[32] AgCCNT to PC, 18 September 1910, NAG, ADM 56/1/7.

[33] Despatches, Subsidiary Nickel Coinage, TNA, CO 96/471; Despatches, Subsidiary nickel coinage, TNA, CO 96/481; Annual Report NEP for 1912, NAG, ADM 56/1/467.

be more appreciated by the people who disliked "the dull dark colour of the copper coins".[34] Portability was also considered for the little cost of transport. They decided to mint them in a form comparable to cowries, with a hole in the centre, "to conform to consumer taste" (Swanepoel 2015, p. 44). It was considered more popular than the former, and it indeed enjoyed more success, at least until the First World War, at which point the supply of coins was reduced.[35] Starting from 1916, experimental issues of currency notes took place in the Gold Coast (McPhee 1926, p. 244). However, in 1919 such an attempt in the Gurensi region was regarded by the District Commissioner as an "imbecile performance" by the Treasury that was not aware of the fact that notes would quickly spoil because of the weather conditions and would not fit in the everyday commercial exchanges of the people.[36]

Coins for Commerce: Colonial Currency in the African Markets

Currency imposition was intended to serve as a way of affirming the colonial state, in that monitoring coinage in the marketplaces was supposed to make its power "both public and binding" (Chalfin 2004, p. 99). Coin circulation was meant to facilitate direct taxation policy, the control over the caravan trade and commerce development (Grischow 2006, p. 45; Guyer and Pallaver 2018; Helleiner 2002). On a regional level, the diffusion of British coins directly influenced the commercial centrality of the colonial settlements and their marketplaces' success and liveliness in the Northern Territories. In the Protectorate, British coins spread mainly around the stations and in the marketplaces of the towns where they decided to settle, where it was easy for the officers to monitor them (Bening 1973, p. 12). For example, this was the case for Zuarungu and its market, where the constabulary and clerks, the few classes of wage

[34] Duplicate letter Book, NAG, ADM 56/1/2.

[35] Annual Report on the Northern Territories for 1912, NAG, ADM 56/1/464; Annual Report NEP for 1912, NAG, ADM 56/1/467; Annual Reports, Annual Report on Navarro-Zuaragu Districts for the year 1917, NAG, ADM 56/1/463.

[36] Navrongo Zuarungu Informal Diary 1919, NAG-T, NRG 8/4/3.

labourers together with porters, further enhanced the diffusion and acceptance of colonial coinage.[37] However, its prosperity was closely associated with their presence, and it experienced a sudden decline after the troops left for the First World War (Cristofaro 2020a).

Coin circulation remained limited to the colonial headquarters. In the rest of the country, the coins were either rejected in the markets, smuggled or melted down. From the moment it was introduced, as already mentioned, silver was reported to have too high a value. Nickel circulation was reported to be successful mostly due to the lesser value of the coins. When it was introduced in the markets, only the lowest denominations were commonly accepted.[38] It remained unpopular, and it was reportedly either melted to make adornments or bracelets or smuggled for cowries across the border.[39] Many officers suspected that melting was one of the principal means through which the local population got rid of coins,[40] but a closer reading of the sources suggest that smuggling and arbitrage were probably more frequent.

The case of the marketplace in Bolgatanga, just 5 kms away from the Zuarungu colonial station, where colonial currency was exchanged without the officers' supervision, suggests this kind of conclusion. Cpt. Nash reported that in this area it was not melting but rather the "export of money" that led to the almost complete disappearance of the coins.[41] The pence were collected and "exported" to both the northern French territories and the southern trade centres in Asante and Gold Coast.[42] Many of the traders from the French territories, conversant with coin rates of exchange, frequented the markets in the British Protectorate to secure

[37] Monthly Report NEP for 1910, NAG, ADM 56/1/441; Company of the G.C. Regt. Stationed in the Northern Territories, PCNEP to AgCCNT, 16 July 1913, NAG, ADM 56/1/59.

[38] Annual Report Northern Territories 1914, NAG, ADM 56/1/479.

[39] Navrongo Station District Diary, entry for 1 June 1915, NAG, ADM 63/5/3.

[40] Annual Report NT for 1910, NAG, ADM 57/1/448; Annual Report Northern Territories for 1916, NAG, ADM 56/1/486; Zouaragu Station Official Diary, entry for 17 August 1919, NAG, ADM 68/5/1.

[41] Annual Reports, Annual report on the Zouaragu District for the year 1911, NAG, ADM 56/1/463; Annual Reports, Annual Report on Zouaragu District for the year 1913, NAG, ADM 56/1/463.

[42] By the end of the nineteenth century merchants were already accustomed to procuring coins the further they proceed southward from Salaga, one of the most attended trade centres in Ghana in that period (Johnson 1965, p. 141).

coinage to use in paying their taxes.[43] On the other hand, those headed south took advantage of local buyers' limited familiarity with exchange rates between cowries and pence to profit from them.[44] In this way, the colonial currency lost most of its purchasing power:

> A Fra Fra gets 3d from a European or anyone else for a fowl- When trying to change this 3d for cowries he finds he can only get 150 cowries; whereas if he had originally sold the fowl in the market for cowries he would probably have got at least 250.[45]

Foreign traders bought coins at convenient prices in the Gurensi markets near Zuarungu, and most probably in Bolgatanga, one of the leading marketplaces in the area, and then spent them in the southern markets at a profit or to pay taxes in the French colonies.[46] In so doing, they were able to take advantage of the overlapping currency zones that they encountered along their journey and make a "marginal gain" on them (Guyer 2004).

The presence of practices such as smuggling, arbitrage, melting, and, in general, refusal of colonial coinage does not equate with the colonial bias that people did not understand money. Quite the opposite, as I will show in the next section, the value and use of colonial coins were well-known.

[43] Duperray notes that in 1911, almost half of the tax collection in the Cercle du Mossi was in British silver coins. The payment of taxes in British coins was indeed allowed in French territories (Duperray 1984, p. 163).

[44] Annual Report on the Northern Territories for 1917–1918, NAG, ADM 56/1/489. Relation among traveling traders and locals were characterized by ambivalence and frauds on both sides. For a discussion of Mossi traders' "arrogant attitude" towards the Gurensi see Zouaragu Station Official Diary, entry for 4 October 1913, NAG, ADM 68/5/1; for an example of Mossi fraud against Gurensi see Record Book for North Mamprusi District, p. 6, NAG, ADM 68/4/3. For a "classic" Gurensi scam against Mossi see District Record Book Navrongo, p. 240, NAG, ADM 63/5/2.

[45] Annual Reports, Annual report on the Zouaragu District for the year 1911, NAG, ADM 56/1/463. Also, in 1920, the exchange rate was disadvantageous. "The chief of Zuaragu came in to complain about the rate of exchange in the local markets. 3d is now only worth 120 cowries, some time ago 3d was worth 250. The Chief's explanation is that the people in this District don't yet know the value of the white man's money, he informed me that the cowries are plentiful. The Chief suggested that there should be a standard rate of exchange laid down", Zuaragu Informal Diary, entry for 17.05.1920 NAG-T, NRG 8/4/10.

[46] Arbitrage was a longstanding and well-known practice among the Yarse and Hausa traders (Schildkrout 1978, p. 36; Tauxier 1912, p. 423).

Fig. 2.1 Cloth traders in Bolgatanga (1940 ca.) (*Source* 511-58-13, Masson I-127-4, courtesy of Photothèque, A.G.M.Afr)

However, due to the coins limited circulation, imprecise and unknown rates of exchange, high value, and reasons related to social approbation, people preferred not to rely solely on this currency (Fig. 2.1).

The "Commensuration" of Colonial Coinage and the Value of Money

The local name given to the smaller denominations of nickel pence is much telling about the currency systems used by the Gurensi. The lower denominations were easier to manage because their decimal system made it possible to convert them into cowries without much effort (the Gurensi numeral system was and still is decimal). For example, the tenth of a penny was called *pia*, meaning ten (cowries); ½ penny was called *pinu*, meaning fifty (cowries); and one penny was *kwobega*, meaning one hundred (cowries).[47] The name of the coin was thus associated with the number of cowries needed to exchange that particular coin, demonstrating "the degree to which the expression of value is embedded in use contexts and ingrained in habit" (Swanepoel 2015, p. 41).[48] Colonial money was hence an ancillary currency, easily convertible into the more popular and widespread cowries. British coins were integrated into the trade transactions as a parallel currency to the cowries, whose functions, value and use were regarded as pretty similar. The cowry was the currency through which Gurensi were able to convert colonial coins to their regime of value and "commensurate" the colonial order of value.[49] In this process, there is at stake not only the conversion between two different means of exchange but also the commensuration between two different regimes of value.[50]

Colonial sources often explained the refusal of British coins with the ignorance of the people. However, this was not the case. As discussed above, people perfectly understood colonial money and were able to convert it easily into cowries. In 1925, the chief of Bolgatanga negotiated the land leasing for the establishment of the new mission of the White Fathers. He proposed an annual rent to be paid in sterling, a decision taken without prior consultation with the British officers (Cristofaro 2020b). The chief was already aware of the use, functions and value of the coins. After the land concession, the missionaries began to build their mission. Since the local chiefs refused to provide forced labour, the missionaries started to hire masons autonomously, offering a daily wage paid in colonial money. Two days later, the applicants' number was so high that they had to stop hiring, not being able to provide coins for

[47] The local name of the colonial coins was first obtained during an interview with the elders of the Kalbeo chief's family (13 February 2018), and then confirmed by other informants.

[48] Something similar happened during the 2007 revaluation of the Ghanaian cedi: in that year (and in the following ones) many traders and buyers continued to express the values of the new notes and coins by using the old ones (Swanepoel 2015, p. 41).

[49] I use here the term "commensuration" as the set of "mechanisms that render equitable and negotiable different orders of value" (Comaroff and Comaroff 2005, p. 107).

[50] I took the notion of "regime of value" as intended by Arjun Appadurai, that is the interrelated political, economic and intellectual fields that determine value regionally and historically (Appadurai 1986).

all.[51] These events suggest that the refusal of colonial coinage was due to the unfitting of the coins in the region's economic landscape rather than the supposed ignorance of the people.

Still in the 1960s money was not necessarily the most significant attribute of a wealthy man. Keith Hart presents cases of entrepreneurs born in the 1920s, the first generation of "businessmen" who had dealt with colonial coins since their childhood (Hart 1975). He presents four main categories of wealthy men in Gurensi society. The first and most respected was the *nera gu'la*, or a man who was "able to gain material wealth in the form of crops, livestock, personal possessions, wives and offspring through stewardship of inherited lineage property and achievements as a farmer, trader or community leader" (Hart 1975, p. 16). Then there was the *bondaana* or the man with his private wealth and the *bom kate*, or the big man, someone generally recognized for his strength. Lastly, there was the *ligeredaana*, or the "money man", the man who possessed much money.[52] Much more than the mere possession of money, the Gurensi regarded the ways a man acquired wealth in the form of livestock, crops and family size, and if these were socially acceptable.[53]

Conclusion

The First World War and the post-war years did not bring radical changes to a system characterized by the circulation of multiple currencies. True, coins circulated much more than in the previous decade. Soldiers, already active agents in spreading colonial coins, were recruited in numbers for the war. They received a salary and a monetary reward that they brought back home when they returned. Moreover, migration also contributed to the spreading of coins. Increasingly from the early 1920s, young Gurensi men started to head south in search of work and new opportunities (Hart 1971; Rouch 1956). This migration was often not permanent, and when migrants returned to their villages in the North, they took with them

[51] I discuss in detail the leasing and settling of the White Fathers in Bolgatanga in Cristofaro (2020b, p. 198).

[52] It is worthy to note that this last category did not have a morally negative connotation.

[53] Still today in Northern Ghana there is a widespread notion of wealth that encompasses a person's material wealth, his social status and reputation and is entangled with notions of health, illness and the symbolic structure of society (Bierlich 2007, p. 155).

what they earned, in this way contributing to the spreading of colonial coins and challenging the ways of wealth accumulation of their fathers.

However, there were substantial shortages of coins that reduced their circulation in the colony (Wrangham 2013, pp. 129–138). Moreover, the reintroduction of direct taxation in the 1930s during the indirect rule seems to have not modified the diffusion and acceptance of coins. Recent studies demonstrate that the payment of taxes in coins remained an unresolved issue also in this period (Kunkel 2019, p. 134).[54] Still in the 1940s, the Northern Territories were reported to suffer from a "currency problem", in that coins were used mainly to pay taxes, and cowries continued to be the main currency of everyday commercial transactions (Hinds 1947; Sutton 1989).

In conclusion, this chapter has shown that British colonial efforts to introduce currency and, therefore, regulate the monetary exchanges in the Northern Territories of the Gold Coast were largely unsuccessful. In the first decades of the twentieth century, the Gurensi area never actually transitioned to the colonial money system. The study of colonial coins' circulation revealed that markets and trade in the Gurensi area lay outside of direct colonial control and operated independently, even though they were incorporated into more extensive West African trade networks. Here, as in the rest of the Protectorate, British coins were inserted into a context of currency multiplicity and became a secondary and parallel currency. People refused to accept colonial coins in most everyday transactions due to their high value. Moreover, smuggling, arbitrage and speculation became profitable practices for traders, affecting the trust people had in that form of currency. Colonial authorities tried to enforce the use of metal coins and banknotes, but these efforts proved vain. Instead, many people continued to operate transactions in a multiple currency system, into which they incorporated colonial currencies.

[54] Much more than spreading coins, the collection of revenues in the 1930s had an important political consequence, in that it put the chiefs in a privileged economic position over their subjects. With the introduction of native treasuries, chiefs became responsible for development projects (such as road maintenance) in their area, and this had to be financed with revenue from direct taxation. In this way, they "emerge[d] as employers of waged labour" (Kunkel 2019, p. 144).

Acknowledgements I wish to thank for their support and comments on earlier drafts: Seiji Nakao, Karin Pallaver, Gerardo Serra. Thanks also to all the participants of the workshop on which this volume is based, in particular to Bamidélé Aly, Akinobu Kuroda, Toyomu Masaki, Admire Mseba and Tinashe Nyamunda for their comments on my paper.

References

Anafu, Moses. 1973. "The Impact of Colonial Rule on Tallensi Political Institutions, 1898–1967." *Transactions of the Historical Society of Ghana* 14 (1): 17–37.

Anquandah, James. 1987. "The Stone Circle Sites of Komaland, Northern Ghana, in West African Archaeology." *The African Archaeological Review* 5: 171–180.

Appadurai, Arjun. 1986. *The Social Life of Things: Commodities in Cultural Perspective*. Cambridge: Cambridge University Press.

Arhin, Kwame, ed. 1974. *The Papers of George Ekem Ferguson. African Social Research Documents*. Leiden: African Studies Center.

———. 1976. "The Pressure of Cash and Its Political Consequences in Asante in the Colonial Period, 1900–1940." *Journal of African Studies* 3 (4): 453–468.

———. 1979. *West African Traders in Ghana in the Nineteenth and Twentieth Centuries*. New York: Longman.

Bening, Raymond B. 1973. "Indigenous Concepts of Boundaries and Significance of Administrative Stations and Boundaries in Northern Ghana." *Bulletin of the Ghana Geographical Association* 15: 7–20.

———. 1975. "Location of District Administrative Capitals in the Northern Territories of the Gold Coast (1897–1951)." *Bulletin de l'Institut Fondamental d'Afrique Noire* 37 (3): 646–666.

———. 1977. "Administration and Development in Northern Ghana." *Ghana Social Science Journal* 4 (2): 58–76.

Bierlich, Bernhard. 2007. *The Problem of Money: African Agency and Western Medicine in Northern Ghana*. New York: Berghahn Books.

Binger, Louis Gustave. 1892. *Du Niger au Golfe de Guinée*. Vol. 2. Paris: Hachette.

Bohannan, Paul. 1959. "The Impact of Money on an African Subsistence Economy." *The Journal of Economic History* 19 (4): 491–503.

Chalfin, Brenda. 2004. *Shea Butter Republic: State Power, Global Markets, and the Making of an Indigenous Commodity*. New York: Routledge.

Clauson, Gerard L. M. 1944. "The British Colonial Currency System." *The Economic Journal* 54 (213): 1–25.

Comaroff, Jean, and John L. Comaroff. 2005. "Beasts, Banknotes and the Colour of Money in Colonial South Africa." *Archaeological Dialogues* 12 (2): 107–132.

Cristofaro, Domenico. 2020a. "From Caravans to Lorries: Shifting Patterns of Mobility and Colonial Roadmaking in Northern Ghana (1896–1936)." *International Journal of African Historical Studies* 53 (3): 289–314.

———. 2020b. "Between African Planning and Colonial Intervention: The Process of Urbanization in Bolgatanga, Ghana (1896–1939)." PhD diss., University of Bologna.

Der, Benedict G. 1998. *The Slave Trade in Northern Ghana*. Accra: Woeli Publishing Services.

Duperray, Anne-Marie. 1984. *Les Gourounsi de Haute-Volta: conquête et colonisation, 1896–1933*. Stuttgart: F. Steiner Verlag Wiesbaden.

Eagleton, Catherine, Harcourt Fuller, and John Perkins, eds. 2009. *Money in Africa*. London: British Museum.

Evans, Philip. 1985. "The Cowrie Economy and the Maintenance of Social Boundaries in Northern Ghana." *Cambridge Anthropology* 10 (2): 29–40.

Gardner, Leigh. 2018. "From Cowries to Mobile Phones: African Monetary Systems since 1800." In *The History of African Development. An Online Textbook for a New Generation of African Students and Teachers*, edited by Ewout Frankema, Ellen Hillbom, Ushewedu Kufakurinani, and Felix Meier zu Selhausen, 16. Bloemfontein: African Economic History Network.

Garrard, Timothy Francis. 1986. "Brass-Casting among the Frafra of Northern Ghana." PhD diss., University of California.

Goody, Jack. 1998. "Establishing Control: Violence along the Black Volta at the Beginning of Colonial Rule." *Cahiers d'Études Africaines* 38: 227–244.

Graeber, David. 2011. *Debt: The First 5,000 Years*. Brooklyn, NY: Melville House Publishing.

Grischow, Jeff D. 2006. *Shaping Tradition: Civil Society, Community and Development in Colonial Northern Ghana, 1899-1957*. Boston, MA: Brill.

Guyer, Jane I., ed., 1995. *Money Matters. Instability, Values and Social Payments in the Modern History of West African Communities*. Portsmouth, NH: Heinemann.

———. 2004. *Marginal Gains: Monetary Transactions in Atlantic Africa*. Chicago, IL: University of Chicago Press.

Guyer, Jane I., and Karin Pallaver. 2018. "Money and Currency in African History." In *Oxford Research Encyclopedia of African History*, 1–29. Oxford: Oxford University Press. https://oxfordre.com/africanhistory.

Hart, Keith. 1971. "Migration and Tribal Identity among the Frafras of Ghana." *Journal of Asian and African Studies* 6 (1): 21–36.

———. 1975. "Swindler or Public Benefactor? The Entrepreneur in his Community." In *Changing Social Structure in Ghana; Essays in the Comparative Sociology of a New State and an Old Tradition*, edited by Jack Goody, 1–35. London: International African Institute.

———. 1978. "The Economic Basis of Tallensi Social History in the Early Twentieth Century." In *Research in Economic Anthropology. An Annual Compilation of Research*, edited by George Dalton, 185–216. Greenwich: Jai Press Inc.

Helleiner, Eric. 2002. "The Monetary Dimensions of Colonialism: Why Did Imperial Powers Create Currency Blocks?" *Geopolitics* 7 (1): 5–30.

———. 2003. *The Making of National Money: Territorial Currencies in Historical Perspective*. Ithaca, NY: Cornell University Press.

Herskovits, Melville J. 1926. "The Cattle Complex in East Africa." *American Anthropologist* 28 (1): 230–272.

Hill, Polly. 1963. *The Migrant Cocoa-Farmers of Southern Ghana. A Study in Rural Capitalism.* Cambridge: Cambridge University Press.

Hinds, James H. 1947. "A Currency Problem—Picturesque Money Customs of the Lobi." *The West African Review* 18: 1428–1430.

Hopkins, Antony G. 1966. "The Currency Revolution in South-West Nigeria in the Late Nineteenth Century." *Journal of the Historical Society of Nigeria* 3 (3): 471–483.

———. 1973. *An Economic History of West Africa*. London: Longman.

Hutchinson, Sharon. 1992. "The Cattle of Money and the Cattle of Girls among the Nuer, 1930–83." *American Ethnologist* 19 (2): 294–316.

Insoll, Timothy, Rachel Maclean, and Benjamin Warinsie Kankpeyeng. 2013. *Temporalising Anthropology: Archaeology in the Talensi Tong Hills, Northern Ghana*. Frankfurt: Africa Magna Verlag.

Johnson, Marion. 1965. *Salaga Papers*. Legon: Institute of African Studies.

———. 1968. "The Nineteenth-Century Gold 'Mithqal' in West and North Africa". *The Journal of African History* 9 (4): 547–569.

———. 1970. "The Cowrie Currencies of West Africa Part I." *The Journal of African History* 11 (1): 17–49.

———. 1986. "The Slaves of Salaga." *The Journal of African History* 27 (2): 341–362.

Kankpeyeng, Benjamin W. 2009. "The Slave Trade in Northern Ghana: Landmarks, Legacies and Connections." *Slavery & Abolition* 30 (2): 209–221.

Kuklick, Henrika. 1979. *The Imperial Bureaucrat: The Colonial Administrative Service in the Gold Coast, 1920–1939*. Stanford, CA: Hoover Institution Press.

Kunkel, Sarah. 2018. "Forced Labour, Roads, and Chiefs: The Implementation of the ILO Forced Labour Convention in the Gold Coast." *International Review of Social History* 63 (3): 449–476.

———. 2019. "Taxation Without Resistance: Native Treasuries in the Northern Territories." *Ghana Studies* 22 (1): 114–145.
Kuroda, Akinobu. 2008. "What Is the Complementarity among Monies? An Introductory Note." *Financial History Review* 15 (1): 7–15.
Lovejoy, Paul E. 1973. "The Kambarin Beriberi: The Formation of a Specialized Group of Hausa Kola Traders in the Nineteenth Century." *The Journal of African History* 14 (4): 633–651.
———. 1982. "Polanyi's 'Ports of Trade': Salaga and Kano in the Nineteenth Century." *Canadian Journal of African Studies/Revue canadienne des études africaines* 16 (2): 245–277.
Maasole, Clifford. 2017. "Tax Collection in Northern Ghana during British Colonial Rule (1898 – 1950)." *Ghana Journal of Development Studies* 14 (2): 267–281.
McPhee, Allan. 1926. *The Economic Revolution in British West Africa*. London: Routledge.
Mtetwa, Richard M. G. 1978. "Myth or Reality: The 'Cattle Complex' in South East Africa, with Special Reference to Rhodesia." *Zambezia* 6 (1): 23–36.
Northcott, Henry P. 1899. *Report on the Northern Territories of the Gold Coast*. London: Harrison and Sons.
Ofonagoro, Walter I. 1979. "From Traditional to British Currency in Southern Nigeria: Analysis of a Currency Revolution, 1880–1948." *The Journal of Economic History* 39 (3): 623–654.
Rattray, Robert S. 1932. *The Tribes of the Ashanti Hinterland*. Oxford: Oxford University Press.
Rouch, Jean. 1956. "Migrations au Ghana (Gold Coast): enquête 1953–1955." *Journal de la Société des Africanistes* 26: 33–196.
Şaul, Mahir. 2004. "Money in Colonial Transition: Cowries and Francs in West Africa." *American Anthropologist* 106 (1): 71–84.
Schildkrout, Enid. 1978. *People of the Zongo: The Transformation of Ethnic Identities in Ghana*. Cambridge: Cambridge University Press.
Scott, James C. 1990. *Domination and the Arts of Resistance: Hidden Transcripts*. New Haven, CT: Yale University Press.
Skinner, Elliott P. 1962. "Trade and Market among the Mossi People." In *Markets in Africa*, edited by Paul Bohannan and George Dalton, 237–278. Evanston, IL: Northwestern University Press.
Sutton, Inez. 1989. "Colonial Agricultural Policy: The Non-Development of the Northern Territories of the Gold Coast." *The International Journal of African Historical Studies* 22 (4): 637.
Swanepoel, Natalie. 2015. "Small Change. Cowries, Coins and the Currency Transition in the Northern Territories of Colonial Ghana." In *Materializing Colonial Encounters. Archaeologies of African Experience*, edited by Francois Richard, 41–69. New York: Springer.

Tauxier, Louis. 1912. *Le noir du Soudan: pays Mossi et Gourounsi: documents et analyses*. Paris: Émile Larose.

Thomas, Roger G. 1983. "The 1916 Bongo 'Riots' and Their Background: Aspects of Colonial Administration and African Response in Eastern Upper Ghana." *The Journal of African History* 24 (1): 57–75.

Wrangham, Elizabeth. 2013. *Ghana during the First World War: The Colonial Administration of Sir Hugh Clifford*. Durham: Carolina Academic Press.

CHAPTER 3

Spheres of Money, Payments, and Credit Systems in the Colony of Senegal in the Long Nineteenth Century

Toyomu Masaki

For a long time, in the field of African studies, the *substantivist* school of economic anthropology, as represented by Karl Polanyi and his followers, has been influential. However, a close look at African behavior regarding money reveals that Africans are just as rational as others. Senegal, which will be the focus of this study, occupies a unique place in Africa: it already had a Western type of issuing bank in the middle of the nineteenth century and experienced the circulation of both *traditional* and *modern*

[1] "Modern money" here simply refers to metal coins and banknotes. While it is true that Europeans introduced these types of money to the African continent, the author does not intend to attribute modernity to Europe and traditionality to Africa by using the term "modern money".

T. Masaki (✉)
Kanazawa University, Kanazawa, Japan
e-mail: tmasaki@staff.kanazawa-u.ac.jp

K. Pallaver (ed.), *Monetary Transitions*,
Palgrave Studies in Economic History,
https://doi.org/10.1007/978-3-030-83461-6_3

monies in parallel for more than several decades until the beginning of the twentieth century.[1] The author has been interested in monetary transitions in Senegal and has wondered what type of conventional financial system had been formed before the introduction of *modern* money and how indigenous people differentiated (or did not differentiate) *traditional* money from *modern* money. The answers to these questions may be helpful in understanding how human beings have recognized an item as money and used it. Furthermore, since *modern* money and some types of *traditional* money were introduced by colonizers, this study may serve to uncover how the monetary spheres of Senegal have been transformed through colonization.

Many scholars have already addressed these questions and provided thoughtful insights. For instance, Karin Pallaver reveals how the people of Uganda accepted colonial money and concludes that this did not entail a simple adoption of outside notions of wealth, but rather Africans created new forms of wealth by reconciling outsiders' views with traditional ones (Pallaver 2015). Relative to Eastern Africa, the monetary transition in West Africa has been investigated by many more researchers. For instance, historians such as Lars Sundström, Philip Curtin, Marion Johnson, Jan Hogendorn, James Webb Jr. and Toby Green uncovered economic transactions involving commodity monies and monetary spheres in different regions of West Africa (Curtin 1983; Green 2019; Hogendorn and Johnson 1986; Johnson 1968, 1970a, b, 1977, 1980; Sundström 1974; Webb 1982, 1999).

The findings of anthropologists and their discussions are also impressive, and they reveal how Africans consciously or unconsciously dealt with money by taking into account issues of rank, power, reciprocity, and gains in African societies (Bohannan 1955, 1959; Geschiere et al. 2007; Guyer 1995, 2004; Geschiere 2007). Furthermore, Lovejoy (1974) shed light on the interregional monetary flows of cowrie shells and silver coins in precolonial Nigeria and revealed the complexity of African monetary systems. For Francophone West Africa, Şaul (2004) and Diallo (2005) explored the transition from cowrie shells to the CFA franc. Paul Bohannan examined such transitions from traditional to colonial currency through the case of the Tiv population in Nigeria as a monetary revolution, and Anthony Hopkins and Walter Ofonagoro redefined this event as a currency revolution (Bohannan 1959; Hopkins 1966; Ofonagoro 1976). However, subsequent research emphasizes that these monetary changes were not drastic enough to be called a revolution (Ofonagoro 1979; Pallaver 2015).

In contrast to anthropologists interested in defining the relationships between money and people in a specific ethnic group or community, economists tend to be preoccupied with the institutional development of broader society and with how a monetary system in a specific region changes through interactions with other societies. The first purpose of this chapter is to present multiple monetary spheres in the colony of Senegal in the Long Nineteenth Century from an economic perspective. Before introducing colonial money, Europeans brought items similar to those that were already circulating as currencies in Africa as a means of exchange for commodities that they sought in Africa. This type of transaction has often been considered a simple form of bartering. However, what actually occurred was more complex than generally believed (Kriger 2017, pp. 23–28). Both parties often exchanged assortments consisting of a variety of goods rather than engaging in one-to-one exchanges. This type of transaction is called *assortment bargaining*, and the commodity that provides the base unit for determining the value of each assortment is known as "imaginary money" or an "interface currency" (Guyer 1995, pp. 8–9). These facts imply that exchanges can take place without money as a mediator. In fact, moneyless credit systems were well developed in West Africa and coexisted with the new method as it was adopted in response to social change (Austin 1993; Stiansen and Guyer 1999).

The second aim of this research is to rethink what money is by showing that the *modern* and *traditional* monetary spheres were not clearly distinguished in this transitional period and that the users of each type of money could not be strictly categorized along European/African lines. Rather, we can say that both Europeans and Africans chose the money that best suited their purposes, regardless of its type.

The period covered in this study starts with the French Revolution and ends with World War I. During this era, France completed its colonization of Senegal. At the same time, France itself experienced a significant transition in its monetary regime. First, at the end of the eighteenth century, a new currency unit, the franc, replaced the old one, the *livre*. Subsequently, Napoléon Bonaparte established the Bank of France in 1800 and the franc *germinal* in 1803.

The French franc coins issued in metropolitan France were used in Senegal and French West Africa (Gadoury and Cousinié 1979; Zay 1892). Although the Bank of Senegal, which was given the privilege of issuing banknotes to the colony of Senegal, was established in Saint Louis in 1854, the banknotes did not drastically replace traditional monies. In addition, several different types of monies coexisted with traditional credit systems. In fact, since Africans were often reluctant to receive *modern* money, Europeans needed to exert much effort to have Africans accept it. This reluctance is often explained as a resistance to colonialism or adhesion to traditional culture. However, I question this argument because humans generally seek to use useful instruments that will deliver the most convenience while considering both the advantages and disadvantages of their use, and Africans are no exception.

This chapter first introduces a brief history of the colonization of Senegal and its socioeconomic transition that occurred in the nineteenth century. Second, it describes several different monies, from commodity monies to banknotes that were used in this period. Third, it describes how the credit system worked in this colony. Finally, it argues for the complexity of the multiple monetary and credit spheres that existed in Senegal during the transition from the precolonial to the colonial era and examines the conditions prompting economic agents to choose an item as "money."

The Establishment of the Colony of Senegal and the Shift in Export Commodities

Although the economic and political relationships between France and Senegal started with the arrival of Dieppe fishermen from Normandy to the coastal area of Senegambia in the middle of the fourteenth century, it was in the 1630s that France officially established its first settlement in Sub-Saharan Africa, Saint Louis, on an island close to the mouth of the Senegal River.[2] Subsequently, France obtained some settlements such as Gorée, Arguin, and Rufisque, although these trading posts were sometimes seized by rival European countries during the revolutions and wars of the eighteenth century. Finally, with the Treaty of Paris of 1814–1815, Saint Louis, Gorée, and some trading posts in the Senegambia region were officially recognized as French territories, while the British obtained

[2] The interaction with Dieppe fishermen in the fourteenth century was officially reported by French administrators in *Annuaire Sénégal et dépendances*, which was published yearly by the colonial government. In 1638, a French factory was established by Thomas Lambert on the Island of Bocos, at the mouth of the Senegal River.

possession of the territory along the Gambia River except for Albreda, which was a French territory by 1857 (Map 3.1).

Throughout more than 500 years of exchange with Europeans, both Saint Louis and Gorée had developed into unique places with a mixed Euro-African atmosphere (Pasquier 1987). Moreover, these two islands functioned as junctions between two worlds: Africa and the rest of the world. European merchants living there focused on imports and exports from and to the outside world. In contrast, trade with the inland areas was left to *Métis* or African merchants, who often formed cliental relationships with African chiefs or Muslim religious leaders in the hinterland. Europeans could not expand their businesses without relying on these merchants.

In 1848, slavery was abolished in all French colonies including Senegal, and a part of the compensation paid to the slave owners was used to establish the Bank of Senegal. By a decree dated August 10, 1872, Saint Louis and Gorée became full-fledged municipalities known as *communes,* and

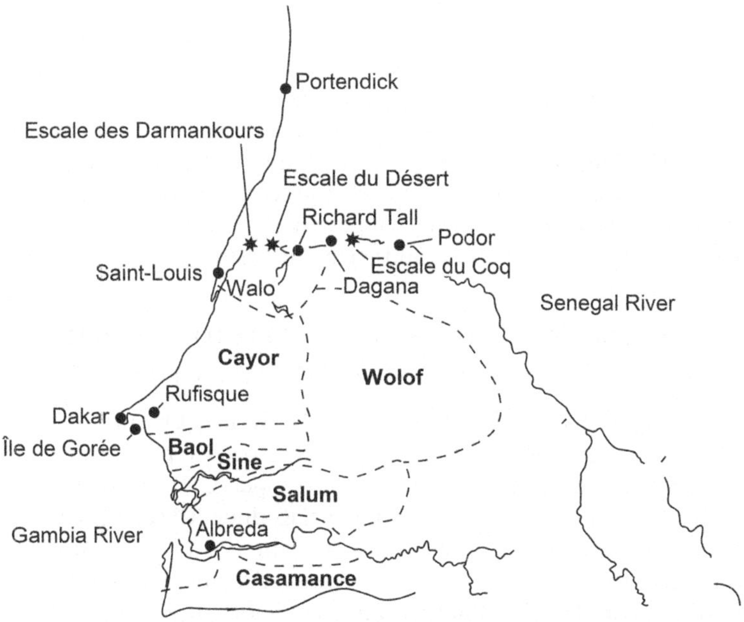

Map 3.1 Senegambia in the mid-nineteenth century

the inhabitants were entitled to the same rights and privileges as French citizens (Idowu 1968). Rufisque (1880) and Dakar (1887) later received the same privilege.

For the remaining areas, France initially adopted a protectorate policy to annex the territories controlled by African chiefs. By the order of January 15, 1890, the colony of Senegal was divided into three types of status: four *communes* (*quatre communes*), territories under direct administration, and territories under protection (*pays de protectorat*), which refer to territories annexed through the signing of treaties of protection with African rulers (Thiam 1997, p. 254). The inhabitants of the territories under protection did not have the privileges that were entitled to those in the four communes, and all powers were vested in the commandant of the *cercle*, a unit of French political administration for French Colonial Africa.

At the beginning of the nineteenth century, the main purpose of European business with Africa shifted from slave trade to legitimate commerce. Gum arabic harvested in the Sahel and traded by North African merchants became the most important Senegalese export product. After the mid-nineteenth century, groundnuts cultivated by African farmers in Cayor, Baol, Sine-Saloum and Casamance became the most sought item in Senegal, replacing gum arabic. Shifts in export products and their suppliers also altered the means of exchange that France brought to Senegal (Marfaing 1991). However, the nature of the local trade system, which was based on credit, did not change considerably, although some modifications were made with changes in the social environment, the structure of the trade network, and payment methods.

Commodity Monies Exported to Senegal: Iron Bars and *Guinée* Cloth

Curiously, cowry shells imported from the Indian Ocean, which were widely circulated in West Africa, have rarely been reported in Senegal. Instead, when Europeans arrived in the Upper Guinea coast, Africans were already using iron bars as money (Rodney 1970, p. 194). Iron smelting technology was developed in the interior of West Africa by at least the fourth century B.C., but iron-producing industries did not exist along the coast (Jemkur 2004, p. 33). Therefore, it is natural that iron became a sought-after material on the Upper Guinean coast. This iron trade created a new form of exchange currency based on the standardized weight and length of an iron bar. In response to this system, Europeans brought similar types of iron bars to Senegambia. For example, Philip Curtin reported that iron bars, each of which was approximately 3 m long, 5 cm wide, and 9 mm thick and weighed approximately 13 kg, were exported from Europe to Senegambia in the middle of the seventeenth century, and cut into approximately 20-cm long rods after arriving in West Africa to serve as a form of currency (Curtin 1975, p. 241). These iron bars served as currencies but at the same time were materials to be melted to make agricultural tools or weapons. However, the currency system using the iron bars collapsed by the end of the eighteenth century due to the depreciation of their value (Curtin 1975, pp. 240–257). Instead, silver coins and *guinée* cloth became important commodities serving currency functions in Senegambia in the nineteenth century. To be precise, silver coins replaced the iron bar currency on the coast, while *guinée* cloth replaced it along the Senegal River.

Guinée refers to a type of Guinea cloth that was often used as a means of exchange for African commodities that Europeans sought (Masaki 2015a). *Guinée* cloth itself came in several types, but the *guinée* transported to the upper Guinea Coast was almost always cotton cloth dyed dark blue with indigo, which was similar to the cotton cloth circulating as money in the western Sahel, known as *baysa-al-nila* in the local language (Masaki 2021; Lydon 2009). Although cloth was mostly of domestic manufacture when used as currency in West Africa, Hogendorn and Gemery emphasized that the single important exception is this *guinée* (Hogendorn and Gemery 1988, p. 131). Unlike the narrow strips that were widely produced in West Africa and that served as money in Senegambia, *guinée* or *baysa* was wide cloth having an approximate length of 15 m and a width of 1–1.5 m (Lydon 2009, p. 251). The inhabitants of the western Sahel appreciated this Indian *guinée* cloth and requested it as a means of exchange for gum arabic, which was in high demand in Europe. Therefore, France transported *guinée* with similar specifications, initially from India and later from Europe, to Senegal. For example, the *guinée* specified by the French Royal Ordinance of 1843 for gum arabic trade along the Senegal River was 1.0 m in width, 16.5 m in length, and 2.3 kg in weight, but the cloth gradually grew smaller and lighter (Masaki 2015a). This *guinée* cloth was transported from Saint Louis to trade centers known as *escales* established along the Senegal River, from where it was brought to the western Sahel and circulated as money. Although some accounts say that French merchants in Gorée transported *guinée* to Gambia as a means of exchange for groundnuts, *guinée* was not an important form of money in southern Senegal.[3] Since the narrow strips of cotton cloth were traditionally used as money in the greater Senegambia, *guinée* was likely sometimes received as money in Gambia. However, French five-franc silver coins mainly served as a means of payment for groundnuts.

These commodity monies are often recognized as one-way money (Johnson 1980, p. 196). However, when there was an organization that encouraged the circulation of money, commodity money also must have circulated. For instance, France penetrated inland West Africa from Saint Louis along the Senegal River. In areas where France had not yet established its control, Africans were, of course, reluctant to accept French currencies. Therefore, France had to provide items that were very similar to the monies that the Africans used, to procure food and services on site. Consequently, the French colonial administration brought *guinée* cloth inland to accomplish its purposes. Furthermore, the colonial government received poll taxes and local tariffs (*oussourou*) with *guinée* cloth, and the *guinée* collected was reused for administrative purposes (i.e., for the payment of customs duties to the heads of villages or ethnic groups).[4] This arrangement proves that not only Africans but also the French colonial government itself officially used commodity monies and that even commodity money circulated under an institution established by colonizers.

In the early nineteenth century, the price of a piece of *guinée* was approximately 20–25 francs in Saint Louis, and it gradually decreased over the course of the nineteenth century reaching approximately 10 francs by the end of the century, except during the American Civil War, when cotton prices soared globally (Masaki 2015a). Charles Cerisier, who was the General Secretary of the Society for Colonial and Maritime Studies (*Société des Études Coloniales et Maritimes*) and a member of the Statistical Society of Paris (*Société de Statistique de Paris*) reported in 1885 that

[3] The minutes of the Bordeaux Chamber of Commerce for 22 June 1875, Chambre de Commerce de Bordeaux, Extraits des Procés-Verbaux, 1875: pp. 531–532; The minutes of the Bordeaux Chamber of Commerce for 20 April 1880, Chambre de Commerce de Bordeaux, Extraits des Procés-Verbaux, 1880: pp. 416–427, Archives Départmentales de la Gironde (ADG), BIB 7 I/M1.

[4] See Arreté of November 27, 1893 and that of February 21, 1895 in Ministère de la marine et des colonies, Bulletin Administratif du Sénégal, each annual volume. About *oussourou*, see Masaki (2021).

a cow and a horse were, respectively, equivalent in value to 7–10 pieces and 50–100 pieces of *guinée* (Cerisier 1885, p. 75). These facts suggest that a piece of *guinée* was a quite large denomination of money. As small change, it was paid per cubit. Furthermore, at that time, one piece of *guinée* still weighted approximately 1.4–2.0 kg, while two five-franc coins (10 francs) only weighted 50 g. In this sense, the transaction costs of *guinée* were very high in terms of portability. Nevertheless, *guinée* was still used as money in Senegal and further inland areas.

A Credit System Developed with Commodity Money: The Case of *Guinée* Cloth

Guinée cloth was not always directly exchanged for commodities on the spot. Rather, it sometimes functioned as a means for trading based on credit. European merchants wisely used and improved upon the traditional African credit system to obtain the African commodities that they sought. At the same time, this system enabled African merchants who did not have enough initial capital to establish their businesses.

In the trade of *guinée* cloth and gum arabic, three main agents, *négociants* (wholesale merchants), *traitants* (middlemen dealers), and North African traders (the *Moors* who provided gum arabic), were involved. As Fig. 3.1 shows, *guinée* was exchanged for gum arabic in markets established along the Senegal River known as *escales*. Until the late nineteenth century, Europeans were not permitted to do business in these *escale*s and left this activity to *traitants*. African *traitants* initially obtained *guinée* in advance from *négociants* in Saint Louis with or without collateral such as gold or silver jewelry or other properties. Next, the *traitants* went to *escale*s with the *guinée* and conducted business with the North African traders. The exchange rates between gum arabic and *guinée* cloth in Saint Louis were determined when the *guinée* was distributed to the *traitants*. Therefore, the *traitants* could make a profit only when the difference between the two exchange rates in Saint Louis and the *escale*s was sufficiently large, and they incurred losses when this was not the case.

A letter sent by the governor of Senegal to the Office of the Trade Policy Regime in Paris in September 1841 offers an overview of this

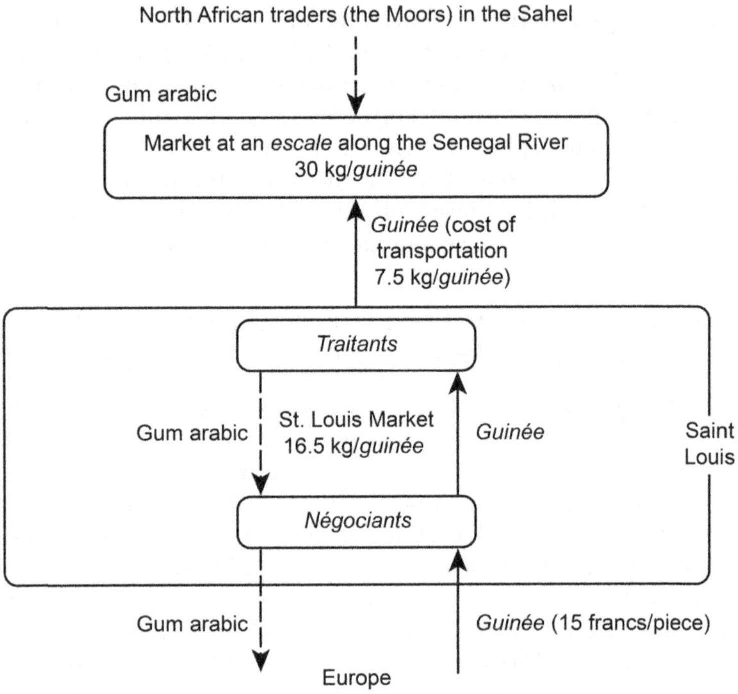

Fig. 3.1 Exchange markets for guinée and gum arabic (kg) and exchange rates (1841) (*Source* Letter, dated September 11, 1841 from the Governor of Senegal to the Office of the Trade Policy Regime (Bureau du Régime Politique du Commerce), Archives national du Sénégal (ANS)/2B18)

business.[5] The *guinée*-gum arabic trade in 1841 was regulated by the government, and the *négociants* sold a piece of *guinée* on credit to *traitants* in Saint Louis for 16.5 kg of gum arabic. The cost of transporting a piece of *guinée* cloth between Saint Louis and an *escale* was approximately equivalent to 7.5 kg of gum arabic. Thus, the total cost of bringing a piece of *guinée* cloth to an *escale* was approximately equivalent to 24 kg of gum arabic. In the same year, in an *escale*, *traitants* could approximately obtain 30 kg of gum arabic per piece of *guinée* cloth, including 10

[5] In a letter dated September 11, 1841 from the Governor of Senegal to the Office of the Trade Policy Regime (Bureau du Régime Politique du Commerce), ANS/2B18.

percent charges, leaving the *traitants* with a profit of 6 kg of gum arabic per *guinée* cloth. In Saint Louis, 1 kg of gum arabic was sold for 1.3 francs, meaning that the *traitants* made a profit of 7.8 francs per piece of *guinée* cloth.[6] Conversely, since the price of *guinée* exported from Europe to Saint Louis was approximately 15 francs, the *négociants* in Saint Louis could make a profit of 6.45 francs from 16.5 kg of gum arabic, which was equivalent to 21.45 francs (16.5 kg × 1.3 francs). Thus, in 1841, both the *traitants* and *négociants* had sound profit margins.

However, if the quantity of gum arabic obtained from a piece of *guinée* cloth in an *escale* was less than the amount agreed upon in Saint Louis, the *traitants* owed the *négociants* a debt. This phenomenon was created by heavy competition among an increasing number of *traitants* and the removal of regulations. According to Bouët-Willaumez, who came to Senegal as a governor in 1843, the number of *traitants* increased from 40 in 1818 to 150 in 1837 (Bouët-Willaumez 1848, pp. 12–13). Therefore, in the 1840s, the colonial government sometimes attempted to regulate the number of *traitants* and the gum arabic trade, though not always successfully (Hardy 1921; Schefer 1921).

Silver Coins: Commodity or "Modern" Money?

Silver coins were legal tender in France, but we can say that Africans initially recognized it as a commodity because they melted the coins down to transform them into accessories. Nevertheless, we can say that silver coins were the only currency that was widely accepted both in Europe and Senegal in this period.

Relative to its prevalence on the eastern side of the African continent, the Maria Theresa thaler was less commonly used in Senegal, but Spanish dollars were circulating widely by the end of the eighteenth century. The British colonial government made this currency an official medium of exchange when it occupied Saint Louis in the late eighteenth century, and France took over the system when it retook Saint Louis in 1779 (Curtin 1975, p. 265). With a law promulgated on March 28, 1803, France adopted a bimetallic system under Napoléon Bonaparte and began to mint a silver coin of 90% fineness. In particular, the five-franc silver coin, known as the *gourde* or *écu*, was easily accepted by Africans because

[6] In this rough calculation, the cost of carrying gum arabic back to the coast seems to be included.

it was almost the same size as that of eight *reales* (Spanish silver coins). In 1864, the purity of the silver coins was debased from 90 to 83.5% except for the five-franc coins, which probably increased the popularity of the five-franc coin, and it ultimately became the most widely circulated silver coin in the Senegambia region (Gardner 2015).

The method used to calculate amounts of money in present-day Senegal is still rooted in the five-franc coin. A five-franc silver coin was called a *dërëm* in Wolof, which is assumed to originate from the word *dirham*, a unit of currency used in North Africa. In present-day Senegal, people call the 50 CFA franc piece a *fukki*, which derives from the Wolof word *fukk*, meaning the number ten. Thus, *fukki* concretely indicates *fukki dërëm*, ten 5-franc coins, or 50 CFA francs. In the same way, the Senegalese call 1000 CFA francs *ñaari teemeeri*, which indicates the number 200, implying 200 five-franc coins. The amount expressed in Wolof thus becomes a fifth of the actual figure because it is expressed based on the number of five-franc coins. This fact indicates the importance of the effects that French five-franc coins had on Senegalese society.

The *Modern* Financial System Developed by Colonizers

In 1854, France established the Bank of Senegal, which was the first issuing bank to appear in Sub-Saharan Africa.[7] The bank started its operation in Saint Louis in August 1855 and opened a new branch in Gorée in 1871, which was transferred to Dakar in 1884. Another new branch was established in Rufisque, a center for groundnut production, in 1899. Finally, the bank was reorganized into the Bank of West Africa (*Banque d'Afrique Occidentale*) in 1901. Although the bank was owned by shareholders, its operation was under the control of the French government.

The Bank of Senegal initially issued banknotes in denominations of 25, 100, and 500 francs and in denominations of 5 francs from 1874. These banknotes were known as local francs and circulated only within the

[7] This section provides an overview of the Bank of Senegal based on Masaki (2015b) with updated information.

colony of Senegal and were printed in France and sent to the bank's headquarters in Saint Louis, from where they were issued with the signatures of the director and auditor of the bank. Metropolitan and local francs were supposed to have equal book values. However, these banknotes were not positively received by the indigenous population. Consequently, the demand for silver coins was much greater than that for banknotes. Table 3.1 indicates the annual movements of banknotes and specie in the vault of the Bank of Senegal for the years 1889/90 and 1896/97. The table shows that there was 8–10 times more demand for specie than banknotes within the same period. A probable reason for this finding is that the denominations of the banknotes were too large for use in daily life. In addition, paper money was easily damaged by the tropical climate and insects in Africa.

The Bank of Senegal also functioned as a commercial bank. The most important services of the Bank were providing credits for the local economy and exchange services. For the first service, the bank discounted local bills of exchange with signatures of two solvent persons.[8] In addition, the bank provided collateral loan services. A report from a shareholder meeting held on July 9, 1872, reveals that the stock of gold or silver deposited for collateral loans reached 200,300 francs, which was equivalent to 13.43% of the bank's total assets at the time.[9] Some African merchants who could not obtain credit from European merchants seemed to rely on this collateral loan service to develop their business with metropolitan France.[10] However, letters giving notice of the repayment day were often ineffective for people who could not read French.[11] Indigenous people were already accustomed to collateral loans by European merchants even before the bank was established, which probably facilitated them to use this service. Furthermore, the revision of the articles of association in 1874 enabled the bank to invest in bonds that local governments in France or in the colonies issued under certain conditions.

For the exchange service, the bank mediated financial settlements between the colony and metropolitan France through a designated bank

[8] One signature could be replaced by collateral such as merchandise, stocks, precious metals, or bonds.

[9] Banque du Sénégal, *Compte-rendu des operations de la Banque présenté au nom du conseil d'administration*, 1871–1872, p. 8, FR/ANOM/FM/ Sénégal/IX66.

[10] Ibid., p. 5.

[11] Ibid.

Table 3.1 The movement of banknotes and specie in the vault of the Bank of Senegal in Saint Louis (francs)

1889/1890	*June 30, 1889*	*Received*	*Disbursed*	*June 30, 1890*
Banknotes	420,925.00	883,340.00	1,032,125.00	272,140.00
Specie	375,869.28	8,444,835.30	8,378,718.63	521,810.29
1896/1897	*June 30, 1889*	*Received*	*Disbursed*	*June 30, 1897*
Banknotes	357,015.00	1,174,775.00	943,225.00	588,565.00
Specie	478,673.94	10,148,955.14	9,958,775.56	668,853.52

Source Banque du Sénégal, *Compte-rendu des operations de la Banque présenté au nom du conseil d'administration*, 1880, France (FR)/ Archives nationales d'outre-mer (ANOM)/ Fonds ministériels (FM)/ Sénégal/IX66; 1897, ANS/Q39

in Paris: initially the Bank of France and, beginning in the 1870s, the Paris Discount House (*Comptoir national d'escompte de Paris*). For instance, for the export business, the bank discounted the bills of exchange that exporters in Senegal drew on importers in France. For the import business, in exchange for local francs that the importers provided, the bank issued a money order (*mandat*), and the recipient of the *mandat* could receive payment for his export in metropolitan francs from a designated bank in Paris (Amaïzo 2001, pp. 120–21). This *mandat* was also used when the bank procured silver coins from Paris.

The value of the bills discounted by the Bank of Senegal from 1865 to 1866 was 555,184.55 francs.[12] Thirty years later, this amount had increased more than nine times to 5,093,006.20 francs.[13] In contrast, although the amount of *mandat* issued by the bank was large from the start, it did not increase as much as that of the bills discounted for local transactions: 1,248,033.97 francs in 1865/1866 and 1,997,920.20 francs in 1895/1896.[14] One of the reasons could be the start of the postal

[12] Banque du Sénégal, *Rapport sur les opérations de la Banque*, 1865–1866, p. 4, FR/ANOM/FM/ Sénégal/IX66.

[13] Banque du Sénégal, *Compte-rendu des operations de la Banque présenté au nom du conseil d'administration*, 1895–1896, p. 7, FR/ANOM/FM/ Sénégal/IX66.

[14] Banque du Sénégal, *Rapport sur les opérations de la Banque*, 1865–1866, p. 10; Banque du Sénégal, *Compte-rendu des operations de la Banque présenté au nom du conseil d'administration*, 1895–1896, p. 9, FR/ANOM/FM/ Sénégal/IX66.

money order service in 1870s.[15] The service first enabled the remittance of money between a colony and metropolitan France and was later expanded to remittances between colonies and the rest of the world.

The maximum amount of remittance per one postal money order was initially fixed at 500 francs (AOF 1918). This amount was almost equivalent to the annual remuneration of indigenous unskilled labor employed by the colonial government.[16] The numbers of postal money orders issued by 1907 in the colony of Senegal and in the colony of Upper Senegal and Niger were 9346 and 6052, respectively, and the average amounts per postal money order for each colony were 79 and 29–30 francs, respectively (AOF 1907, Chap. 9). These statistics indicate that a significant number of postal money orders were used but that the amount for each remittance was comparatively modest.

The Development of a Credit System Without the Intermediation of Money

By the establishment of the Bank of Senegal in 1854, banknotes and a formal financial institution were introduced in Senegal, but traditional credit systems without money as a mediator did not disappear; instead, such systems continued to exist in a different way in response to social and economic changes. In the mid-nineteenth century, groundnuts became the most important Senegalese export commodity. Among farmers in the groundnut cultivation area, silver coins were popular as a means of payment for their harvests. However, until the late 1870s when the Latin Monetary Union converted to a *de facto* gold standard, silver coins were particularly in short supply in Senegal (Masaki 2016). Even after this point, the Bank of Senegal could not soundly provide sufficient silver coins to satisfy the demand created by the rapid expansion of groundnut production.

[15] From July 1, 1874, postal money order services were opened to the public, but they were temporarily suspended by the Minister of Finances on May 5, 1876 and restarted with the decree of 26 June 1878, see AOF (1907).

[16] According to the local budget determined for 1880, the annual remuneration of a handyman employed by the court of justice was 480 francs, and that of a surveillant agent of a prison was 500 francs. Sénégal et Dépendances, Budget local exercise 1880, p. 12, 16, FR/ANOM/FM/Sénégal/IX7.

To obtain African commodities, Europe-based import–export companies had established an extensive and tight purchasing network by the end of the nineteenth century (Guiraud 1938; Marfaing 1991, 1992; Péhaut 1986; Thiam 2007). Each network formed a hierarchy with a general agent at the top, known as a *comptoir*, based in Saint Louis or Dakar. The *comptoir* also had regional branches (*factoreries*) in some important interior cities. Furthermore, each regional branch had several local agencies under its umbrella further inland. At the bottom of the hierarchy, African dealers served as intermediaries between a local agency and groundnut farmers and were often based in stores known as *boutiques* and sometimes went to trading places (*escales*) established close to the farmers. In principle, the *comptoirs* in Saint Louis or Dakar were subsidiaries of a European-based company, but the further down the hierarchy one went, the more African merchants or dealers were involved in this system. In addition, after the First World War, Syro-Lebanese immigrants took up the role of mediating between the *comptoirs* and African dealers. Groundnuts collected by a store were sent to the *comptoir*, moving up this hierarchy, and silver coins and imported goods moved downward to the stores. European trading companies provided a set of different types of merchandise to the dealers in exchange for groundnuts. Cotton cloth, arms, and alcohol were often noted as popular products among indigenous people.

The import–export business requires sufficient initial capital to sustain the business until the merchandise can be transformed into cash. Therefore, African dealers who did not have enough capital often had to borrow in advance from European companies the merchandise or silver coins required to purchase groundnuts. These dealers paid off the debt with groundnuts after the harvest, and if they could not pay off the debt, the collateral they had deposited was confiscated. A similar phenomenon occurred in the transactions between African merchants and farmers, where African farmers often had to borrow seeds and food (rice or millet) in advance from African dealers to sustain themselves until the harvest (Thiam 2007, p. 223). Sometimes, the farmers even borrowed cash to pay taxes or purchase necessities (Thiam 2007, p. 230), and they paid off the debt with groundnuts at the harvest. The African farmers at the bottom of the hierarchy often suffered from high borrowing costs.

Some African dealers accumulated profits by wisely navigating this credit system. First, the dealers often asked for collateral from peasants to provide credit, and when the farmers defaulted, they sold the collateral at a higher price than the lending portfolio. Jewelry, cotton cloth and livestock were often used as collateral. Second, the dealers often made multiple transactions in a season. In Senegal, groundnuts are planted in June and harvested in November. For instance, suppose that the merchandise that the African dealers borrowed from the merchants at a higher position in this hierarchy was first exchanged for local products such as millet. These products were lent to groundnut producers in June, and the loans were repaid in groundnuts in December (Marfaing 1991, p. 337; Thiam 2007, p. 118). Even in this simple example, African dealers were afforded two chances to secure net margins per season. In fact, independent African dealers accumulated profits by rotating numerous times the capital or credit that they borrowed from the merchants above them in the hierarchy before paying it back (Fall and Sow 1992; Marfaing 1991; Sow 1992; Thiam 2007).

Of course, it was essential for African dealers to obtain groundnuts from farmers at a better rate than their repayment rate to European merchants; otherwise, they would accumulate deficits. Generally, a high-return business entails a high degree of risk. In reality, both African farmers and dealers often suffered from accumulated debt. Therefore, the colonial administration attempted to regulate this system several times. Finally, France introduced a system to establish a mutual-aid fund (*Société indigenes de prevoyance*) for each *cercle* in 1910 and an agricultural loan bank for Senegal, known as *Crédit Agricole*, by decree on 23 May 1926; however, the system was unable to completely resolve this issue (Thiam 2007).

As we have seen, providing European products as a means of payment for African commodities has often been considered nothing more than a means of simple bartering by outsiders. However, what actually occurred was more complex than bartering. Furthermore, the products were not exchanged on site but were traded over a long period of time. In this sense, such an exchange should be recognized as a credit system without the intermediation of money.

Coexistence of Multiple Spheres of Money, Payment, and Credit Systems as an Outcome of the Rational Behaviors of Economic Agents

The following is an overview of the monetary spheres of the colony of Senegal and its dependent areas in the long nineteenth century. First, indigenous people had their own monetary system before contact with Europeans. Therefore, the Europeans first introduced commodity monies that were similar to the monies used in the area in the precolonial period as means of payment for African commodities they sought. Iron bars and *guinée* cloth were the most frequently mentioned commodity monies imported from outside of the African continent to Senegal. Among them, iron bars became less popular during the era of the French Revolution due to the depreciation of their value and were hardly in use in the nineteenth century in Senegal. On the other hand, *guinée* cloth functioned as money until the beginning of the twentieth century. Especially in areas where coins or banknotes were not circulating, the colonial government allowed Africans to pay their poll taxes with *guinée* cloth and reused this tax revenue as a part of its expenditures. This fact indicates that not only Africans but also Europeans relied on commodity money in Senegal.

In the middle of the nineteenth century, France established the Bank of Senegal. However, the indigenous populations were reluctant to accept banknotes. Africans did not refuse the banknotes because they were too novel or because they were introduced by the colonizers. In fact, the commercial banking services were frequently used not only by Europeans but also by Africans. Rather, the large European trading houses in Senegal did not need to rely on the services provided by the Bank of Senegal because they could make settlements through the headquarters in Europe and import silver coins on their own ships from Europe to Senegal (Lydon 1997). In contrast, Africans, including those who did not know how to read French, used the bank services, even providing their gold or silver jewelry as collateral to the bank. The bills of exchange that the bank provided facilitated commercial payments and credit facilities within the colony and economic transactions with France, regardless of the backgrounds of the users.

French silver coins were the only form of money that was positively and widely accepted in both metropolitan France and African communities. The coins were provided by the Bank of Senegal as well as the French merchants themselves. In the late 1870s, the value of silver had greatly depreciated in Europe, and France moved from bimetallism to a limping standard system. Consequently, a massive export of silver coins to the country's colonies started. France wisely obtained its wanted products with its unwanted coins.

How did Africans handle these completely different types of money: *guinée* cloth, banknotes, and silver coins? A report published in Bordeaux in 1879 states that people living along the southern reaches of the Senegal River and Africans living near French posts preferred to be paid in five-franc silver coins because they were easy to carry and exchange (Négociants Sénégalais 1879). The North African traders also preferred to be paid in silver coins when they were trading between Saint Louis and Gorée, but they switched to *guinée* before they returned to the desert because it was the only means of payment that allowed them to obtain livestock or foodstuffs there (Négociants Sénégalais 1879). In this regard, Kobayashi (2019, pp.102-110) presents an interesting interpretation of the exchange between *guinée* and millets in Senegal based on the complementarity among monies established by Akinobu Kuroda (Kuroda 2003, 2008a, b). However, further investigations are needed to determine whether millets functioned as small change in Kuroda's context. In 1911, the French colonial administration reported that emigrants who left the Nioro *cercle* in the colony of Upper Senegal and Niger to work on farms and construction sites sent money to their families in their hometowns by postal money order (AOF 1911). A manual for post office employees in those days provides instructions on how to assist illiterate service users (AOF 1918). These accounts imply that the Africans who could not read French letters and their families in inland West Africa recognized francs as their money and used the modern cash transfer system; they also show that there was not a distinct monetary zone for Africans and another for Europeans.

In Senegal, the advanced credit system in which some commodities were handed over in advance for the purpose of obtaining future harvests was also well developed. This system can be recognized as a form of bartering in the sense that European goods were exchanged for African commodities, but it should also be recognized as a credit system without the intermediation of money. Although this system did not require money itself as a means of payment for goods, it increased the money supply in society through a money creation mechanism involving multiple rotations of credit facilities in the market. Of course, the expansion of credit without the expansion of the real economy destabilizes the economy itself. The recession that occurred at the end of the nineteenth century resulted in many bankruptcies, and some independent African merchants also became mere employees of European companies. Thus, the Senegalese economy was sufficiently capitalistic even before there was substantial circulation of *modern* money.

Conclusion

This chapter first showed that several different types of money and means of settlement coexisted in Senegal, the oldest French colony in West Africa, in the Long Nineteenth Century. Next, it provided that the monetary transition from commodity monies to *modern* money happened gradually and was not revolutionary even in Senegal, which had an issuing bank by the middle of the nineteenth century. Each money or monetary institution had both advantages and disadvantages, and each monetary sphere was not identical but not completely distinct. The chapter showed that, in this complex context, the economic agents in Senegal in the middle of the nineteenth century chose the most suitable money for their purposes and the Africans did not confine themselves to the use of commodity currencies. The colonial government also used commodity money in areas where silver coins and banknotes were not adequately available.

Money is expected to maintain its value from when economic agents receive it to when they pay with it. Indeed, iron bars that lost their value were no longer circulated as money by the beginning of the nineteenth century. The same result occurred for *guinée* cloth at the beginning of the twentieth century when the colonial government decided not to accept commodity monies. In this regard, Antony Hopkins also points out that the traditional currency system was in decline by 1880 in Southern Nigeria due to cowrie inflation and the demonetization of foreign silver coins rather than a result of colonizers' efforts (Hopkins 1966). Unlike commodity monies, which have no central organization to control their issuance, stabilizing the value of *modern* money has been relatively easy, and this type of money has continued to be used for quite a long time. However, African national currencies tend to depreciate relative to developed countries' currencies. This fact has driven Africans to be more positive to have new monies (e.g., virtual and mobile currency) than people in developed countries. Although money that has a higher value than its face value is held and does not circulate in the market, money that is losing value is also unwanted and is replaced with other alternatives by market forces.

It is not surprising that the economic conditions faced by economic agents in Senegal were very different from those in Europe. Consequently, such agents' choices or attitudes regarding money were necessarily different from those assumed in Western society, as anthropologists often point out. However, this conclusion does not imply that Africans do not make rational choices about money in the market.

Acknowledgements This work was supported by JSPS KAKENHI Grant Numbers JP19H01513 (PI: Takeshi Nishimura) and JP20K01805 (PI: Toyomu Masaki). This study is a major revision and restructuring of a paper entitled "Multiple Monies in Senegambia (1815–1901) — Indian Cotton, Silver Coin, and Paper Money," which was presented at the World Economic History Congress 2015 (Session: The interaction between the multiple payment systems and the emerging banking infrastructures in global and historical comparison, chaired by Mina Ishizu, Christiaan van Bochove, and Takeshi Nishimura).

References

Amaïzo, Yves Ekoué. 2001. *Naissance d'une Banque de la Zone Franc: 1848-1901: Priorité aux propriétaires d'esclaves*. Paris: L'Harmattan.

AOF. 1907. *Les postes et télégraphes en Afrique occidentale*. Paris: Crété.

———. 1911. *Rapport d'ensemble annuel*. Paris: AOF.

———. 1918. *Instruction n° 1 à l'usage du personnel des postes et des télégraphes*. Paris: De Oberthur.

Austin, Gareth. 1993. "Indigenous Credit Institutions in West Africa, c.1750–c.1960." In *Local Suppliers of Credit in the Third World, 1750–1960*, edited by Gareth Austin and Kaoru Sugihara, 93–159. London: Palgrave Macmillan.

Bohannan, Paul. 1955. "Some Principles of Exchange and Investment among the Tiv." *American Anthropologist* 57: 60–70.

———. 1959. "The Impact of Money on an African Subsistence Economy." *The Journal of Economic History* 19 (4): 491–503.

Bouët-Willaumez, Louis Edouard. 1848. *Commerce et traite des noirs aux côtes occidentales d'Afrique*. Paris: Imprimerie Nationale.

Cerisier, Charle. 1885. "Les colonies françaises." *Journal de la société statistique de Paris* 26: 69–88.

Curtin, Philip. 1975. *Economic Change in Precolonial Africa. Senegambia in the Era of the Slave Trade*. Madison, WI: University of Wisconsin Press.

———. 1983. "Africa and the Wider Monetary World, 1250-1850." In *Precious Metals in the Later Medieval and Early Modern Worlds*, edited by John F. Richards, 231–268. Durham: Carolina Academic Press.

Diallo, Booubacar S. 2005. "Des cauris au franc CFA." In *Mali-France regards sur une histoire partagée*, edited by Pierre Boilley, 405–431. Paris: Karthala.

Fall, Babacar and Abdoul Sow. 1992. "Les traitants saint-louisiens dans les villes-escales du Sénégal 1850–1920." In *Commerce et commerçants en Afrique de l'Ouest*, edited by Boubacar Barry and Leonhard Harding, 155–190. Paris: L'Harmattan.

Gadoury, Victor and Georges Cousinié. 1979. *Monnaies coloniales françaises: 1670–1980*. Monte-Carlo: Gadoury.

Gardner, Leigh. 2015. "The Curious Incident of the Franc in the Gambia: Exchange Rate Instability and Imperial Monetary Systems in the 1920s." *Financial History Review* 22: 291–314.

Geschiere, Peter. 2007. "Regional Shifts—Marginal Gains and Ethnic Stereotypes." *African Studies Review* 50 (2): 43–56.

Geschiere, Peter, Mitzi Goheen and Charles Piot. 2007. "Introduction: Marginal Gains Revisited." *African Studies Review* 50 (2): 37–41.

Green, Toby. 2019. *A Fistful of Shells: West Africa from the Rise of the Slave Trade to the Age of Revolution*. Chicago, IL: University of Chicago Press.

Guiraud, Xavier. 1937. L'*arachide sénégalaise*. Paris: Librarie technique et économique.

Guyer, Jane I. 1995. "Introduction: The Currency Interface and Its Dynamics." In *Money Matters: Instability, Values and Social Payments in the Modern History of West African Communities*, edited by Jane I. Guyer, 1-33. Portsmouth, N.H. & London: Heinemann & James Currey.

———. 2004. *Marginal Gains: Monetary Transactions in Atlantic Africa*. Chicago, IL: The University of Chicago Press.

Hardy, Georges. 1921. *La mise en valeur du Sénégal de 1817 à 1854*. Paris: E. Larose.

Hogendorn, Jan S. and Henry A. Gemery. 1988. "Continuity in West African Monetary History? An Outline of Monetary Development." *African Economic History* 17: 127–146.

Hogendorn, Jan and Marion Johnson. 1986. *The Shell Money of the Slave Trade*. Cambridge: Cambridge University Press.

Hopkins, Antony G. 1966. "The Currency Revolution in South-West Nigeria in the Late Nineteenth Century." *Journal of the Historical Society of Nigeria* 3 (2): 471–483.

Idowu, H. Oludare. 1968. "The Establishment of Protectorate Administration in Senegal, 1890–1904." *Journal of the Historical Society of Nigeria* 4 (2): 247–267.

Jemkur, Joseph F. 2004. "The Beginnings of Iron Metallurgy in West Africa." In *The Origins of Iron Metallurgy in Africa: New Light on Its Antiquity: West and Central Africa*, edited by Hamady Bocoum, 33–42. Paris: UNESCO.

Johnson, Marion. 1968. "The Nineteenth-Century Gold 'Mithqal' in West and North Africa." *The Journal of African History* 9 (4): 547–569.

———. 1970a. "The Cowrie Currencies of West Africa. Part I." *The Journal of African History* 11 (1): 17–49.

———. 1970b. "The Cowrie Currencies of West Africa. Part II." *The Journal of African History* 11 (3): 331–353.

———. 1977. "Cloth Strips and History." *West African Journal of Archaeology* 7: 169–178.

———. 1980. "Cloth as Money: The Cloth Strip Currencies of Africa." *Textile History* 11: 193–202.

Kobayashi, Kazuo. 2019. *Indian Cotton Textiles in West Africa*. Cham: Palgrave Macmillan.

Kriger, Colleen E. 2017. *Making Money: Life, Death, and Early Modern Trade on Africa's Guinea Coast*. Athens: Ohio University Press.

Kuroda, Akinobu. 2003. *Kahei shisutemu no sekaishi [A World History of Monetary System]*, Tokyo: Iwanami Shoten.

———. 2008a. "What is the complementarity among monies? An introductory note." *Financial History Review* 15(1): 7-15.

Kuroda, Akinobu. 2008b. "Concurrent but non-integrable currency circuits: complementary relationships among monies in modern China and other regions." *Financial History Review* 15(1):17-36.

Lovejoy, Paul E. 1974. "Interregional Monetary Flows in the Precolonial Trade of Nigeria." *The Journal of African History* 15 (4): 563–585.

Lydon, Ghislaine. 1997. "Les péripéties d'une institution financière, la Banque du Sénégal, 1844–1901". In *AOF, réalités et héritages: Sociétés ouest-africaines et ordre colonial, 1895–1960*, edited by Charles Becker, Saliou M'baye, and Ibrahima Thioub, 475–91. Dakar: Direction des Archives du Sénégal.

———. 2009. *On Trans-Saharan Trails: Islamic Law, Trade Networks, and Cross-Cultural Exchange in Nineteenth-Century Western Africa*. New York: Cambridge University Press.

Masaki, Toyomu. 2015a. "Jukyuseiki ni senegaru ni hakobareta indosan menpu gine:furansu ga kaizaishita shokuminchikankoeki no jittai to sonohaikei [The Export of Indian Guinée to Senegal via France: Inter-Colonial Trade in the Long Nineteenth Century]," *Shakai Keizai Shigaku [Socio-Economic History]* 81: 239–260 [in Japanese]. An English translation is found in *Modern Global Trade and the Asian Regional Economy*, edited by Tomoko Shiroyama (Singapore: Springer, 2018).

———. 2015b. "Senegaruginko (1853-1901) setsuritsu no haikei to sono-jittai [Institutional backgrounds and the facts about La Banque du Sénégal (1853-1901)]." *Kokumin-Keizai Zassi [Journal of Economics & Business Administration, Kobe University]* 211(1):39–57.

Masaki, Toyomu. 2021. "Indian *guinée* cloth, West Africa, and the French colonial empire 1826–1925: Colonialism and imperialism as agents of globalization." *Economic History of Developing Regions* (forthcoming).

Marfaing, Laurence. 1991. *L'evolution du commerce au Sénégal 1820-1930*. Paris: L'Harmattan.

———. 1992. "L'implantation des maisons de commerce au Sénégal et la réaction du commerce africain 1885-1930." In *Commerce et commerçant en Afrique de l'Ouest: Sénégal*, edited by Boubacar Barry and Leonhard Harding, 309–346. Paris: L'Harmattan.

———. 2016. "Movements of Silver Coins between France and Senegal 1833–1925: Evidence from French Trade Statistics." Discussion Paper Series No. 26, Faculty of Economics and Management, Kanazawa University, Kanazawa, Japan.

Négociants Sénégalais. 1879. *Le Sénégal et les guinées de Pondichéry: Note présentée à la commision supérieure des colonies*. Bordeaux: G.Gounouilhou.

Ofonagoro, Walter I. 1976. *The Currency Revolution in Southern Nigeria: 1880–1948*. Los Angeles: African Studies Center, University of California.

———. 1979. "From Traditional to British Currency in Southern Nigeria: Analysis of a Currency Revolution, 1880–1948." *The Journal of Economic History* 39 (3): 623–654.

Pallaver, Karin. 2015. "'The African Native Has No Pocket': Monetary Practices and Currency Transitions in Early Colonial Uganda." *The International Journal of African Historical Studies* 48 (3): 471–499.

Pasquier, Roger. 1987. "Le Senegal au milieu du XIXème siècle: La crise économique et sociale." PhD diss., Université de Paris Sorbonne.

Péhaut, Yves. 1986. *Les oleagineux dans le monde*. Paris: Economica.

Rodney, Walter. 1970. *History of the Upper Guinea Coast: 1545–1800*. New York: Monthly Review Press.

Şaul, Mahir. 2004. "Money in Colonial Transition: Cowries and Francs in West Africa." *American Anthropologist* 106 (1): 71–84.

Schefer, Christian. 1921. *Instructions générales données de 1763 à 1870 aux gouverneurs et ordonnateurs des établissements français en Afrique occidentale*. Paris: Société de l'histoire des colonies française.

Sow, Mariam. 1992. "Le crédit aux commerçants Sénégalais." In *Commerce et commerçants en Afrique de l'Ouest*, edited by Boubacar Barry and Leonhard Harding, 243–308. Paris: L'Harmattan.

Stiansen, Endre and Jane I. Guyer. 1999. *Credit, Currencies, and Culture: African Financial Institutions in Historical Perspective*. Uppsala: Nordiska Afrikainstitutet.

Sundström, Lars. 1974. *The Exchange Economy of Pre-Colonial Tropical Africa*. New York: St. Martin's Press.

Thiam, Iba D. 1997. "Le combat des populations africaines pour la démocratie, l'égalité et la justice, 1895–1960. L'exemple du Sénégal." In *AOF: Réalités et héritages: Sociétés ouest-africaines et ordre colonial, 1895–1960*, edited by Charles Becker, Saliou Mbaye, and Ibrahima Thioub, 250–263. Dakar: Direction des Archives du Sénégal.

Thiam, Samba. 2007. *Les indigènes paysans entre maisons de commerce et administration coloniale: Pratiques et institutions de crédit au Sénégal (1840-1940)*. Aix-en-Provence: Presses Universitaires d'Aix-Marseille-PUAM.

Webb, James L. A., Jr. 1982. "Toward the Comparative Study of Money: A Reconsideration of West African Currencies and Neoclassical Monetary Concepts." *International Journal of African Historical Studies* 15 (3): 455–466.

———. 1999. "On Currency and Credit in the Western Sahel, 1700–1850." In *Credit, Currencies and Culture: African Financial Institutions in Historical Perspective*, edited by Jane I. Guyer and Endre Stiansen, 38–55. Stockholm: Nordiska Afrikainstitutet.

Zay, Ernest. 1892. *Histoire monétaire des colonies françaises d'après les documents officiels*. Paris: Typographie de J. Montorier.

[illegible]

[illegible]. 19[illegible]. [illegible] [illegible] Gender, [illegible]

[illegible], Ernst. 19[illegible]. The [illegible] [illegible] 2000. [illegible]

[illegible] Polanyi, Karl [illegible] [illegible] [illegible]

CHAPTER 4

The Maria Theresa Thaler in Italian Eritrea: The Impact of Colonial Monetary Policies During the First World War

Alessandro De Cola

On 30 July 1916, the regional commissioner in Massawa Paolo Teodorani wrote in a report to the regent of the government of Eritrea Giovanni Cerrina Feroni, that a "radical monetary reform" would represent "an act of true and final colonial conquest".[1] The commissioner was writing at the beginning of the worst currency crisis that the colony had faced since the arrival of the Italians, a crisis that was sparked by the beginning of the First World War. At the eve of the WWI, Eritrea had been an Italian colony for almost 25 years. When the Italians occupied

[1]Commissariato Regionale di Massaua a Governo della Colonia Eritrea, 30 July 1916. Industria commercio moneta 1886–1924, Archivio Storico Diplomatico del Ministero degli Affari Esteri (ASDMAE), Archivio Eritrea (AE) Pacco 51.

Present Address:
A. De Cola (✉)
University of the Free State, Bloemfontein, Republic of South Africa

K. Pallaver (ed.), *Monetary Transitions*,
Palgrave Studies in Economic History,
https://doi.org/10.1007/978-3-030-83461-6_4

Massawa, on the Red Sea, in 1885, this port town was a node of multiple trade networks that connected large and small commercial centres and in which a multiple currency system was in use. Among them, glass beads from Venice that were treaded through Cairo were employed as currency in Massawa and some inland locations. Together with beads, salt bars were also an important means of exchange for the caravan trade (Pankhurst 1968, pp. 357–391). Alongside these *commoditycurrencies*, Indian rupees, Egyptian piastres and Maria Theresa thalers (MTT) were also in use in the ports along the coast (Pankhurst 1968, pp. 460–475). The MTT was a 28 g 833/1000 fine silver coin, first issued in the Austro-Hungarian empire in 1751, that gained a wide circulation in the Red Sea, being employed in the trade of pearls, mother of pearls, coffee, rubber and resins (Alamanni 1891, p. 219). After the death of Empress Maria Theresa in 1780, her son, Joseph II, decided to allow the minting of the coin for private companies that required them to trade in the Red Sea and Indian Ocean markets (Tschoegl 2001, p. 445). Therefore, at the time of the Italian occupation, the MTT was already crucial in connecting local and transregional trade networks, and the Italians had to accept its circulation to support commerce in the area. Thus, a shortage of this coin in the Red Sea region during the First World War provoked the concern of Italian authorities in the colony of Eritrea.

In the framework of African monetary history, few studies have paid attention to the financial consequences of the First World War in Africa.[2] During the First World War, the gold standard system collapsed, leaving the world currencies free to float (Eichengreen 2019, pp. 44–45). The rising prices of precious metals on international markets and the high demand for currency in Europe itself—a result of rising volumes of industrial production supporting the war effort—caused a lack of currency in most European colonies (Pallaver 2015). As Karin Pallaver has recently shown, the shortage of currency in the British East African colonies caused difficulties in paying carriers and soldiers coming back from the front (Pallaver 2019a). In West Africa, the lack of circulating currency during the war caused a significant part of the indigenous population to revert to the use of commodity money, such as cowries (Killingray 1978, p. 45; Michel 2014, p. 167). Moreover, the currency crisis led to the formulation of new monetary policies that, together with the post-war

[2] For a review of the studies regarding the financial impact of the First World War see Pallaver (2015).

trade depression, produced turmoil among the indigenous population and colonial settlers (Pallaver 2019b). As Wambui Mwangi shows, the study of currency crises is a tool to analyse how power is renegotiated by colonial subjects, and between them and the colonial governments (Mwangi 2001). For this reason, the study of the financial consequences of the First World War and its impact on currency circulation in Eritrea can be a workbench to analyse both the functioning of the Eritrean monetary system, and the way in which different actors dealt with colonial monetary policies. Moreover, the resilience of pre-colonial monetary systems during the First World War shows that the introduction of colonial currencies did not produce a swift passage to a new currency and social order but was rather a slow and non-linear transition.

The WWI caused increasing demand on the Eritrean population in terms of the production for the war effort. In a recent volume about the impact of the First World War on north-east Africa (Bekele et al. 2019), Massimo Zaccaria focussed on the economic impact of the war on Eritrea through the history of the first canned meat factory in the colony, which had signed a contract for the supply of this product to the Italian army (Zaccaria 2018). The factory demand for cattle at reduced prices put strong pressure on the local people's reserves of livestock. And this, together with the shortage of circulating currency and the rise of commodity prices, sparked protests in some districts of the colony (Zaccaria 2018, pp. 206–208). In addition to this, Italian attempts to enhance the agricultural production of the colonies in order to support the war effort and achieve self-sufficiency had a disruptive impact, and produced a general popular unrest (Zaccaria 2019, pp. 29–32).

The classic studies on the monetary history of Eritrea have noted that the WWI produced a dramatic scarcity of circulating MTTs in the colony, but no work has addressed this specific period in detail (Mauri 1967, pp. 131–146, 203–208, 1980, 1998, 2003; Pankhurst 1963; 1968; Tuccimei 1999, pp. 138–152, 223–237).[3] However, as this chapter contends, an analysis of monetary circulation and colonial currency policies during the First World War can be an illuminating window to understand the role that the MTT played in the economy of Eritrea and

[3] Richard Pankhurst analysed the fluctuations of the quotation of the MTT in relation to its scarcity and to the rising price of silver in Ethiopia during the First World War (Pankhurst 1968, pp. 486–488).

to provide insights in the functioning of transregional trade in the Red Sea region.

Recently, Steven Serels has analysed the colonial monetary systems of the Southern Red Sea Region—encompassing Italian, French and British colonies—and argued that the instability brought on by the introduction of colonial currencies in the area provoked a loss of wealth among indigenous people (Serels 2019). According to him, one of the factors bolstering this instability was the strong depreciation of European currencies during the First World War (Serels 2019, p. 156). Pallaver (2018) has specifically analysed the consequences of the First World War on the monetary system of the Italian colonies of Somalia and Eritrea, and explained that the Italian failure to replace the MTT was largely due to the lack of understanding of the functioning of the local monetary system and of the role of the MTT. Akinobu Kuroda provides an interesting explanation of the success of the MTT in the region (Kuroda 2007, 2020, pp. 154–170). Through the analysis of trade volumes and exchange rates from 1935 to 1941, Kuroda shows that the MTT operated as a "buffer money" that connected different market levels, facilitating the "vertical" conversion between small denomination currencies—such as salt bars, cartridges and, later, 10 lire notes—and international trade currencies, such as the pound sterling. At the same time, the interregional circulation of thalers allowed the "horizontal connection" among markets located in different regions. A shortage of thalers disrupted the connection among markets, causing a reduction in the volume of exchanged commodities and a rise in prices. Kuroda argues that the reason why the MTT was so successful was that it circulated in a complementary relationship with other currencies in a multiple currency system—such as the one of the Red Sea region—where "a combination of monies can do what a single money cannot" (Kuroda 2007, p. 109). Owing to this "non-substitutability among monies", colonial policies did not manage to eliminate the Maria Theresa thaler from circulation (Kuroda 2007, p. 107).

This chapter contributes to the history of the financial impact of the First World War on the Italian colony of Eritrea, by analysing the consequences of the MTT shortage during the war and of the colonial policies implemented to face it. This will contribute to clarifying the reasons for the success of the MTT in the region, as well as the continuous failures of the attempts to replace it. During the war, the lira progressively lost value, whereas the value of the MTT continued to rise. As a consequence, this chapter will show that the section of the Eritrean population that most suffered in relation to the war impact on currency were the labourers who worked for the colonial state and received their wages in lire.

Italian Monetary Policies During the First World War and Their Consequences

The period from the eve of the First World War to the interwar years represents a turning point in the history of Eritrea. During the first decades since the Italian occupation, most of the colonial budget had been deployed for the expeditions in the inland and the war with Ethiopia, while the colony had been administered by the military (Podestà 1996, pp. 204–205, 243–244). Following a period of administrative reorganisation that had started with the appointment in 1897 of the first civilian governor, Ferdinando Martini, Italian colonial administrators were trying to transform the colony into a commercial hub (Podestà 2004, pp. 172–176) (Map 4.1).

The railway connecting the port town of Massawa to the capital, Asmara (2200 m above the sea level), was completed in 1911 (Colosimo 1919, p. 108). The first branch of the Bank of Italy was opened to the public in Asmara on 2 February 1914, followed by a second one in Massawa on 15 April 1914 (Mauri 1967, pp. 161–163, 165; Tuccimei 1999, pp. 89–91).

Before the bank opened its doors to the public, with a seventy-five-page report, the new director of the Asmara branch, Luciano Cristoforis, described the colony's economic and financial situation to Bonaldo Stringher, director of the Bank of Italy. In his report, Cristoforis acknowledged that the MTT was "the base for every negotiation" and that its import from Austria was on the rise. Given the importance of the MTT for local and interregional commerce, he stated that placing the control of its circulation in the hands of the Bank of Italy's agencies was necessary for fighting speculation.[4] The fluctuations of the value in lire of the MTT had been problematic for the government of the colony since the

[4] Cristoforis al Direttore Generale della Banca d'Italia Bonaldo Stringher, 16 September 1913, Archivio Storico della Banca d'Italia (ASBI), Affari coloniali, pratiche—Ramo Banca 305, Relazione 1913, p. 22.

Map 4.1 The Italian colony of Eritrea in the Red Sea region. Political and administrative borders are represented as they were at the end of the First World War

first years of Italian occupation. The time needed to import the Austrian coins from Trieste exposed the government to important losses, as their value would not be the same once they arrived in the colony.[5] This had caused problems in the management of the colonial budget over the years,

[5] Nota del Ministero del Tesoro, 14 December 1886, ASDMAE, AE Pacco 60.

as this kind of losses had to be taken into account.[6] On the contrary, some merchants operating in the colony were able to gain from these fluctuations, exploiting their knowledge of the regional markets and their transregional connections to convert the MTTs in other currencies when it was more advantageous for them. This was particularly true for the Indian merchants operating in the colony, dealing in MTT and converting them in money orders to send rupees to Bombay when it was more convenient to do so.[7] However, at the time of the opening of the first branch of the Bank of Italy in Eritrea, the agents of the bank realised they lacked the necessary knowledge about the regional currency market to directly compete with local actors to buy and sell MTTs on the spot. Thus, in February 1914, given the unpredictability of the MTT quotation, Stringher asked the director of the branch in Asmara not to employ the MTTs held in bank deposits to speculate in the exchange market.[8]

The situation changed after the outbreak of the First World War, when the agencies of the bank in Eritrea were requested to have a more active involvement in the management of the MTT circulation. On 21 August 1914, the director of the Massawa branch, Silvio Pacetti, wrote to the director of the Asmara branch that.

> The exodus of the thalers to Aden and Bombay has started, and it is supposed to last, till the [war] events allow the circulation of our steamships . . . in these seas [i.e. the Red Sea]. This is the only means the Banyans[9] have to send the payments for their purchases. For now, these shipments do not have a significant effect on the market, because the thalers they have sent till now had already been hoarded by them; but,

[6] Relazione sulla Colonia Eritrea sull'impianto di una agenzia della Banca d'Italia in Asmara, Cav. Introna, 1906, ASBI, Affari coloniali, pratiche—Ramo Banca 305, p. 55.

[7] Ibid., p. 38.

[8] Direzione Generale a Direttore della filiale di Asmara, 13 February 1914, ASBI, Filiale Asmara Pratiche—Ramo Banca 110.

[9] This name describes people originating from different parts of the Indian subcontinent, mostly of (but not limited to) Hindu religion. The term comes from "Hindu Vania", which were the members of the Gujarati commercial caste. A common trait of the so called "banyans" was their belonging to networks encompassing the whole Indian Ocean, and their business organisation model (Clarence-Smith 2001, pp. 335–336; Miran 2009, p. 137).

in the long term, it is believed here that [the shipments] will produce a substantial increase in the price of this coin.[10]

The price of the MTT was destined to rise even sooner than Pacetti predicted. Due to the need to protect precious metal reserves, the coinage of new MTTs by the Austrian mints was totally interrupted, and new imports of MTTs from Trieste into the Italian colony became impossible (Tschoegl 2001, p. 448). The governor of the colony Giuseppe Salvago Raggi was concerned about the impact that a shortage of MTTs could have on Eritrean trade. On 5 September 1914, in order to stop the outflow of MTTs and speculation, he issued a ban on the export of the MTTs by sea.[11] However, the measure was not enough to stop speculation, and in a letter to the director of the Asmara branch, the Massawa agent of the Bank of Italy reported that the bulk of MTTs in Massawa was concentrated in the hands of a few merchants, who were waiting for the right moment to sell.[12] In fact, the "banyans" were still able to control the MTT market: their share in the local currency market was so important that the quotation of the MTT would drop when the "banyans" decided to sell their thalers in order to acquire lire for their businesses.[13] At that point, the Bank of Italy was still far from having a hold on the local exchange market.

During the first year of the First World War, Italy maintained a neutral position. After one year of diplomatic and economic pressures by the British, Italy decided to timidly enter the conflict by declaring war on Austria on 23 May 1915 (Marcuzzi 2018). Soon after, the British requested a more active Italian involvement against the Ottoman Empire, including the participation in a blockade in the Red Sea, in order to cut supplies to the Arabian coasts of Asir and Hejaz, which were then

[10] L'Agente, filiale di Massaua, al Direttore, filiale di Asmara, Massawa, 21 August 1914, ASBI, Sottofondo Filiale Asmara, Pratiche—Ramo Banca, 110.

[11] *Decreto governatoriale*, 5 settembre 1914 n. 2049, see *Bullettino Ufficiale della Colonia Eritrea*, Supplemento al n. 42, Asmara, 24 October 1916.

[12] Direzione filiale di Massawa a Direttore della filiale di Asmara, 14 November 1914, ASBI, Sottofondo Filiale Asmara, Pratiche—Ramo Banca, 110.

[13] Direzione filiale di Massawa a Direttore della filiale di Asmara, 21 August 1915, ASBI, Filiale Asmara, Pratiche—Ramo Banca, 110.

controlled by the Turks and the Germans.[14] A partial blockade started in November 1915 and was eventually more strictly enforced in May 1917. The blockade helped the Italians to limit the illegal export of thalers from the colony. At the same time, however, it also worsened economic conditions as it hindered the colony's supply of foodstuff and cattle (Zaccaria 2018, pp. 203–206).

By the beginning of 1916, the scarcity of MTTs had caused a significant reduction in the colony's reserves. Consequently, in April, the government asked the agents of the Bank of Italy to buy 100,000 MTTs on the internal market.[15] Nonetheless, problems of currency circulation continued. Therefore, the government of the colony decided to employ some more drastic policies. On 1 July 1916, a decree was issued by Giovanni Cerrina Feroni, that prohibited merchants from fixing the price of goods in MTT and banned negotiations in MTT in public marketplaces.[16] In explaining the reason for his decision, Cerrina Feroni stressed that the new rules were a way to push local traders to employ the lira—that was legal tender—rather than the MTT, that was "a non-legal" tender.[17]

In order to not undermine interregional trade, the ban on MTT negotiation was not enforced on the merchants engaged in the caravan trade connecting the colony with Ethiopia and Sudan.

However, the reports of the regional commissioners on the effects of the new decree did not confirm Cerrina Ferroni's expectations. One month after the issuing of the decree, the regional commissioner Paolo Teodorani wrote from Massawa that "many MTTs pass to the Arab coast and Aden, where there is a high demand for them and they can be sold at high rates".[18] In a second report sent on 16 September 1916, Teodorani

[14] German War, Turkey, Jeddah War Supplies, Italy, Trade and Treaty, Foreign Office to Sir. R. Rodd (Rome), 3 March 1915, British Library (BL), India Office Records (IOR), L/PS/10/466, no. 253.

[15] Direzione di Finanza a Direttore della filiale della Banca d'Italia di Asmara, 11 April 1916, ASBI, Filiale Asmara, Pratiche—Ramo Banca, 110.

[16] *Decreto governatoriale*, 1° luglio 1916 n. 2589; see Circolare. Cerrina Feroni ai Commissariati Regionali, Asmara, 1° luglio 1916, ASDMAE, AE Pacco 51.

[17] Cerrina [Feroni] ai Commissari regionali tutti, Asmara, 6 July, 1916. ASDMAE, AE Pacco 51.

[18] Commissariato Regionale di Massaua a Governo della Colonia Eritrea, 30 July 1916, ASDMAE, AE Pacco 51.

acknowledged that every commercial transaction was negotiated in relation to the MTT value, despite the decree forbidding it. Moreover, he confirmed that the "banyans, as usual" gathered as many thalers as they could in order to export them to India, where the demand for silver continued to rise. To do this, the Indian merchants continued to import goods whatever the price, knowing that they could earn significant gains through the use of MTT in payments and money-exchange.[19]

In order to curb speculation, a new set of rules was issued by the new governor, Giacomo De Martino, on 24 October 1916.[20] The new decree prohibited any kind of payment with MTTs in local markets and declared a fixed exchange rate for government fees at 2.50 lire per MTT, and payments made by the government—such as wages and orders—at 2.65 lire per MTT. The fixed exchange rate of 2.50 lire per MTT was also applied to the hiring of transport services by camels and porters.[21] The most important change introduced by the decree was the concession of the monopoly of money-changing services to the Bank of Italy that, for this purpose, opened the office of the *Gestione Talleri* (Thalers Management Office).[22] Negotiations in MTT were still allowed for foreign trade, and the MTTs could be exchanged by the agencies of the Bank of Italy and the post offices. The exchange rate for this kind of transactions was periodically set by a commission nominated by the government of the colony.[23] However, every money exchange was to be authorised by the regional commissioners. The buyer had to deliver to the agency of the bank a form signed by the commissioner reporting the quantity of MTTs requested, the reason for the exchange, and the amount of goods intended to be bought with the MTTs.[24]

[19] Commissariato Regionale di Massaua a Governo della Colonia Eritrea, 16 September 1916, ASDMAE, AE Pacco 51.

[20] "Decreto governatoriale, 24 ottobre 1916 n. 2653" in *Bullettino Ufficiale della Colonia Eritrea*, Supplemento al n. 42, Asmara, 24 October 1916.

[21] Ibid.

[22] Gestione Cambio talleri M.T., Direzione Finanza a Direttore della Banca d'Italia (Asmara), 24 October 1916, ASBI, Filiale Asmara, Pratiche—Ramo Banca, 137.

[23] *Bullettino Ufficiale della Colonia Eritrea*, n. 42, 19 ottobre 1916.

[24] *Bollettino Ufficiale della Colonia Eritrea*, Supplemento al n. 42, 24 October 1916.

Most of the regional commissioners were sceptical about the impact that these measures would have in curbing speculation, which was producing a sizeable depreciation of the lira in relation to local prices. One of the most negative reactions to the new regulations came from Ludovico Pollera, commissioner of the Barka region. The Barka region and the bordering region of the Gash-Setit were lacking infrastructure and were mostly inhabited by pastoralist people who often crossed the borders of Ethiopia and Sudan with their herds and kept their savings in MTT. The ban on negotiations in MTT produced a burdensome premium for the exchange of MTTs by these groups, "for the exclusive benefit of the money-changers".[25] As a consequence, some of the people living in these regions, "not having any Eritrean money [Eritrean thaler[26] subdivisions and lira coins], cannot buy *dura*".[27] Ludovico Pollera pointed out that the availability of MTTs was essential to the import of *dura* from Ethiopia, the silver coin being the only one accepted beyond the borders of the colony.[28] Another concern for Pollera was represented by the effect of the regulations on the fundamental services of the Beni Amer camel-drivers.[29] In fact, the fixed exchange rate of 2.50 lire per thaler constituted a loss for the camel-drivers, as the price of MTT continued to rise well above the 2.50 exchange rate fixed by the government throughout the war period.

According to the commissioner of Asmara, Giuseppe Cavalli, the retailers in the local markets used to plan the amount of money they

[25] Commissario Gasc-Setit a Governo Asmara, Agordat, 2 July 1916, ASDMAE, AE Pacco 51.

[26] The minting of the *tallero eritreo* had been the first Italian attempt to introduce a new coin to replace the MTT, in 1890. It was issued with a fixed exchange rate of 5 lire to 1 *tallero eritreo*, which was the main reason for its failure, as it was overvalued compared to the MTT (Pollera 1926, pp. 63–64). On the other hand, its subsidiary silver coins, valued 4/10 (2 lire), 2/10 (1 lire) and 1/10 of an Eritrean thaler (0.50 cents of a lira), widely circulated in the colony together with 10 and 5 lira cents, as the MTT lacked any divisional coin (Rossetti 1914, p. 33).

[27] From the Arabic *ḏura*, *Sorghum vulgare* or *bicolor* was the staple food of the Horn of Africa. Commissario Gasc-Setit a Governo Asmara, Agordat, 3 July 1916, ASDMAE, AE Pacco 51.

[28] Commissario Gasc-Setit a Governo Asmara, Agordat, 2 July 1916, ASDMAE, AE Pacco 51.

[29] Commissariato Regionale del Barca, al Governo della Colonia, Agordat, 26 July 1916, ASDMAE, AE Pacco 51.

wanted to earn according to the daily exchange rate of the MTT. Even if the prices were expressed in lire, the sellers fixed them according to the amount of MTT they owed to the *nəggāde* (the heads of the caravans), operating the interregional wholesome trade.[30] Moreover, according to Commissioner Cavalli, the new regulations, together with the shortage of MTTs due to the halting of new imports from Austria, produced concern in the population. Those who had MTTs tended to hoard them, which, according to Commissioner Cavalli, represented "a new psychological-economical factor" worsening the state of monetary circulation.[31] This situation fostered, according to him, the activities of speculators "to the detriment of those who, being paid with the Italian currency (and among these especially those working for the colonial administration that once used to be paid in thalers), are forced to pay more those goods that experience an artificial rise in their MTT price [on the market], while the [wholesale] price has not changed".[32]

A report from the regional commissioner of the Dancalia region, Dante Odorizzi, explains how the new measures indirectly affected wage labourers. The commissioner reported that ever since the new regulations had been in force, the price of the MTT in the market had gradually risen from 2.50 to 3.00 lire. Local merchants kept calculating the price of goods on the basis of this increased value of the thaler, thus causing the rise in prices. As a consequence, the price of a bag of *dura* increased from 30 MTT (when the value of the thaler was 2.50 lire) to 36 MTT, when the thaler's value rose to 3 lire. And this, according to the commissioner, happened within three days without any variation in the supply of *dura*: "On the Red Sea shore, the *dura* is like gold... the amount of money needed to buy it changes according to exchange rate".[33] The new regulations, which forced the fixing of prices in lire, facilitated this kind of speculation. Moreover, the price of the MTT in the port town of Assab

[30] Governatore dell'Hamasien a Direttore Affari Civili, Asmara, 17 August 1916, ASDMAE, AE Pacco 51.

[31] Ibid.

[32] Governatore dell'Hamasien a Direttore Affari Civili, Asmara, 17 August 1916, ASDMAE, AE Pacco 51.

[33] Commissariato regionale della Dancalia, risposta alla circolare 7 agosto 1916 all'Uff. Governo Affari Civili, Assab, 1 September 1916, ASDMAE, AE Pacco 51.

was largely dependent on the quotation in Aden, being the trade there strongly dependant on the market of Aden. For an Indian merchant who knew the exchange rate of the MTT on the market of Aden, it was quite easy to calculate the profits he could obtain by exploiting the difference in exchange rates. In Aden, the exchange rate of the MTT was calculated in relation to the rupee, with a fixed rate of 15 rupees to the pound. Given the fixed exchange rate of the rupee, the Indian merchants simply needed to keep up to date with the daily exchange rate of the MTT in Aden, expressed in rupee, and that of the pound, expressed in francs (at that time at par with the lira).[34] When Odorizzi was writing, in Aden 100 MTTs were valued at 153 rupees, and one pound was valued 29.80 francs (or lire). Therefore, the exchange rate used by the Indian merchants in Assab was 2.93 lire per MTT.[35] This value was slightly higher than the official exchange value the government used for the payments of wages, which was 2.65 lire per MTT.[36] As a consequence, this represented a downside especially for those employed by the government, the majority of whom were *ascari* (indigenous troops). The low ranks were earning a wage of 1.00 to 1.25 lire per day, and when the MTT reached the exchange rate of 3 lire per thaler at the end of August 1916, they had lost almost one third of their purchasing power, because the prices in the markets were still handled in MTT.[37] At first, the Government of Eritrea did not help to solve the problems affecting its indigenous wage labourers. According to Cerrina Feroni, an adjustment of the salaries in line with the rising cost of living would have been proof that "[the Government was] regulating the wages according to the quotation of the MTT, which, instead, should

[34] The parity between francs and lire was guaranteed by the Latin Monetary Union agreements, signed by four countries in 1865. These agreements established the use of 0.835 silver for the coins minted by the involved countries, thus equalising the exchange rate of the national currencies (Eichengreen 2019, p. 14).

[35] Commissioner Odorizzi reported the formula in this way: "L. 28.80:15 × 153:100 = 2.93 L."; 1 pound = 15 rupee = 29.80 francs (lire) so 1 rupee = 1.92 lire; 100 MTT = 153 rupees, so 1 MTT = 1.53 rupee. To calculate the price of the MTT in lire according to its price in rupee, it was sufficient to solve this calculation: 1.53 × 1.92 = 2.93 ca. See Commissariato regionale della Dancalia, risposta alla circolare 7 agosto 1916 all'Uff. Governo Affari Civili, Assab, 1 September 1916, ASDMAE, AE Pacco 51.

[36] Ibid.

[37] Commissario Regionale dell'Hamasien al Governo della Colonia, 23 August 1916, ASDMAE, AE Pacco 51.

not have any influence on the Eritrean monetary system anymore".[38] Following pressure from the Italian military officers, the government had to find a different solution to the problem of the declining purchasing power of wage labourers.[39] From April 1918, the MTT started to be exchanged by the Bank of Italy at a special fixed rate for the *ascari* that was more convenient for them (3.5 lire per thaler instead of 6). The difference for every exchange was paid by the treasury of the government of the colony.[40]

The price of the MTT continued to rise for the entire period of the First World War: from the pre-war value of about 2.50 lire, in 1918 it reached 6 lire per MTT (see Fig. 4.1).

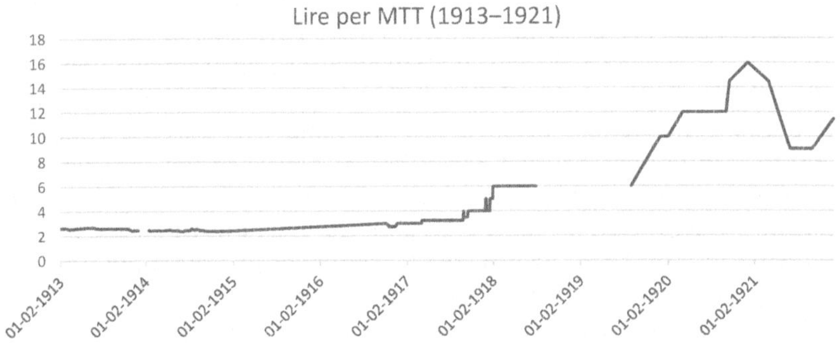

Fig. 4.1 Quotation of the MTT in lire in Eritrea for the period 1913–1921[41] (*Source* "Massaua, Talleri M.T. Prezzo medio settimanale, 1913", ASBI, Filiale Asmara, Pratiche—Ramo Banca, 110; "Movimento Talleri M.T. 1914", ASBI, Filiale Asmara, Pratiche—Ramo Banca, 110; "Gestione Talleri 1916–1918", ASBI, Filiale Asmara, Pratiche—Ramo Banca 137)

[38] Direzioni Affari civili e Reggente del Governo della Colonia Eritrea a Commissario regionale dell'Hamasien, Asmara, 25 August 1916, ASDMAE, AE Pacco 51.

[39] Examples of protests by Italian officers advocating a solution for the loss of purchasing power of the indigenous troops can be found in Comando del Regio Corpo di Truppe Coloniali dell'Eritrea, Assab, 24 August 1916, ASDMAE, AE Pacco 51.

[40] Governo dell'Eritrea, Affari Economici e Finanziari al Direttore della Banca d'Italia di Asmara, 11 March 1918, ASBI, Filiale Asmara, Pratiche—Ramo Banca, 137.

[41] There are no data available for the period September 1918–August 1919, see note 46.

This rise was the result of a combination of internal and external factors. Besides the scarcity of MTTs due to the halting of minting, speculation and hoarding, the value of the coin itself increased due to a significant rise of the price of silver on the international markets.[42]

In order to face the scarcity of currency, it was decided to send banknotes to Eritrea (Di Fausto 1918, p. 119). However, the banknotes were not readily accepted and, on some occasions, the colonial government had to force their use on the local people.[43] As we can see from the complaints of the Ethiopian traders to the Italian administration, the main reason was that the banknotes did not circulate in the bordering countries and could not be used in interregional trade.[44]

In October 1918, the government of the colony made again legal the free exchange of the MTT on the market and its use in trade negotiations. However, this news was received with scepticism and suspicion by traders operating in the markets, as they feared that this was a strategy of the Italian government to force them to release the MTTs that they had hoarded, thus slowing down the refuelling of local markets with silver coins.[45]

At the end of the war, the government of Eritrea tried to take advantage of the lack of silver coins by attempting another replacement of the MTT with a new silver coin with a free-floating value. The *tallero d'Italia*, firstly issued by the mint of Rome on 31 May 1918, had the same physical features of the MTT, with a personification of Italy engraved on the face instead of Empress Maria Theresa's profile (Mariani 1918). However, the

[42] The rise of the international price of silver was the consequence of several different factors, including a decrease in the supply of silver from Mexico following the Civil War, and the rise in demand due to the growth of global industrial activity in preparation for the First World War (Leavens 1939, pp. 136–139).

[43] Gente dell'Hamasien, di Dembelas, di Cheren che vanno nel Gasc e Setit per acquistare bestiame senza autorizzazione, Commissario Gasc e Setit to Direzione Affari Civili, 3 April 1920, ASDMAE, AE Pacco 876/72.

[44] Promemoria, Asmara, 27 December 1919, ASDMAE, AE Pacco 859/72; Abraha Teferri di Tigrai, Reggente del Governo a Commissario di Adi Ugri, 29 December 1919, ASDMAE, AE Pacco 859/72. Another explanation for their failure was that the banknotes were not suitable for the environmental conditions of the colony, nor for indigenous hoarding practices (Pollera 1926, p. 76).

[45] Calmiere tallero di Maria Teresa, Pro-memoria sul decreto che riguarda la trattazione in talleri, Asmara, 14 October 1918, ASDMAE, AE Pacco 827/164.

new coins did not circulate in Ethiopia and were always valued at least 2.00 lire less than the MTT on the markets.[46] Their lower quotation, together with the issuing of an insufficient number of new thalers (only 510,000 for a population of about 300,000[47]), was probably at the base of their failure. Alberto Pollera[48] noted how the jewellers preferred to buy *talleri d'Italia* to melt them, as they were less expensive than the MTTs and contained about the same amount of silver, and according to him this practice made the Italian coin rapidly disappear (Pollera 1926, p. 73).

The Maria Theresa Thaler in a Regional Perspective

The lack of MTTs, together with the Italian control on their use in transactions, also affected interregional commerce. For the Ethiopian *nəggāde* it was not advantageous to change their thalers at the official rate fixed by the Italian colonial government that was always lower than the market rate.[49] Moreover, the *nəggāde* needed MTTs for their return journeys, in order to pay tributes and fees in Ethiopia.[50] They, therefore, tended to trade in those markets where they could more easily obtain MTTs, choosing them on the base of the information they could gather from

[46] Agente filiale di Adi Caieh a Filiale Asmara, 20 September 1920, ASBI, Filiale Asmara, Pratiche—Ramo Banca, 138. The *Gestione Talleri* office of the Bank of Italy was temporarily closed on 15 October 1918 ("being the free circulation of the MT thaler restored") only to be reopened on 25 August 1919, in order to manage the buying and selling of MTTs and Italian thalers on behalf of the colonial government. See Relazione Annuale 1918, ASBI, Affari coloniali—Pratiche 305, Relazioni Asmara, p. 26; "*Decreto governatoriale*, 25 agosto 1919 n. 3363," in *Bullettino Ufficiale della Colonia Eritrea*, Supplemento al n. 20, Asmara, 25 August 1919.

[47] The most accurate census at that time had been produced in 1905, and reported 274,944 people (Ministero delle Colonie 1913, p. 43).

[48] Alberto Pollera, Ludovico's brother, had been a commissioner too and was a prolific scholar of Eritrean and Ethiopian history, economy and consuetudinary laws (Sòrgoni 2001).

[49] Agenzia commerciale Dessie a Governo dell'Eritrea, Dessie, 10 August 1916, ASDMAE, AE Pacco 51.

[50] Commissario Regionale della Dancalia, 1 August, 1916, ASDMAE, AE Pacco 51.

other merchants operating in the area.[51] When the MTT was not allowed to be freely exchanged in the Eritrean markets, they were forced to turn to the colonial administration to change the lire they had collected, before starting their return journey.[52] The administration could not refuse to sell them MTTs in exchange for their lire, because the Italian colony needed to import foodstuffs for the entire period of the war.[53] Hence the outflow of MTTs continued.

The data on the caravan trade during the war further show the interconnectedness of the Red Sea economic system and the effects of the policies of currency circulation on the regional trade system.

The first information that stands out from these data is the inversion of the direction of the caravan trade between Eritrea and Ethiopia. Before the war, the exports from Eritrea to Ethiopia exceeded the imports. The main export items were cotton fabrics, silk waste, oil and Indian rice.[54] From 1916, Ethiopia implemented a ban on the export of MTTs to confront their over-valuation due to the outflow of silver thalers (Pankhurst 1968, p. 487). The Ethiopian currency system was entirely based on silver coins, and, as a consequence, it was less exposed than Eritrea to the fluctuations of the MTT exchange rate with the gold standard currencies circulating in the European colonies. This situation fuelled speculation, as in Ethiopia the quotation of the MTT remained lower compared to that in Eritrea and in Aden. For this reason, it became convenient to buy MTTs in Ethiopia to sell them on those markets

[51] Agenzia commerciale Dessie a Governo dell'Eritrea, Dessie, 10 August 1916, ASDMAE, AE Pacco 51. In 1920, the agent of the bank of Italy in Adi Keyh, wrote that telegraphic services were widely used by the *nəggādе* in Mekelle, Ethiopia, to stay up to date about the state of trade in Eritrea, the exchange rates in the markets and the availability of MTTs. Riservata. Al direttore della filiale di Asmara, Adi Keyh, 20 September 1920. ASBI, Filiale Asmara, Pratiche—Ramo banca 138, Gestione Talleri 1918–1922.

[52] Direzione Affari Civili a Direzione Affari Economici, Asmara, 26 April 1918, ASDMAE, AE Pacco 827/164.

[53] Starting from 1917, the imminent arrival of a *nəggādе* with his caravan in the colony was communicated by the Italian commercial agents in Ethiopia and published on the pages of the official bulletin of the colony. In this way the merchants of the colony were allowed enough time to request the commissioners for the authorization for the buying of the necessary MTTs to pay the *nəggādе*. See, for example, Direzione Affari Economici e Finanziari. Arrivo di Carovane, *Bullettino Ufficiale della Colonia Eritrea*, Asmara, 27 September 1917.

[54] Relazione sulla Colonia Eritrea sull'impianto di una agenzia della Banca d'Italia in Asmara, Cav. Introna (1906), ASBI, Affari coloniali—pratiche, 305, pp. 39–40.

where their quotation was on the rise (Pollera 1926, p. 30). The MTT export ban, and the Italian need for supplies to support the war effort, reversed the trade balance with Ethiopia.[55] The value of the imports from Ethiopia went from 2,319,000 lire in 1911 to 22,020,299.33 lire in 1918, whereas the exports from Eritrea to Ethiopia rose from 3,071,000 lire to 12,500,224 lire.[56] The most important items imported into the colony were hides and skins, due to the high demand for the manufacture of boots for the army (Colosimo 1919, pp. 315–316).

These data need to be interpreted in the light of the fact that the total amounts of imports and exports were swollen by the rise in the price of the MTT in relation to the lira discussed above. At the same time, the colonial statistics did not capture the trade that did not pass through the markets and caravanserais controlled by the government, due to the total absence of customs offices at the border with Ethiopia.[57] Nonetheless they show two ways in which Maria Theresa thalers continued their exodus from the colony during and after the war, notwithstanding Italian policies. The first was through caravan commerce itself. Imports from Ethiopia had to be paid for in MTT, which was the only currency accepted there. The second was smuggling. Looking at caravan trade statistics for the year 1918, another loophole stands out. The figures on the caravan trade with Sudan recorded in Eritrea by the Italians did not match with those recorded by the British authorities on the other side of the border: the value of the exports recorded in Eritrea for the year 1918 was 157,575 lire, while in Sudan the British recorded 306,840 lire of imports from Eritrea, hence almost double the figure reported by the Italians. According to an accurate report by the Bank of Italy written in Keren, the border with Sudan was the route preferred by Indian merchants to export MTTs outside Eritrea, because of its porous nature. The report describes the route that Indian merchants took to reach and pass the Sudanese borders in order to get to Port Sudan and send the smuggled

[55] The main exports from the colony to support the war effort had been: tinned meat, 12 million pieces; hides, 18 million lire; *doum* nuts: ca. 50,000 q; potassium chloride, ca. 50,000 q. (Colosimo 1919, p. 322).

[56] "Relazione Asmara 1913," ASBI, Affari coloniali – pratiche, 305, pp. 32–34. Movimento carovaniero con l'oltre confine, Asmara, 18 September 1919, ASDMAE, AE Pacco 859.

[57] Ibid.

thalers to Aden and Bombay.[58] Another very detailed report, written in October 1921, sheds light on the circulation of MTTs once they had left the western coast of the Red Sea. According to this report, only a small quantity of MTTs exported by the "Banyans" to Aden and Bombay were melted and/or re-coined. MTTs were instead exchanged in Aden with Arab merchants for coffee, hides and dates. In turn, the Arabs used the MTT to buy imported *dura*. When the *dura* harvest in Yemen was good, the Arabs used to hoard MTTs as they did not need them to import the *dura* from the western shore of the Red Sea. On the contrary, during bad harvests, the thalers used to go west, back to the port of Massawa. Even this case shows that the MTTs were used to fuel interregional trade in particular. Finally, those MTTs that reached Bombay were traded with merchants from the Persian Gulf in exchange for pearls and dates.[59]

The shipment of MTTs to the Arabian Peninsula was allowed again by the Italian government in August 1920.[60] In Ethiopia, the ban on the export of MTTs was removed in May 1921, owing to the pressures that European traders had put on *Ras* Tafari.[61]

At the end of the First World War, a brief economic boom was followed by a slump, as the global economy struggled to reallocate resources and adjust production to the demands of a peacetime economy (Feinstein, Temin, and Toniolo 2008, pp. 6–20). From January 1921, Massawa was hit by a devastating series of earthquakes, and the caravan trade was hampered by the lowering prices of goods. This meant that caravans could not cover the entire costs of the trading expedition towards the market centres of the interior (Tuccimei 1999, p. 95). Furthermore, the exports from the colony to Italy were dramatically reduced, due to the drop in demand for commodities to supply the wartime production. For example, *doum* nuts that were mostly used during the war to produce buttons for

[58] Agenzia di Cheren al Direttore dello Stabilimento di Massaua, Keren, 30 December 1921, ASBI, Filiale Asmara, Pratiche—Ramo Banca, 138.

[59] Gestione Talleri Massaua a Direttore Filiale di Asmara, Massawa, 11 October 1921, ASBI, Filiale Asmara, Pratiche—Ramo Banca, 138.

[60] Esportazione di talleri per via di mare, Direzione dei Servizi Finanziari della Colonia Eritrea a Banca d'Italia (Gestione Talleri), Asmara, 15 August 1920, ASBI, Filiale Asmara, Pratiche—Ramo Banca, 138.

[61] Crisi commerciale. Quistione esportazione talleri. Regia Legazione d'Italia in Etiopia a Ministro Affari Esteri, Addis Ababa, 14 January 1921, ASDMAE, Archivio Storico del Ministero dell'Africa Italiana (ASMAI) I Posizione 50/1.

the troops' uniforms, were no longer requested by Italian factories.[62] The end of the war therefore resulted in a reduction in exports to Italy, and in general trade as well. The office of the *Gestione Talleri* was closed on 31 December 1921, "considering the reasons that led to [its] foundation ceased [to exist]".[63]

After the war, a period of political and economic transformation of the colony began. A more aggressive political and commercial strategy made its influence felt both in Ethiopia and on the opposite shores of the Red Sea (Quartararo 1979, p. 813; Zaccaria 2012, pp. 294–299). A multiple currency system, that included the MTT, continued to fuel the economic life of the Italian colony of Eritrea. But it was only in 1936, after the Italian invasion of Ethiopia, that the office of the *Gestione Talleri* of the Bank of Italy resumed its operations as a way to control the circulation of the MTT in Ethiopia, where it still was the cornerstone of local monetary circulation.[64]

Conclusion

The chapter has analysed the impact that WWI had on currency circulation in the Italian colony of Eritrea. The exceptional currency crisis that engulfed the region during the war, along with the greater attention the colonial government paid towards currency circulation, provides an unprecedented number of documents on the monetary system of Eritrea that can be used to highlight its interregional ramifications. As already observed by Kuroda (2007) for Ethiopia in 1935–1941, the chapter has shown that also in Eritrea, during the First World War, the Maria Theresa thaler was essential for the steady functioning of regional trade. The fact that local prices continued to be calculated in MTT highlights the dependence of the Eritrean market on the network of regional markets. At the same time, the chapter has shown how the MTT was necessary to facilitate the transportation of goods across colonial borders. The Italians were aware of the crucial importance of the MTT for interregional trade but, at the same time, they wanted to protect the value of the

[62] Relazione 1921, Asmara, 26 January 1922, ASBI, Affari coloniali—Pratiche, 305.

[63] Gestione talleri: trimestre 1 luglio-30 settembre 1921, Governo dell'Eritrea, Direzione di Finanza a Gestione Talleri, Asmara, 16 December 1921, ASBI, Filiale Asmara, Pratiche—Ramo banca, 138.

[64] *Ordinanza Governatore A.O.I*, Repertorio n. 41, Addis Ababa, 10 August 1936.

lira in the colony. This was challenged by the rise of commodity prices during the First World War, worsened by the uninterrupted use of the ever scarce and costly MTT as a unit of account in local markets. The policies implemented by the Italians to face the monetary crisis produced different consequences for different actors. Notwithstanding the ban on negotiations in MTT, those who were involved in trade across colonial borders (such as the *nəggāde*) continued to demand the Austrian thalers, exploiting the Italian need for food supplies. The Indian traders earned from the smuggling of the MTTs outside the colony, using their transregional networks and their knowledge of the regional currency market. The local retailers were forced to illegally fix the price of goods taking into account the quotation of the MTT, it being a *buffer* money employed by their wholesale suppliers. Finally, far from tackling speculation, the Italian policies hit those who were more bound to the colonial monetary system, earning a wage in lire and losing their purchasing power, namely those employed by the administration, and, in particular, indigenous soldiers.

Acknowledgements This chapter presents some of the results of a research financed by the Gerda Henkel Stiftung, as part of the project "Monetary Transitions: The Introduction of Colonial Currencies in East Africa and their Impact on Indigenous Societies and Economies" (AZ 37/F/16), principal investigator: Prof. Karin Pallaver. I wish to thank the participants in the International Workshop "Monetary transitions in colonial Africa" for their comments on the subject presented here. Earlier versions of this paper have been presented at the 14th Meeting of the African Economic History Network (AEHN), Barcelona, at the Ramblers Seminar organised by the International Studies Group (ISG), Bloemfontein, and at the Laboratory for the Economics of Africa's Past (LEAP), Stellenbosch. My gratitude goes in particular to Prof. Johan Fourie, Prof. Antony G. Hopkins, Prof. Ian Phimister and Prof. Dieter Von Fintel for their advice.

References

Alamanni, Ennio Quirino Mario. 1891. *La colonia eritrea e i suoi commerci*. Turin: Fratelli Bocca.

Bekele, Shiferaw, Uoldelul Chelati Dirar, Alessandro Volterra, and Massimo Zaccaria, eds. 2019. *The First World War from Tripoli to Addis Ababa (1911–1924)*. Addis Ababa: Centre français des études éthiopiennes.

Clarence-Smith, William G. 2001. "Indian and Arab Entrepreneurs in Eastern Africa (1800–1914)." *Publications de la Société française d'histoire des outremers* 2 (1): 335–349.

Colosimo, Gaspare. 1919. *Relazione al Parlamento sulla situazione politica economica ed amministrativa delle colonie italiane*. Rome: Tipografia del Senato.

Di Fausto, Amanto. 1918. "Relazione n.13. Sistema monetario." In *Problemi del dopoguerra. Relazione del governo dell'Eritrea*. Ministero delle Colonie, 117–122. Rome: Tipografia nazionale Bertero.

Eichengreen, Barry. 2019. *Globalizing Capital: A History of the International Monetary System* (Third Edition). Princeton, NJ; Oxford: Princeton University Press.

Feinstein, Charles H., Peter Temin, and Gianni Toniolo. 2008. *The World Economy Between the World Wars*. Oxford: Oxford University Press.

Killingray, David 1978. "Repercussions of World War I in the Gold Coast." *The Journal of African History* 19 (1): 39–59.

Kuroda, Akinobu. 2007. "The Maria Theresa Dollar in the Early Twentieth-Century Red Sea Region: A Complementary Interface between Multiple Markets." *Financial History Review* 14 (1): 89–110.

———. 2020. *A Global History of Money*. London: Routledge.

Leavens, Dickson H. 1939. *Silver Money*. Bloomington, IN: Principia Press.

Marcuzzi, Stefano. 2018. "A Machiavellian Ally? Italy in the Entente (1914–1918)." In *Italy in the Era of the Great War*, edited by Wanda Wilcox, 99–121. Leiden; Boston, MA: Brill.

Mariani, Lucio. 1918. *Il nuovo tallero italiano*. Rome: Tipografia dell'Unione Editrice.

Mauri, Arnaldo. 1967. *Il mercato del credito in Etiopia*. Istituto di Economia Aziendale dell'Università Commerciale "L. Bocconi," Milano. Milan: Giuffrè.

———. 1980. "Le credit dans la colonie italienne d'Erythree, 1882–1935." *Revue Internationale d'Histoire de la Banque* 20/21: 170–198.

———. 1998. "The First Monetary and Banking Experiences in Eritrea." *African Review of Money Finance and Banking* 1/2: 67–84.

———. 2003. "Eritrea's Early Stages in Monetary and Banking Development." Working Paper 3, Rochester, NY.

Michel, Marc. 2014. *Les Africains et la Grande Guerre. L'appel à l'Afrique (1914–1918)*. Paris: Karthala.

Ministero delle Colonie. 1913. *Relazione sulla colonia Eritrea del R. Commissario Civile Deputato Ferdinando Martini per gli esercizi 1902–1907*. Vol. 1. Rome: Tip. della Camera dei Deputati.

Miran, Jonathan. 2009. *Red Sea Citizens. Cosmopolitan Society and Cultural Change in Massawa*. Bloomington; Indianapolis: Indiana University Press.

Mwangi, Wambui. 2001. "Of Coins and Conquest: The East African Currency Board, the Rupee Crisis, and the Problem of Colonialism and the East African Protectorate." *Comparative Studies in Society and History* 4 (4): 763–787.

Pallaver, Karin. 2015. "War and Colonial Finance (Africa)." In *1914-1918-online. International Encyclopedia of the First World War*, edited by Daniel Ute, Peter Gatrell, Oliver Janz, Jones Heather, Jennifer Keene, Alan Kramer, and Bill Nasson. Berlin: Freie Universität Berlin. https://encyclopedia.1914-1918-online.net/article/war_and_colonial_finance_africa. Accessed on September 26, 2021.

———. 2018. "Da moneta straniera a moneta nazionale: Prima Guerra Mondiale, politiche coloniali e circolazione monetaria in Eritrea e Somalia'. In *Africa. Storia, Antropologia, Economia, Migrazioni*, edited by Donatella Strangio, 95–124. Roma: Edizioni Nuova Cultura.

———. 2019a. "Pockets Full of Rupees, but Bodies Very Weak: The Carrier Corps and Their Demobilization at the End of WWI in East Africa." *Afriche e Orienti* 3: 79–96.

———. 2019b. "A Currency Muddle: Resistance, Materialities and the Local Use of Money During the East African Rupee Crisis (1919–1923)." *Journal of Eastern African Studies* 13 (3): 546–564.

Pankhurst, Richard. 1963. "The Maria Theresa Dollar in Pre-War Ethiopia." *Journal of Ethiopian Studies* 1 (1): 8–26.

———. 1968. *Economic History of Ethiopia, 1800–1935*. Addis Ababa: Haile Sellassie University Press.

Podestà, Gian Luca. 1996. *Sviluppo industriale e colonialismo. Gli investimenti italiani in Africa orientale 1869–1897*. Milano: Giuffrè.

———. 2004. *Il mito dell'Impero. Economia, politica e lavoro nelle colonie italiane dell'Africa orientale 1898–1941*. Torino: Giappichelli.

Pollera, Alberto. 1926. *La vita commerciale etiopica e la circolazione monetaria Eritrea*. Tivoli: A. Chicca.

Quartararo, Rosaria. 1979. "L'Italia e lo Yemen. Uno studio sulla politica di espansione italiana nel Mar Rosso (1923–1937)." *Storia Contemporanea* 10 (4): 811–871.

Rossetti, Carlo. 1914. *Il regime monetario delle colonie italiane*. Rome: Tipografia dell'Unione Editrice.

Serels, Steven. 2019. "The Circulation of Modern Currencies and the Impoverishment of the Red Sea World 1882–2010." In *Currencies of the Indian Ocean World*, edited by Steven Serels and Gwyn Campbell, 141–164. New York: Palgrave Macmillan.

Sòrgoni, Barbara. 2001. *Etnografia e colonialismo: l'Eritrea e l'Etiopia di Alberto Pollera: (1873–1939)*. Torino: Bollati Boringhieri.

Tschoegl, Adrian E. 2001. "Maria Theresa's Thaler: A Case of International Money." *Eastern Economic Journal* 27 (4): 443–462.

Tuccimei, Ercole. 1999. *La banca d'Italia in Africa: introduzione all'attività dell'istituto di emissione nelle colonie dall'età crispina alla Seconda Guerra Mondiale*. Bari: Laterza.

Zaccaria, Massimo. 2012. "Agenzie commerciali, compagnie di navigazione e näggadras: la definizione dello spazio coloniale nell'Eritrea italiana'. In *Votare con i piedi: la mobilità degli individui nell'Africa coloniale italiana*, 273–312. Macerata: EUM.

———. 2018. "Feeding the War: Canned Meat Production in the Horn of Africa and the Italian Front." In *The First World War from Tripoli to Addis Ababa (1911–1924)*, edited by Shiferaw Bekele, Uoldelul Chelati Dirar, and Alessandro Volterra, 193–224. Addis Ababa: Centre français des études éthiopiennes.

———. 2019. "'Not a Hectare of Land Shall Remain Uncultivated This Year!' Food Provisions for Italy and the Role of the Colonies, 1917–1918." *Afriche e Orienti* 3: 25–41.

PART II

Money Forms, Politics and Banking in the Transition

CHAPTER 5

Gold, Currency and Stamps: The Rejected Plans for a State and Public Bank in Early Colonial Zimbabwe (1896–1907)

Tinashe Nyamunda

Introduction: Colonisation, Monetary Transitions and Economic Encounters, 1890–1896

Currently facing severe challenges with its monetary system which has never really been stable since independence, post-colonial Zimbabwe has consistently been teetering on the brink of economic collapse from the late 1990s onwards. A number of studies have begun tracing the possible causes of these challenges, correctly noting how its various currencies are extremely unstable, always fluctuating against the United States (US) dollar (Bond and Manyanya 2003; Nyamunda 2021; Nyamunda and Sibanda 2020). Managing currencies on the basis of a key currency peg is

T. Nyamunda (✉)
Department of Historical and Heritage Studies,
University of Pretoria, Pretoria, South Africa
e-mail: tinashe.nyamunda@up.ac.za

K. Pallaver (ed.), *Monetary Transitions*,
Palgrave Studies in Economic History,
https://doi.org/10.1007/978-3-030-83461-6_5

a product of highly problematic monetary arrangements, and is, in some ways sketched here, a legacy of how colonial economies were constructed and developed. This has resulted in a lack of imagination in terms of alternative monetary models that would best avoid the limitations of these global anchor pegs whose host countries use their status to control the global economy.

In analysing global economic relations, scholars pay far less attention to the economic impact of these currency block areas on peripheral countries in relation to their interest in contemporary floating currency dynamics (Palludeto and Abouchedid 2016). At present, they are more interested in and are laying heavier emphasis on, for instance, the question of whether the US dollar will remain an international anchor currency or this role will move to the Chinese renminbi (Eichengreen and Lombardi 2017, pp. 56–57; Gourinchas 2019). In some of these studies, there is a tacit acceptance of the necessity of a global key currency to allow smooth trade and the stability of the international exchange system. There is also an assumption that these global anchor currencies, although products of different forms of historical change as Paul Bohannan has suggested, occur naturally and are taken up by traders and states who benefit from network-increasing returns (Bohannan 1959). But as the case of Southern Rhodesia will illustrate, this is sometimes inaccurate. This paper articulates the ways in which sterling, a British anchor currency, was imposed on colonial Zimbabwe and its effects in the early experiences, particularly of its white settlers. It is hoped that the analysis will invite other scholars to consider that some dominant northern perspectives about colonial money being critical to civilisation and economic development can be challenged by the experiences within the colonies themselves, thereby providing an alternative southern perspective (Connell 2007; Morrell 2016).

The local monies, now relegated to the spectrum of soft currencies and their economies now problematically designated as *emerging*, trace their origins to the violent process of colonisation, imposition of colonial currencies, and as empires retreated, the remnants of colonial tools of exchange and extraction. The colonial anchor invariably shifted at different times from the official colonial to the USA relations of power and exchange. Colonial currencies were thus violently imposed in Southern Rhodesia with lasting legacies. Sometimes, in order to broadly appreciate the origins of contemporary challenges, historical origins may be a good starting point. The chapter uses a particular perspective: that of white settlers and not necessarily African communities as an angle that can show the extent to which colonial currencies were inefficient even when employed by those used to imperial exchange systems.

Tracing the British South Africa Company (BSAC) state's attempts to establish a currency ordinance and State and Public Bank of issue in Southern Rhodesia between 1896 and 1907, this chapter examines the foundations of a peripheral currency in the context of an emerging colonial economy. It suggests that "An Ordinance to Regulate Banking and Note Issue" (hereafter the Banking Ordinance) drafted among the first legislation of the Legislative Council (Leg.Co) that was established in 1898 had the potential to steer economic development in the nascent colony, independently of its imperial master, Britain.[1] But operating on the basis of a Royal Charter, the BSAC's authority on the southern Zambezia plateau, which was renamed Southern Rhodesia through an 1898 Order in Council, could be extended only to the limits prescribed by imperial legislation. The chartered company was established by Cecil John Rhodes in London in 1889 for the purpose of securing charters in order to allow its shareholders to benefit from the profits of mining in colonial territories. Although its earliest major shareholders included Rhodes, Barney Barnato, Alfred Beit and others, it was a public company that was floated on the London Stock Exchange from which it raised significant finance to fund its colonial exploration and other activities. Until its charters expired, it took the form of both a registered exploration mining and land company in Northern and Southern Rhodesia as well as that of a company government that was legally obliged by the terms of its charters to conform with imperial legislation despite the ambitions of its directors and the aspirations of the colony's white settler community. The Banking Ordinance represents early forms of negotiations between white settlers in the colony with BSAC officials and imperial legislators in London over the direction of the colony's currency and economy. A study of the challenges of implementing an imperfect monetary standard in a context where the conditions were not appropriate created tensions that reveal fractures between the imperial state and colonial society. It shows how, even in those early years of colonial settlement, feelings of white political and economic autonomy arose in response to their encounter with colonial context, but also how the broader monetary and economic

[1] An Ordinance to regulate Banking and Note Issue, National Archives of Zimbabwe (NAZ), A11-2/15/1-2. The file contains information and correspondence on the making of the Ordinance, the role of the Leg.Co and how it was eventually thrown out in 1907.

interests always took higher priority to the experiences of the resident white colonial community, never mind the colonised indigenous inhabitants. At the centre of imperial considerations was the mode of exchange that would facilitate the smooth extraction of primary commodities from the colonies.

Southern Rhodesia's attempt to pass a bank ordinance and establish a State and Public Bank provides an opportunity to examine the complexity of money, finance and banking. It looks at colonial systems of exchange as tools of colonial economy and state-making that position them as technologies of imperial power which facilitated financial exclusion as one of the main strategies of colonial encroachment, racial hierarchies and subjugation. It is a discourse that requires examining specific cases to fully appreciate, not only the origins of banking in Africa, but also its enduring legacies even in a postcolonial context. What follows is based on the study of monetisation and early banking experiences of Southern Rhodesia between 1896 and 1907. It adopts a peculiar monetary angle as a way to show the complexities of colonial economy and state-making of the BSAC. Located within a history of establishing a new colony and an encounter between indigenous societies and white settler pioneers, the chapter examines the struggle of establishing effective colonial occupation and the challenges of imposing colonial administrative systems with a particular focus on the economy. The focus on gold, currency and stamps is informed by the insistence of the British that despite numerous problems in establishing a colonial monetary system such as coin shortages, its imperial gold standard took precedence over all else. As such, the local white settler community came up with inventive strategies to cope with the problems, for example the use of stamped coupons. But the entanglement of these factors, the imperial gold standard, colonial currencies and coping mechanisms such as the use of stamped coupons as currency all demonstrate to what extent monetisation was a fraught process, rather than a revolutionary and substantial innovation that changed the course of African development as suggested by some scholar engaged in this chapter.

The chapter is divided into two sections and a conclusion. The first section challenges the notion that colonial monetisation produced a revolution in Africa that side-lined precolonial makeshift currencies for more efficient colonial currencies that made international trade sound. It introduces the case of Southern Rhodesia arguing that the introduction of colonial currency was neither sudden, revolutionary, nor did it make trade more efficient. The section uses the case of white settlers, themselves predominantly of British origin, to demonstrate the extent to which even their economic activities and transactions were disrupted, how they confronted coin shortages and limited banking services, as well as attempting a more permanent local solution by considering the idea to create a local state bank. The second section examines how, when the Legislative Council (Leg.Co)—a body established to run the white colonial affairs of Southern Rhodesia—was established, amongst its first ordinances was one to regulate banking and note issue, and to create a state bank. Although this ordinance was passed in the Leg.Co in 1899, it was simply kept in Britain and never ratified until it was thrown out in 1907. The chapter analyses, using the lenses of imperial sterling interests and local colonial encounters, why the ordinance was kept floating for seven years in a context where challenges continued to disrupt exchange in Southern Rhodesia. The section examines the power matrices at imperial and colonial level and how they informed the introduction of a currency in a British colony, including how these formed the earliest antecedents of settler disillusionment and feelings for colonial political and economic autonomy.

Currency, Colonial State and Economy Formation: Settler Experiences to 1898

The introduction of sterling currency and banking in early colonial Zimbabwe can be analysed within the context of scholarship of (i) currency hierarchies in centre–periphery relationships; and (ii) the introduction of so-called "modern" banking in Africa. Alex Pallutedo and Saulo Abouchedid have observed that in the structuralism and dependency scholarship that demonstrate the unequal power and economic relations between the centre and the periphery, issues involving money and international finance are relatively absent (Pallutedo and Abouchedid 2016). Yet, as illustrated in this chapter, not only can examining the hierarchy of money in centre–periphery relationship facilitate a better understanding of economic imbalances between the Empire's centre and the colonial periphery, but tracing the foundations of such connections in specific contexts is crucial to mapping the making of such relationships. In doing so, the chapter challenges the colonial notions that colonial monetisation and establishment of banks had a modernising effect which installed civilised exchange practices.

Central banking on the continent has been viewed as an important institution that was introduced on the eve of independence to help *emerging* economies establish autonomy in the context of an international liberal economic order in the post Second World War period. The monetary and banking sector is an important component of any economic system that provides the institutional capacity for economic activities in the form of credit facilities, loans, investments and a variety of other specialized activities (Chimombe 1982, p. 6; Seidman 1986). Orthodox economists generally view banks as performing the crucial role of intermediation, acquiring funds from surplus economic units and channelling them towards deficit units. In more simple terms, banks use people's savings to finance lending at interest, preferably to stimulate investments and consumption (Kim 1993, p. 35). Central banking, in this context, is established to regulate the monetary and banking sector through such policies as banking registration and supervision, money supply and interest rate management. In this explanation, money and banking are therefore ostensibly viewed as neutral facilities and tools for economic development. The study of contexts such as early colonial Africa and especially in settler colonies, in which versions of these banks were ultimately introduced, can provide a counter-narrative to these assumptions. The ways in which expatriate commercial banks operated in the colonies, more as institutions for the dissemination of currency and limited services to white settler communities, reveals the close connections they had to particularly the City of London and more general imperial interests.

Africa, and works on Africa, rarely feature in the scholarly outputs on the history of money. Where focus is given to them, it is usually with reference to their being recipients of *benevolent* European inventions. The transition towards colonial monetisation was originally described in the 1950s by Paul Bohannan as facilitating "modern money" (Bohannan 1959, p. 501; Latham 1971). "The shift to gold in Europe", Antony Hopkins suggests with reference to its influence on the making of a colonial monetary system in West Africa, "also carried implications for the underdeveloped world as a result of the penetration of Western technology and trade in the period following the industrial revolution" (Hopkins 1970, p. 101). Capturing the accepted conventions of the 1970s, he added that,

> The interests of the leading Western nations lay in ensuring that the currencies of countries engaged in international trade were soundly based, readily convertible, and otherwise compatible with the workings of the gold standard so that world commerce could be conducted and expanded with smooth efficiency. Many smaller countries, the junior trading partners of the dominant powers found it necessary to overhaul their diverse and often antiquated monetary systems, and some were unable to adapt to the requirements of the industrial world and its new gold standard without external assistance. (Ibid.)

The 1970s argument that colonial monetisation revolutionised exchange and made it efficient has endured to date, even if challenged by some scholars, including Jonathan Parry and Maurice Bloch as well as Jane Guyer (Guyer 1995; Parry and Bloch, 1989). But, as the case of Southern Rhodesia illustrates, that argument is highly problematic.

Guyer and Pallaver convincingly challenge evolutionary theories of money informed by "the externally provoked changes coming from centres of power to the peripheries" (Guyer and Pallaver 2018, p. 3) They argue that, because of "the [centuries old] prominence of international trade in the supply of currency goods to Africa, the continent is not marginal to global currency history" (Ibid., p. 2). Rather than precolonial exchange being archaic and unstable, dealing with multiple currencies and different stages of transitions or shifts over time allowed Africans to be inventive with different currency objects "both within and between systems in which the role of monetary authorities was local and specific, rather than national and international. . ." (Ibid.). Far from being evolutionary, currencies for European colonies were motivated by economic reasons, "including the reduction of transaction costs, the construction of colonial economies, and the increase in control over macroeconomic conditions" (Pallaver 2015, p. 271). Building upon historiographies that describe colonial monetisation "as an encounter of different regimes of value that gave rise to processes much more nuanced and complex than the replacement of precolonial currencies with coins and notes", Pallaver contributes towards scholarship that demonstrates that the imposition of colonial money was not an abrupt occurrence but "a gradual transition that encompassed the co-existence, sometimes for decades, of multiple currencies, circulating in different currency circuits and often performing different functions" (Ibid., pp. 473–474).[2]

It is convincing, as Pallaver submits, that "the monetary system that resulted from this transition was not a replacement of the old currency system with a new one, but rather the result of convergence of different systems of value and monetary practices", (Ibid., p. 474) especially where encounters with Africans were concerned. However, this study attempts to broaden this argument and suggest that there were initial attempts to trigger this "evolution" which failed, resulting in a gradual transition because of resistance, not just among Africans, but among early European settlers as well. Whereas a number of studies examine early colonial currency interfaces with African communities, this chapter considers how the colonial encounter informed currency practices by early white settlers within colonies such as Southern Rhodesia. In the context of Southern Rhodesia, the imperial state utilised its legislation to impose the use of a bloc currency in an attempt to centrally discipline and control exchange to their advantage. Bloc currency is used to refer to how colonial money fell into imperial monetary areas such as the sterling area that fully backed British colonial currencies, the Franc zone for French colonies and the Portuguese escudo monetary zone for example.[3] However, as the imperial state assumed greater control of the colonies and their peoples through various mechanisms over time, they achieved a degree of currency control as demonstrated by their success in bringing these colonies into the sterling orbit. But unlike the stability suggested by currency revolution scholars like Bohannan, this imposition instead destabilised African enterprise while granting increased access to extraction of colonial resources to Europeans through colonial currencies and economic formations.

The imposition of imperial currencies was destabilising to African livelihoods in the colonies, including in settler colonies. In the colonial setting of early Southern Rhodesia, economic encounters influenced colonial thinking about how the economy should be arranged. What became clear to the pioneer settler community and the white immigrants that settled later was the ways in which imperial interests and settler experiences were

[2] Pallaver builds upon the studies by, for example, Comaroff and Comaroff (2005), Şaul (2004), and Naanen (1993).

[3] For a more in depth explanation of colonial monetary areas, see Narsey (2016), Mata (2020), and Sylla (2020).

sometimes at variance, forcing them to disagree on how to make the colonial state and economy. Nowhere is this point clearer than the attempts by the early settler community and chartered government to establish economic autonomy in the colony through establishing a state bank, a policy that contradicted the British policy of consolidating all imperial trade in sterling.

To grasp the objectives of imperial monetary impositions on Southern Rhodesia, the ways in which the colony was established and its administrative machinery formed are crucial considerations. The principal actor in the colonisation of the Zimbabwe plateau was Cecil John Rhodes. Challenging claims by scholars such as John Gilbert Lockhart and Christopher Montague Woodhouse, John S. Galbraith and others who suggested that Rhodes did not pursue Empire for profit, but instead used his wealth to secure it, Ian Phimister argues that Rhodes was "a capitalist, who in many respects, utilized British imperialism for the benefit of his private fortune" (Galbraith 1973, p. 175; Lockhart and Woodhouse 1963, p. 142; Phimister 1974, p. 75). The colony was a product of Rhodes interests in what became the mining complex of Southern Africa (Phimister 1974).

Because of his penchant to secure finance from the City of London, Rhodes was a product of the British gentlemanly capitalist class who, Peter J. Cain and Antony G. Hopkins observed, "had a clear understanding of the market economy and knew how to benefit from it" (Cain and Hopkins 1986, p. 505). These gentlemanly capitalists pursued "making" money rather than "working for money" which they viewed as culturally inferior. But to make money, capitalists became gentlemen if, among other income streams in agriculture and urban property, "they were rentiers drawing on other types of investment, whether public or private" (Ibid., p. 506). For Rhodes, the mining in the colonies and speculation on the London stock exchange facilitated this. But the use of British sterling in the colonies would be critical, not just in his fortunes, but more importantly in preserving British financial hegemony which had been established in the 1870s (Balachandran 2008).

Phimister traces how Rhodes made his fortune in Kimberly and at the Rand, but eventually sought to expand his enterprise on the Zimbabwean plateau. Driven by the desire to make a fortune from his expanding mining empire and hoping that the new colony would be the next step in this direction, Rhodes established the BSAC to colonise the southern *Zambezia* region that became Southern Rhodesia (Phimister 1974). Through the Rudd concession signed with King Lobengula and the Royal Charter granted by the British Crown, Rhodes secured all land and minerals within the colony, triggering the colonial enterprise, and the pursuit of money-making by the company officials in the colony. However, for this enterprise to function, the company had to take up the burden of administration as well as provide political, economic, social and other forms of security for the settler population that would move there. Also, the colonial administrators assembled legal and economic institutions modelled on South Africa and Britain as the basis of their colonial authority. Among the institutions such as Roman-Dutch law and private property, a monetary system was established (Mseba 2016).

The first structures of a colonial state and economy were set up as the pioneer column settled in Mashonaland from September 1890. Ordinance number 3 (1891) established sterling based currency "in terms of which the standard coinage in the colony of the Cape of Good Hope became the standard coinage to be used within the territorial limits set out in the ordinance, namely Mashonaland" (Nyamunda and Mseba, forthcoming). Thereafter, Ordinance number 6 (1894), extended the territories in which this currency would be legal tender to cover the rest of Southern and Northern Rhodesia and Nyasaland (Ibid.). Minted by the Royal Mint in London, sterling silver coinage became the means of exchange within the colonies, and between the colonies and the imperial centre. As such, British colonial administration principally exercised authority on the colonial currency of Southern Rhodesia and its other central African colonies. The currency and banking infrastructure were set up well before the BSAC established the Leg.Co and other state institutions. The Department of the Administrator was in fact only established in 1894 and a Leg.Co in 1898.

Prior to the establishment of a bank, quasi-banking services were provided by non-banking institutions such as the Mashonaland Agency. Its core business was the provision of services in prospecting and exploratory work, the general management of mines as well as the advancement of loans on claims and it also included "the general business of banking and financial agents".[4] Although the agency served the pioneer business community, it was not a bank as defined by the British

[4] See one of its daily adverts in the *Rhodesia Herald*, 5 November 1892. The Mashonaland adverts regularly advertised in this paper.

Bank Act of 1844 and had no account with the Bank of England. Customers' funds could not be insured, and at best, the Mashonaland Agency was merely a financial agent that banked funds with South African banks on behalf of its clients.[5] It could therefore not secure the monetary stock needed to alleviate the cash shortages in the new colony. However, until the arrival of a bank, the Mashonaland Agency and the secretary to the BSAC administration, F. Rutherford Harris had to ensure that funds reached people from the Cape and Mafikeng bank.[6] Moreover, the nascent credit system based on South African cheques issued in the absence or shortage of coins was not sustainable. Many of the cheques issued bounced. Henry argues that this was because life in the early days was "rough and ready" with undercapitalised adventurers that sought to get rich quickly from the wealth of the rumoured second rand (Henry 1953, p. 89). As the cheques were drawn on Mafikeng based banks, they took two weeks to be transported, and if dishonoured, took another two weeks before the holder of the cheques knew of it. These conditions slowed down the rate of development of settler business enterprises. Despite these challenges, the first stockbroking firm was set up in 1891 to facilitate share trading. This was followed by the Standard Bank which was established in 1892 followed by other expatriate commercial banks (Karekwavanane 2003).

The Standard Bank of South Africa set up a branch in June 1892. They were followed by the African Banking Corporation in 1893 and the Bank of Africa in 1895 which were taken over by the Barclays Bank when it opened its Southern Rhodesia branch in 1922. But the banks had coins only when delivered into the colony, and shipments were extremely inefficient. Moreover, there were many risks when transporting the specie to the colony by road, not least because of thieves. Reminiscing about one incident where messengers were sent to deliver money, W. Pywell, a bank official, recalled that,

> A few years ago, two natives were sent in charge of £500 in gold coins to the bank and were about 10 days overdue . . . the party expected the worst to have happened. Native police were sent to scour the country but

[5] Ibid.

[6] Letters and correspondence to the Treasury, NAZ T2/29/24–27. It also shows how the chief magistrate was also responsible for ensuring that money arrived to its recipients from Mafikeng.

> without avail. One morning, much to our surprise, two natives turned up at the bank, the one limping very badly, and unrolled a small tin box which was rolled up in their blankets, and found to contain £500. One boy had been bitten by a snake and was laid up at a native village, his mate remaining with him until he was able to travel.[7]

These logistical difficulties and other dangers resulted in erratic supplies that disrupted transactions. Moreover, the banks were limited only to providing deposit and withdrawal services and not financing ordinary individuals. As a result, without access to finance in an early colonial setting, undercapitalised miners and farmers either utilised forced or ultra-cheap African labour. Even though the newly imposed colonial currency and the classification of settlers at the apex of the British colonial project in Southern Rhodesia would materially benefit them at the expense of Africans, the imposed monetary system was not immediately beneficial to them, and would take at least half a decade before the institution came close to being more efficient.

Within the ranks of the pioneer column were fortune seekers, especially prospectors who hoped to strike it rich once they "discovered" a "Second Rand". But the wealth they would make from mining ventures was informed stipulations of the Royal Charter at the imperial level, and BSAC policies in the colony. Most of the gold mined was sold to London in sterling, hence the need for British silver coinage in Southern Rhodesia. For its statutory role, the BSAC would benefit from "taxing", or acquiring 50 per cent of the proceeds of those sales. Later, this share was reduced to 25 per cent in 1903 before it was ultimately removed (Phimister 1974, p. 71). The BSAC government took up the role of governance. Many early settlers were involved in prospecting, and if they found gold, would usually sell their claims to larger mining companies such as Globe and Phoenix. The colonial project in the early days was based on a mining model and revenue sharing agreement between the miners and the company state. Having imposed colonial rule through violence, especially after the defeat of the Ndebele in 1893 and the Ndebele and Shona people in 1897, it became apparent that Southern Rhodesia did not hold the anticipated volumes of gold and what existed was contained in reefs that were difficult to exploit. Instead, what emerged was a speculator's paradise until the bubble burst in 1902, paving the way for the

[7] Reminiscences of W. Pywell, Standard Bank official, NAZ, ST2/1/1.

reconstruction of the mining industry and a shift by the company government towards developing the land resources of the new colony (Phimister 1974). But for the emerging colonial economy to function, a colonial monetary system had to be established.

At the core of the colonial economic system that was being established was European enterprise that would be sustained by ultra-cheap African labour. Contrary to the suggestion that colonial capitalist enterprise produced a modern economic framework based on white commercial agriculture, mechanised mining and secondary industrialisation that would voluntarily lead to a shift among Africans from traditional subsistence farming, scholars such as Giovanni Arrighi have shown how primitive accumulation was instead the origin of settler colonial projects (Arrighi 1966, pp. 37–39).[8] To establish a "monetary sector" as stipulated by the provisions of the Royal Charter and early colonial legislation, the colonised Africans had to be systematically coerced into the colonial economy. For example, as Charles van Onselen has shown, the whites, who could not afford to pay labourers, depended on the state's use of *Chibaro* (forced) labour (Van Onselen 1976). The process of establishing a colonial monetary system on which a colonial settler economy developed did not happen overnight and it took at least forty years to accomplish, with the final stage being the passing of the Magna Carta of white rule, the Land Apportionment Act (1930). This Act accelerated the seizure of land in a process that began in the 1890s and continued beyond 1930. The imposition of currency-based taxes gradually forced Africans who could not rely on the proceeds from the sale of their produce into unrewarding wage labour. Once they had little option but to work for settler enterprises, Africans were transformed into poor wage-earners who worked in the mines, farms and urban centres. But this process of African proletarianisation took close to half a century to establish. Africans had hitherto resisted through complex processes "mediated by contestations and conversations, rejection and acceptances, negotiations and complicity" (Ndlovu-Gatsheni 2008, p. 39).

At the outset, African resistance to colonial economy-making was not just a result of resisting a specific monetary system, but rather an opposition to its enforcement in a context where the colonial state

[8] For a comparative study in the context of India, see Levien (2015).

rendered other forms of exchange illegal. It was the way in which colonial legal tender was used to suppress African exchange traditions and economic activities and force them into an exploitative and unequal colonial system. The use of coins pre-existed colonialism as part of plural forms of exchange, but the imposition of colonial legal tender transformed economic relations between the coloniser and the colonised. Some Africans chose to resist colonial economic encroachment and stick to their precolonial exchange cultures such as barter or the exchange of iron implements. They only adopted colonial coinage for tax and other specific purposes. Others invariably were forced to integrate them in their lives to pay taxes and buy newly imported European goods, even though they were discriminated against and excluded from using the services of the colonial expatriate commercial banks. The case of an African man named Diamond, a messenger for the Standard Bank in Salisbury in the 1890s, who tried to copy the banking concept and apply it among Africans is illustrative. According to J. A. Henry,

> Diamond is credited with having started the first native 'bank' in the territory. It was a private bank in the strictest sense of the word. Perhaps it was the ease with which he saw people hand over their money to the bank tellers that bred the idea, and no doubt his prestige as 'bank boy' helped him with starting his bank at the location . . . He was entrusted by guileless depositors with their funds, which were stored in a large padlocked trunk sunk into the floor of Diamond's hut. Unfortunately, his trusting clients found in due course that he had utilised their money for his own private ends. The inevitable 'run' on the bank ensued and as a result Diamond spent some of his time in the gaol. (Henry 1953, p. 134)

Diamond's actions reflect African innovation to adapt and mimic European institutions in contexts where they were imposed on them and where black people were excluded from accessing their services. The failure to access banks left them with little choice but to hold on to their money until they could meet their cash obligations, causing further cash shortages. This was a problem that local white administrators could do little to help as they did not control monetary policy, the purview of the Bank of England, or determine money supply, which was left to the expatriate commercial banks.

The process of colonial monetisation on the basis of British sterling lines also directly affected white settler economic transactions in Southern Rhodesia. The major problem with securing a stable monetary system was with first, the supply of sustainable quantities of currency, and secondly, having banks and policies that would become the foundation of a sound financial system. All of these processes were managed by the Bank of England. Before the establishment of a branch of the Standard Bank in Southern Rhodesia in 1892, the nearest bank was at Mafikeng, the extra territorial headquarters of the British Bechuanaland. The journey there was long and arduous making currency supplies erratic. As a result, quasi-banking services were performed by non-banking institutions such as the Mashonaland Agency. Yet the agency was not a bank as legally defined by the British Bank Act (1844) and it held no account with the Bank of England, but with commercial banks in the Transvaal Republic. Because of this, the BSAC Secretary, F. Rutherford Harris worried about the security of depositors' funds. P. G. Swanson recounted that, "There were no fixed deposits, but substantial floating ones on government accounts and the personal accounts of the officials. These officials were paid by the treasury paying in a lump sum monthly with a list of the accounts to which it was to be credited: the [South African based] bank[s] advising the payees".[9] Clearly, an unstable supply of currency disrupted commerce. Even after the establishment of banks, the challenge of sustaining coinage supplies remained a big hindrance to transactions (Henry 1953, p. 34).

Throughout the 1890s cash shortages were so disruptive that the first editor of the *Mashonaland Herald and Zambezian Times*, W. E. Fairbridge, recounted going about selling the paper. But because of coin shortages, he had frequently accepted payment in kind, "sometimes a packet of candles, a pot of marmalade and even an old spade".[10] An early settler, K.A Byrne, recounted that, "[n]o one paid cash for anything—all business was done on credit. One signed cards for all drinks and accounts were rendered monthly".[11] The early settler communities opted to exchange cheques which often took over two weeks before they could be redeemed. However, they were often doubtful and sometimes bounced. Cheques were usually refused in individual exchanges. Others utilised barter as in the example of a white miner and his black servant. Because of cash shortages, he once paid his worker what he considered

[9] P.G Swanson's reminiscences in NAZ, ST2/1/1.

[10] Quoted in Henry (1953, p. 15).

[11] A respondent K. A. Byrne quoted in Reminiscences on the operations of the Standard bank, NAZ ST2/1/1. These were prepared for, but never actually included in the book published by Amphlett (1914).

to be a hefty wage; a blanket and an old shirt.[12] The shortages were so serious that in August 1891, the *Mashonaland Herald and Rhodesia Times* published a suggestion that the BSAC issue at a low rate of commission, 10s, £1 and £5 stamp coupons to circulate in place of cash pending the arrival of a bank.[13] Years later in 1895, Hugh Marshall Hole as Civil Commissioner of Bulawayo issued stamped coupons in place of cash to resolve cash shortages. He himself had faced problems of accessing cash. Hole explained how he found it difficult to purchase commodities at an auction. With a BSAC cheque" of £5.3s.4d., he bought a bag of potatoes for 17s.6d. for which the auctioneer gave him a pair of second hand boots valued at £2.10s, and a bottle of Cape Brandy for £1. To settle the balance Hole was offered "the choice of another bottle of brandy or a doubtful cheque of £0.5s" (Hole 1928, p. 27). As these examples illustrate, instead of a smooth assemblage of Cape and British sterling, the early settler communities had to barter, prompting them to imagine local solutions to these challenges.

Periods of conflict exacerbated shortages. During the Anglo-Ndebele War, the government had to protect the Bulawayo bank branches by sending the BSA police to protect the premises and assist in building *forts* around them. The African Banking Corporation and Bank of Africa would bring their valuables to the Standard Bank which had more secure strong rooms.[14] In response, the white community and the banks demanded that the government should issue token coupons to circulate, a request that was initially ignored.[15] However, in 1895, the Legal Tender Regulations were passed to allow the banks to issue their own notes.[16] The "Salisbury issue", as they were called, were to be issued as a temporary measure in the context of the 1896 Chimurenga War. Such conflicts, logistical challenges and other problems show how the establishment of a colonial monetary system became a long process and not a rapid event.

[12] A responded K. A. Byrne quoted in Reminiscences on the operations of the Standard bank, NAZ, T2/29/24.

[13] *The Mashonaland Herald and Rhodesia Times*, 29 August, 1891.

[14] According to various accounts, for example Bryne and Swanson, Reminiscences of the operations of the Standard bank, NAZ, ST2/1/1.

[15] Anonymous commentary in *The Rhodesia Herald*, 18 January, 1899.

[16] The Currency Media of Rhodesia, NAZ, D3/9/1, p.12.

The use of sterling currency was supposed to rapidly incorporate colonies into the orbit of the imperial economy. As the mining industry of Southern Rhodesia developed, the two northern territories were set up to provide labour for Southern Rhodesia, upon which the south-central mining complex was to be based. Theoretically, as the miners discovered gold and big capital came in, the sale of gold would have been transacted in sterling. But the reality on the ground was much different. In terms of securing workers, instead of providing cheap labour, Africans took up opportunities to supply agricultural commodities to emerging mining communities. But the major problem was the availability of the actual currency itself. Scholars such as Arrighi, van Onselen and Phimister have stressed the use of taxation for labour coercion and incorporating Africa into the wage economy. There's no doubt that coin shortages complicated this process (Arrighi 1970; Phimister 1988; Van Onselen 1976). The imperial centre, given its responsibility of ruling a large global empire never prioritised the currency issues of Southern Rhodesia. The supplies were erratic and expatriate banks could do little to manage the situation. Not only did this disrupt the process of colonial monetisation, it also affected fortunes of business enterprises. The pressure was put on the company government to come up with solutions that would help local white settlers and make Southern Rhodesia an attractive destination for more white immigrants. The local BSAC administrators would not have wanted their efforts to turn the colony into a white man's country disrupted by the logistical challenges of coinage supply and the absence of reliable banking.

Monetary Challenges, Colonial Legislation and the Plans for the State and Public Bank

The imperial project of sterling-backed monetisation in Southern Rhodesia was disrupted by the shortage of specie. This led settlers to consider erecting a local financial infrastructure. To achieve this, they pushed the BSAC for elected representation, demanding a Leg.Co to be established. The colony's white population could not rely on Bank of England policies to finance local colonial development or expatriate commercial banks to meet their coinage needs. The constraints that militated against banking operations saw a public call to action. An economist

W. Fosciety,[17] first suggested the idea to have a state or public bank created for the colony. Although there is limited information on him in the archives that I could find except references to him as an economist, Fosciety's ideas seem to have significantly influenced the Leg.Co to consider a local Banking Ordinance. Following his arguments in favour of the establishment of a public bank is a way to understand the motivations of the white settlers in an early colonial setting of Southern Rhodesia, especially the ways their economic encounters influenced the decisions they made. Fosciety had written to Rhodes himself saying that,

> Has not the time arrived when it would be alike beneficial to the public in Rhodesia and to the Chartered Company to establish a public or state bank in connection with, or as agents to the Chartered Company? And with this object in view . . . [I] lay before you a few particulars for perusal at your leisure, showing the principles on which such an institution should be conducted to ensure safety to the public and profit to the Chartered Company, as well as providing a favourable investment for capitalists.[18]

The private banks failure to resolve the cash shortages and provide credit was the chief driving force. This influenced Fosciety to suggest the establishment of a Bank that would not only supply local currency, but also determine financial policies such as the lending interest rates which would stimulate local investment into different sorts of businesses.

The State and Public Bank would regulate the printing of notes with security features on them as opposed to doubtful ones that had been printed by a company called Argus.[19] Because few people trusted its notes, many people hoarded coins and smuggled them to South Africa to earn a profit. Fosciety hoped that the bank would have to operate on the principles laid down for the regulation of the Bank of England,

> which have proved . . . to be in the best interests of all classes of the community, especially with regards to note issue as a circulating medium

[17] Apart from some archival references to him, there is no biographical references that I could find on Fosciety, except that he was an economist whose ideas influenced the Leg.Co to consider a local Banking Ordinance.

[18] Letter from Fosciety to C.J Rhodes, 24 August, 1896 in BSAC correspondence, NAZ T2/1/1.

[19] Ibid.

> and there is no reason why the Chartered Company should not derive the same benefit to issue bank notes as that which the British nation derives by the arrangement made with the Bank of England . . . As with the Bank of England, this state bank should be separated into two separate departments, the one exclusively confined to the issue, circulation, and payment of notes, and the other to the ordinary business of a bank of deposit and discount.[20]

The State Bank would be empowered to print banknotes for sovereigns, or for gold bars. The notes would be disseminated to the commercial banks for issuance to their clients. Once the gold or sovereigns were available, sovereigns would be paid out to redeem notes that people would have used in periods of coin shortages. This would, Fosciety thought, ensure the safety of commerce in the country and would not allow any private bank to have control over such currency.

Fosciety was aware that it would be difficult at first to fix a strictly convertible currency. It would not be determined by legislative enactment but the natural laws of equilibrium would decide an approximate amount. The difficulty would be reduced if the Chartered Company was represented on the board of such a bank. These suggestions were made in a colony that was less than seven years old. Fosciety encouraged the establishment of a local mint and the passing of an ordinance that would compel the State Bank to give banknotes for all gold coins brought in the colony.[21] The price, that would sustainably support the gold mining industry, would produce a profit of "£3 7d. 9s. per ounce of . . . pure gold", just as in the case of the Bank of England.[22]

The trading of gold was at this time under the two private banks that had been awarded gold buying licenses and established assay offices the previous year, the Standard Bank (whose Southern Rhodesia branch was set up in 1892) and the African Banking Corporation (which opened its doors in the colony in 1893). Concerning the ordinary business of the bank of deposit and discount "which so materially affects the monetary and commercial world" Fosciety felt that,

[20] Ibid.

[21] Ibid.

[22] Ibid.

> It should be compulsory under heavy penalty to publish quarterly, or at least half yearly statement of assets and liabilities of all banks in the country, as it is most desirable that not only the Chartered Company but the public generally should have constant means of knowing the general character of any bank's proceedings and the state of business generally in the country, which cannot be fairly estimated in the absence of such correct returns. This department should be unfettered by any legislative enactments and left to the entire discretion of an approved board of directors to conduct the same as with the bank of England . . .[23]

In the 1890s, commercial banks refused to redeem notes for gold. Instead, they paid out notes of other branches and sent out of the country every sovereign that they got. Fosciety argued that this was a risk for any country to run as trade would be paralysed in the event of the failure of the bank.[24]

A newspaper commentary in 1896 showed that Fosciety's suggestions received wide support amongst the white community. It noted that, "such a scheme should not be unnecessarily delayed, as with the railways here, as we hope in about eighteen months or so the demands of such an institution will be felt and we are well aware that there will be no difficulty in the presence of such a bank".[25] Given the wide appeal the issue had, Rhodes replied to Fosciety's suggestions, noting they were under serious consideration.[26] The idea, however, was quickly rejected by the BSAC in 1896. The Board was especially opposed to the proposal of retaining the gold produced in Southern Rhodesia and the building of a mint to produce coins. This would have disrupted the BSAC's business model of selling the colony's gold to England. Critically, the Board also recognised that local minting of coins would not be accepted in Britain. This was the preserve of the Royal Mint in London from which the Monarchy derived a seigniorage profit (Newlyn and Rowan 1954, p. 67). Most importantly, it was still too early to establish such an institution in a nascent colony. However, once a Leg.Co was established to represent settler interests, Fosciety's ideas would re-emerge, revealing the extent to which Company

[23] Ibid.

[24] Ibid.

[25] Quoted in commentary, *The Rhodesia Herald*, 30 September, 1896.

[26] Letter from Rhodes to Fosciety, not dated (n.d.), in BSAC correspondence, NAZ T2/1/1.

and imperial centre interests were sometimes at variance with those of the local white settlers.

As Fosciety's idea of a local bank of issue was rejected, coinage shortages worsened in the colony. The colony's administrators, forced as they were to use the very little silver coinage that reached Southern Rhodesia, had to improvise coping mechanisms in long periods of shortages. During the Jameson raid of 1896 and the Anglo-Boer War of 1899–1902, for example, there were crippling shortages of coins. R. C. Smith illustrates how the Boer forces had occupied Vryburg in the Cape, invaded Mafikeng and seized the railway line for nearly 100 miles therefore cutting communications between the Cape and Southern Rhodesia (Smith 1968, p. 54). This was the normal route for the conveyance of supplies including currency, especially silver which quickly disappeared from circulation. Smith highlights how this coin scarcity threatened to denude the farms and mines of African labourers whose wages were supposed to be paid regularly (Ibid). To avoid such a problem, the civil commissioner of Bulawayo, Hugh Marshall Hole, introduced the use of postage stamps affixed to a card/coupon as a temporary currency. Despite some initial hesitancy, the coupons bearing an order on the fiscal officer—who was Hole himself as the civil commissioner—to pay the value of the stamps if presented on or after 1st August, 1900, were adopted. Once the cash shortages were resolved, the coupons would then be redeemed (Henry 1953, p. 55).

The use of currency stamps was again seen as a temporary measure to offset coins shortages. However, at a quick glance, the coupons performed the role that the state bank would have played, by issuing notes as fiat money that was convertible when gold or silver coins became available. What is interesting is how the imperial state was fully aware of the actions of Marshall Hole in confronting the challenges. But there is no evidence to suggest that London tried to stop this. In fact, the British never immediately threw out the ordinance to regulate banking and note issue so as not to deflect the spirits of white settlers in Southern Rhodesia, especially during the Anglo-Boer War and its immediate aftermath. Given the crippling coin shortages, the British did not want to appear insensitive. So they held out and allowed the temporary measures to take effect while never considering a form of a more permanent state bank that would have issued notes to play a similar role as the stamped currencies. Instead, in the interests of preserving sterling as a key colonial currency, they only allowed the colony enough room to confront shortages, and not much else.

The currency stamps, or the "Marshall Hole notes", were issued in denominations of 3d., 6d., 1s., 2s., 2/6d. and 10s. and were in the form of small cards, on the front of which was printed:

> THE CIVIL COMMISSIONER, BULAWAYO
> Please pay in cash to the person producing this card the face value of the stamp affixed thereto, if presented on or after the 1st of August,1900. This card must be produced for redemption no later than 1st October 1900.
> (Signed) H. MARSHAL HOLE
> Secretary.[27]

On each card was affixed a postage stamp denoting the denomination. The stamps that were used were the BSAC's 1896–1897 issue of 3d., 6d., 1s., 2s., 2/6d. and 10s. stamps and the 6d. and 1s. denominations of 1898. They were issued to a total face value of £20,000 and all but £1000 of this amount was redeemed.[28] Despite initial resistance to "worthless stamp cards", the settlers quickly accepted them as they needed to pay their African employees. Africans sometimes resisted the coupons because they mistrusted their authenticity. There were cases where some employers used old stamps and forged cards to escape paying their workers.[29] This led the Africans to demand payment in coin which they had the propensity to hold in the face of such shortages. Although in this case the government had acted as a quasi-monetary authority, it was still limited by the absence of empowering legislation. In any case, however, to some extent, these notes helped to ease the problems caused by the shortages of coins.

The state and the settlers needed to adapt to situations that they could not control. In Southern Rhodesia, the monetary transitions to colonial currency proved problematic on a number of levels. First, only sterling was passed off as legal tender, and all other forms of money criminalised. The colonial state was attempting to demonetise any precolonial African currencies which they argued where makeshift or "primitive". The imperial state never considered whether the transacting community of

[27] The Currency Media of Rhodesia, NAZ S111, p. 15.

[28] Ibid.

[29] *The Rhodesia Herald*, 9 August, 1900.

Southern Rhodesia accepted this currency. As such, power was at the centre of the imposition. To ensure compliance among Africans, legislation was passed to enforce acceptance; for example, taxes were required to be paid mostly in the form of coins. Also, commodities imported from Europe would be sold mostly in cash, if it was available. To justify this move, the imperial state gave the impression that using sterling which was regulated by the international gold standard would create efficient trade. But, as the experience of Southern Rhodesia demonstrates, this was at the expense of local settlers and African communities. Even if the white community was well-positioned to benefit materially through primitive accumulation which involved the utilisation of forced and ultra-cheap black labour to produce commodities sold to Britain in sterling, currency shortages disrupted their activities. So the transition was not smooth and produced interesting dynamics. As the attempts to create a state bank shows, the settler community had little confidence in Britain's capacity to supply coins. Moreover, the State Bank would have provided not only local banknotes, but also the capacity to regulate how banks would lend to the settler society, a function the imperial state was not ready to grant in a nascent colony. This would also have provided economic autonomy in a colony that Britain still wanted access to and control over in order to exploit. The extraction of agricultural produce and minerals was dependent on Britain's control of currency arrangements. The State Bank Ordinance had to be stopped to retain control of settler activities in the colony, as well as Southern Rhodesia's economy.

The challenges faced by the settler community influenced their conviction to consider the suggestions made by Fosciety in 1896. Once the Leg.Co was established in 1898, they acquired a representation that could challenge the company officials in government affairs. Thus, the settlers introduced the matter of a State and Public Bank among their first order of business. The issue of the contrasts between BSAC and settler interests had been among the major sources of contention that resulted in settler community demanding representation in a Leg.Co. The new settler representatives quickly moved to draft an Ordinance that would regulate banking and note issue.[30] This Ordinance sought to ensure the circulation of banknotes as a solution to augment the currency supplies. In a way, the issue of currency stamps had shown how a monetary system controlled by

[30] The correspondence on these issues and the draft bill can be found in Correspondence responses to Ordinance to regulate Banking, NAZ A11-2/15/1-2.

the government could guard against such problems as coin shortages. At the opening of the first Legislative Council meeting in 1899, the senior Administrator, W.H. Milton, introduced this bill among others.[31] On the second reading of the bill in council, Sir Thomas Scanleen, former prime minister of the Cape Colony (1881–1884), who had become legal advisor to Rhodes and member of the Leg.Co, said that the bill was "intended to apply the leading principles of the Cape Bank Act of 1891. Clause 17 provides for the issue in Rhodesia of the notes of the value of £1, £5 and £10, and clause 14 safeguards the interests of the public by compelling the banks to deposit securities against note issues".[32] These clauses reflect some of the issues that Fosciety had suggested in his proposal for a state bank. The bill also dealt with the custody of dies and the legal tender of notes. In the event of any bank failing to take up its notes, the BSAC would pay in gold the notes outstanding.

The attempts by the Leg.Co to regulate banking and note issue as well as establish a bank of issue went contrary to the interests of Britain. Gopalan Balachandran has demonstrated the connection between international financial arrangements, the role of markets, the place of colonies in this matrix and how the British Empire consolidated and incorporated them into the spread of institutions such as the gold standard which it controlled (Balachandran 2008). Phimister took the example of Rhodes and the BSAC's exploits in Southern Rhodesia to demonstrate the ways in which the colony was a market for extractives such as gold from which the company speculated on the stock market creating personal sterling fortunes for the directors (although not for the shareholders who never enjoyed a dividend until 1924). To ensure, as Hopkins observed, smooth trade between Britain and its colonies, in which the Empire purchased gold at prices it determined in sterling, Southern Rhodesia had to be integrated into the Empire-wide sterling network. Only this way would Britain retain its apex position at the helm of the international gold standard, at least until 1931 when it finally abandoned it. The point from all of this, is that Southern Rhodesia would never have successfully created its own system that excluded it from these imperial financial arrangements.

[31] Opening speech by W.H. Milton, *Southern Rhodesia Legislative Council Debates*, 15 May 1899.

[32] Quoted in *Legislative Council Debates*, 19 May 1899.

The sterling arrangements in which the Bank of England determined policies for, and shipped coins to the colonies disrupted commerce, not just among African colonial subjects, but settlers as well. Legally bound by monetary legislation and restricted to British coinage, Southern Rhodesia's financial arrangements disrupted trade and slowed progress for the white settler community. Settlers felt neglected and only managed through inventive alternatives such as barter, using cheques and stamped coupons as well as traded with quasi financial institutions such as the Mashonaland Agency. Although the Leg.Co was allowed to establish the Department of the Treasury in 1903 to manage the colony's finances, it was limited to doing this through the existing expatriate banks and through sterling. But in terms of shortages of coins and how they disrupted trade, the struggle continued. The only way the settlers could consider resolving these problems was through passing their own legislation that allowed them to establish extra-imperial institutions through the ordinance to regulate banking and note issue as well as establish the State and Public Bank of issue. But this challenged the whole point of British economic imperialism and its global control of the gold standard.

To safeguard its financial and political authority within the colonies, certain policies and legislation could not be passed without British government consent. This illustrates Crick's observation that "the exercise of responsibility for currency arrangement was always subject to a reserved power of the home government" (Crick 1965). So, although the Ordinance to Regulate Banking and Note Issue was unanimously passed in the Leg.Co, matters relating to monetary arrangements had to receive royal assent first. This was because most British colonies were backed by the sterling and the coloniser was sensitive to the fact that any monetary developments in the colony had a bearing on the metropole. As such, the British Treasury preferred to retain control on all matters relating to money. The proposed Ordinance would have given Southern Rhodesia a huge measure of autonomy hence it failed to receive royal assent. Although London initially suggested changes to the ordinance that would reduce this autonomy, it was finally thrown out altogether in 1907.[33]

[33] Letter for Sir William of the London office responding to L. Michell, the administrator of Southern Rhodesia, 7 January, 1907, in Correspondence responses to Ordinance to regulate Banking, NAZ A11–2/15/1–2.

Conclusion

Political power is at the heart of international economic relations (Kirshner 2003). The United States has enjoyed this apex position since the Bretton Woods arrangements in 1944 which elevated the US dollar to the position of an international key currency. Many countries determine the value of their currencies and measure their gross domestic products on the basis of US dollar valuations. At the time when Zimbabwe was colonised and came under BSAC administration, Britain enjoyed this position. The powers that control global economies are determined to retain their position as long as they can.[34] So when Southern Rhodesia, a nascent colony, germinated the idea to create an independent financial authority which issued its own currency, it was unsurprising that the proposed banking and currency legislation they drew up was never approved in Britain.

The experience of attempting to establish an autonomous currency and banking system in Southern Rhodesia reveals interesting factors about colonialism. As noted above, Hopkins suggests that the adoption of imperial-based "sound and readily convertible" currencies facilitated smooth transactions (Hopkins 1970, p. 101). He argued that this resulted in the elimination of "antiquated" precolonial currencies.[35] But the experiences of Southern Rhodesia point to a different conclusion. A.S. Mlambo stresses that, "it is in many ways a story of how a small immigrant white minority arrogated to themselves the right to determine the pace and direction of the nation's development at the expense of the majority and how the African majority struggled to ascertain their rights" (Mlambo 2002, p. 3). As illustrated in this chapter, the adoption of a colonial currency was not an event, but a drawn out process characterised by very serious coinage shortages that disrupted trade and complicated colonial economic development. Even the introduction of expatriate banks did not resolve this problem. In fact, most of the colonial community, including white settlers, resorted to barter, stamped coupons and other methods of *primitive* accumulation such as forced labour to chase their production targets. Moreover, even if white settlers were agents of the imperial state

[34] For a more comprehensive discussion of how super powers control international financial arrangements, see for example, Cohen (1998).

[35] Ibid.

arrogating to themselves the control to steer the trajectory of development, they were also affected by encounters of currency shortages and disrupted trade that they resorted to trying to pass legislation that would have given them financial autonomy from Britain.

The second point is that the economy is a function of international power relations. Sterling facilitated the extraction of gold and other minerals from the colonies in a currency that the British controlled and in which the BSAC could derive profit from their speculative activities on the London Stock markets. The settlers, who were certainly more privileged because of the position of power that they held, were directly affected by colonial encounters. The colonised Africans were at the bottom of this financial pyramid and bore the most significant brunt of an imposed legal tender that was in short supply and which was issued by banking institutions they had no access to (Arrighi 1970; Van Onselen 1976). Successive policies were passed designed to reduce them into ultra-cheap wage labourers who could only access this money from their white employers in order to pay tax obligations even if they could barely sustain their families. The frustration for the white settlers was that, at their level, they did not receive sufficient support to make the colonial enterprise more efficient for themselves.

The struggle of the white settlers to get the British government to approve the ordinance that would have provided some degree of financial autonomy and a level of stability reveals interesting power dynamics. In this case, currency supplies were never stable, trade was never conducted with smooth efficiency and often disrupted, and the return to barter and other methods of exchange were certainly not antiquated. If anything, as the process of colonial monetisation proceeded in fits and starts over a period of almost fifty years, it was the inventive strategies of resistance, accommodation, adaptation, and some degree of acceptance among the white settlers and black colonial subjects that facilitated economic transactions and transitions. Even after the proposed ordinance was rejected in 1907, the currency supply challenges persisted well into the 1940s. What was at the heart of the use of the legal tender regulations was imperial power over what currency to be used, rather than which was more efficient and *modern* enough to facilitate smooth exchange and expanded trade. In any case, trade was also a function of imperial power.

The whole point of colonialism was to secure certain strategic markets and the imposition of imperial block currencies facilitated the extraction of resources. Crucially, the experiences of the Leg.Co members created a legacy among the colony's white politicians of challenging imperial policies that they did not agree with. This created a sense of ownership of the colonial territorial space for the settlers who felt that the development of the country was because of their activities. By 1923, the Leg.Co had successfully campaigned to make Southern Rhodesia a white man's country ruled as a settler colony (Phimister 1984). This created the antecedents for the white settler rebellion against Britain in 1965, when the Rhodesian government refused to accept Britain's insistence on the inevitability of black majority rule. Even after the draft ordinance was thrown out, the white settlers continued to demand monetary autonomy, ultimately securing the permission to create a currency board in 1938, a regional central bank in 1956, and a Rhodesian central bank in 1965 (Mseba 2016; Nyamunda 2017a, b). But at the centre of all of these developments remained British economic power which retained its southern African colony's currency under full sterling cover until the 1965 Unilateral Declaration of Independence by Southern Rhodesia. However, the foundation of imperial financial control was laid by the Royal Charter and cemented by subsequent imperial legislation that supported the rejection of the settler demands for financial authority through the ordinance to regulate banking and note issue.

References

Amphlett, George T. 1914. *History of the Standard Bank of South Africa: 1862–1913*. Glasgow: Robert Maclehose and Company Ltd.

Arrighi, Giovanni. 1966. "The Political Economy of Rhodesia." *New Left Review* 39: 35–65.

———. 1970. "Labour Supplies in a Historical Perspective: A Study of the Proletarianization of the African Peasantry in Rhodesia." *The Journal of Development Studies* 6 (3): 197–243.

Balachandran, Gopalan. 2008. "Power and Markets in Global Finance: the Gold Standard, 1890–1926." *Journal of Global History* 3 (3): 313–335.

Bohannan, Paul. 1959. "The Impact of Money on an African Subsistence Economy." *The Journal of Economic History* 19 (4): 491–503.

Bond, Patrick, and Masimba Manyanya. 2003. *Zimbabwe's Plunge: Exhausted Nationalism, Neoliberalism and the Search for Social Justice*. Harare: Weaver Press.

Cain, Peter J., and Antony G. Hopkins. 1986. "Gentlemanly Capitalism and British Expansion Overseas I. The Old Colonial System, 1688–1850." *The Economic History Review* 39 (4): 501–525.

Chimombe, Theresa. 1982. "The Role of Banks and Financial Institutions in the Accumulation and Reinvestment of Capital in Zimbabwe." M. Phil diss., University of Zimbabwe.

Cohen, Benjamin J. 1998. *The Geography of Money.* New York: Cornell University Press.

Comaroff, Jean, and John L. Comaroff. 2005. "Colonising Currencies: Beasts, Bank Notes, and the Colour of Money in South Africa." In *Commodification, Things, Agency and Identity: The Social Life of Things Revisited*, edited by Wim Van Binsbergen and Peter L. Geschiere, 63–82. Leiden: Brill.

Connell, Raewyn. 2007. *Southern Theory: The Global Dynamics of Knowledge in Social Science.* Sydney: Allen and Unwin.

Crick, Wilfred F. 1965. "The Framework of Inter-relations." In *Commonwealth Banking Systems*, edited by Wilfred F. Crick, 1–53. Oxford: Clarendon Press.

Eichengreen, Barry, and Domenico Lombardi. 2017. "RMBI or RMBR? Is the Renminbi Destined to Become a Global or Regional Currency?" *Asian Economic Papers*: 16 (1): 35–65.

Galbraith, John S. 1973. "Cecil Rhodes and His 'Cosmic Dreams': A Reassessment." *The Journal of Imperial and Commonwealth History* 1 (2): 173–189.

Gourinchas, Pierre-Olivier. 2019. "The Dollar Hegemon? Evidence and Implications for Policy Makers." Paper presented at the 6th Asian Monetary Policy Forum, May 31, in Singapore.

Guyer, Jane I., ed. 1995. *Money Matters. Instability, Values and Social Payments in the Modern History of West African Communities.* Portsmouth, NH: Heinemann.

Guyer, Jane I., and Karin Pallaver. 2018. "Money and Currency in African History." In *Oxford Research Encyclopedia of African History.* Oxford: Oxford University Press.

Henry, James A. 1953. *Sixty Years North of the Limpopo.* Salisbury: Standard Bank of South Africa.

Hole, Hugh M. 1928. *Old Rhodesian Days.* London: Macmillan.

Hopkins, Antony G. 1970. "The Creation of a Colonial Monetary System: The Origins of the West African Currency Board." *African Historical Studies* 3 (1): 101–132.

Karekwavanane, George. 2003. "A History of the Zimbabwe Stock Exchange: The Formative Years." *Zambezia* 30 (1): 9–34.

Kim, Taheo. 1993. *International Money and Banking.* London and New York: Routledge.

Kirshner, Jonathan. 2003. "Money Is Politics." *Review of International Political Economy* 10 (4): 645–660.

Latham, Anthony J. H. 1971. "Currency, Credit and Capitalism on the Cross River in the Pre-Colonial Era." *The Journal of African History* 12 (4): 599–605.

Levien, Michael. 2015. "From Primitive Accumulation to Regimes of Dispossession: Six These on India's Land Question." Paper presented at Johns Hopkins University, March 17, in Baltimore, MD.

Lockhart, John, and Christopher M. Woodhouse. 1963. *Rhodes*. London: Hodder and Stoughton.

Mata, Maria E. 2020. *The Portuguese Monetary Escudo Zone: Its Impact on Colonial and Post-Colonial Africa*. London: Palgrave.

Mlambo, Alois S. 2002. *White Immigration into Rhodesia*. Harare: University of Zimbabwe Publications.

Morrell, Robert, 2016. "Making Southern Theory: Gender Researchers in South Africa," *Feminist Theory* 17 (2): 191–209.

Mseba, Admire. 2016. "Money and Autonomy in a Settler Colony: The Politics of Monetary Regulation in Colonial Zimbabwe." In *The Cultural History of Money and Credit: A Global Perspective*, edited by Chia Y. Hsu, Thomas S. Luckett and Erika Vause, 51–65. Lanham, MD: Lexington Books.

Naanen, Ben. 1993. "Economy Within an Economy: The Manilla Currency, Exchange Rate Instability, and Social Conditions in South-Eastern Nigeria, 1900–48." *The Journal of African History* 34 (3): 425–446.

Narsey, Wadan. 2016. *British Imperialism and the Making of Colonial Currency Systems*. Basingstoke: Palgrave Macmillan.

Ndlovu-Gatsheni, Sabelo J. 2008. "Mapping Colonial and Cultural Encounters, 1880s–1930s." In *Becoming Zimbabwe: A History from the Pre-Colonial Period to 2008*, edited by Brian Raftopoulos and Alois S. Mlambo, 115–140. Harare: Weaver Press.

Newlyn, Walter T., and Rowan, David C. 1954. *Money and Banking in British Colonial Africa*. Oxford: Clarendon Press.

Nyamunda, Tinashe. 2017a. "British Sterling Imperialism, Settler Colonialism and the Political Economy of Money and Finance in Southern Rhodesia, 1945–1962," *African Economic History* 45 (1): 77–109.

———. 2017b. "Money, Banking and Rhodesia's Unilateral Declaration of Independence," *The Journal of Imperial and Commonwealth History* 45 (5): 746–776.

———. 2021. "'Open for Business' but bankrupt: Currencies, the 'New Dispensation' and the Zimbabwean Economy," *Journal of Asian and African Studies* 56 (2): 204–217.

Nyamunda, Tinashe, and Admire Mseba. Forthcoming. "Money in South-Central Africa, 1890–1931: Africans, Imperial Sterling and Colonial Economy Building," *African Studies Review*.

Nyamunda, Tinashe, and Geraldine Sibanda. 2020. "The Making of Zimbabwe's Currency and Economic Crisis: International Financial Architecture, Nationalism and Economic Policies." In *The Oxford Handbook of Zimbabwean Politics*, edited by Miles Tendi, JoAnn McGregor, and Jocelyn Alexander,

Oxford: Oxford University Press. https://www.oxfordhandbooks.com/view/10.1093/oxfordhb/9780198805472.001.0001/oxfordhb-9780198805472-e-15.

Pallaver, Karin. 2015. "'The African Native Has No Pocket': Monetary Practices and Currency Transitions in Early Colonial Uganda." *International Journal of African Historical Studies* 48 (3): 471–499.

Palludeto, Alex W. A., and Saulo C. Abouchedid. 2016. "The Currency Hierarchy in Centre-Periphery Relationships." *Analytical Gains of Geopolitical Economy* 30B: 53–90.

Parry, Jonathan, and Maurice Bloch, eds. 1989. *Money and the Morality of Exchange*. Cambridge: Cambridge University Press.

Phimister, Ian. 1974. "Rhodes, Rhodesia and the Rand." *Journal of Southern African Studies* 1 (1): 74–90.

———. 1984. "Accommodating Imperialism: The Compromise of the Settler State in Southern Rhodesia, 1923–1929." *The Journal of African History* 25: 279–294.

———. 1988. *The Economic and Social History of Zimbabwe to 1948: Capital Accumulation and Class Struggle*. London: Longman.

Şaul, Mahir. 2004. "Money in Colonial Transition: Cowries and Francs in West Africa." *American Anthropologist* 106 (1): 71–84.

Seidman, Ann. 1986. *Money and Public Finance in Africa*. London: Zed Books.

Smith, Cherer R. 1968. *Rhodesia. A Postal History*. Salisbury: Mardon Printers.

Sylla, Ndongo S. 2020. "Colonialism Without Colonies: France, Africa and the CFA Franc." *Review of African Political Economy*, February 18. https://roape.net/2020/02/18/colonialism-without-colonies-france-africa-and-the-cfa-franc/. Accessed on 21 April 2021.

Van Onselen, Charles. 1976. *Chibaro, African Mine Labour in Southern Rhodesia, 1900–1933*. London: Pluto Press.

CHAPTER 6

Beyond Imperial Interests: Settler Regimes, Capital and Africans in Colonial Southern Africa's Currency Politics to 1920

Admire Mseba

In February 1893, representatives of the South African Republic (the Transvaal), Natal, the Orange Free State and the Cape Colony convened in Pretoria to induce the various governments to enter into a convention to establish "a truly South African mint" (*The Star* 1928). "The diversity of the coinages then in circulation", the convention's dignitaries argued, was undesirable. "It is not more diversity, but more unity that we want in the general affairs of South Africa" the mint conference attendees stressed. Pursuant to this vision, the conference members proposed "that the existing mint—established by the South African Republic in 1890—should be reconstituted on a new basis as an interstate Mint which would mint a uniform and truly national currency" (*The Star* 1928).

A. Mseba (✉)
University of Missouri-Columbia, Columbia, MO, USA
e-mail: amkgt@missouri.edu

K. Pallaver (ed.), *Monetary Transitions*,
Palgrave Studies in Economic History,
https://doi.org/10.1007/978-3-030-83461-6_6

Curiously, however, "the conference adjourned without coming to an agreement" and the South African territories would remain without a uniform currency until the formation of the Union of South Africa in 1910 (*The Star* 1928). Even then, the new South African currency circulated alongside the currency of the former South African Republic.[1] Indeed, it was not until 1920 that South Africa adopted a single, uniform, currency. Both, Union and South African Republic currencies, also circulated as legal tender in the British High Commission territories of Bechuanaland (Botswana), Basutoland (Lesotho) and Swaziland (Eswatini). At the same time, a combination of British and Cape Colony and, after 1910, British and South African coins, circulated as legal tender in Britain's Southern African territories of Southern Rhodesia (Zimbabwe), Northwest and Northeastern Rhodesia, the latter amalgamating into Northern Rhodesia (now Zambia) in 1911.

Why, despite their understanding that a uniform currency was desirable, did the rulers of Southern Africa in the late nineteenth and early twentieth century fail to provide one? Why did some of these currencies circulate in some but not in other territories even within Britain's Southern African empire? How did the economies and societies of Southern Africa influence currency questions in the region? This chapter attempts to answer these questions.

The chapter focuses on the multiple interests that informed the adoption, use and rejection of certain currencies in Southern Africa from the mid-seventeenth to the early twentieth century to illuminate the broader questions of money and the making of imperial and colonial

[1] By the time of the consummation of the Union of South Africa in 1910, the British possessions in Southern Africa were firmly tied to the sterling. An 1881 Order-in Council enabled the full application of the 1870 Imperial Coinage Act at the Cape, fixing the weights and fineness of sterling coins that would be legal tender in the colony. Subsidiary coins were kept at par with the sterling. Two years later, in 1882, another Order-in-Council extended the Imperial Coinage Act (1870) to Natal, setting its metallic currency on a sterling basis. Subsequent Orders-in Council extended the Cape and sterling coinages to Southern Rhodesia (1891), Bechuanaland, Basutoland and Swaziland. But as will be seen in this essay, from the 1880s onwards, in many of these territories the South African Republic gold sovereign also circulated as legal tender. This sovereign was brought to these territories by migrant labourers returning from the Witwatersrand mines. Meanwhile, the South African Republic introduced its own coinage, a pound, in 1874. For its part, the Orange Free State never introduced its own coinage and so, there, both the South African Republic and the sterling based Cape Coinage circulated as legal tender.

relations. Various scholars (Hazelwood 1952; Krozewski 2001; Mseba 2005; Nyamunda 2015, 2017a, b) have shown how asymmetrical power relations allowed the British to dictate broader questions of finance and, especially after the Second World War, manipulate colonial currencies for their own benefit. With a colonial currency fully backed by and pegged to the pound sterling, these scholars show, Britain turned to the empire to purchase goods in a move that allowed it to save on its dollar expenditures. At the same time, she accumulated dollar reserves by compelling the colonies to deposit dollar export receipts in London. Most of this scholarship (Hazelwood 1952; Newlyn and Rowan 1954; Krozewski 2001; Hinds 2001; Schenk 2010; Sutton 2015; Narsey 2016) illuminate the imperial calculus in the making of colonial currencies and especially its pegging to the pound sterling.

However, it was not only the power of the financial and imperial elites in London which informed decisions about currency in the colonies. South African scholarship has, for example, long demonstrated the class tensions and accommodations that informed currency questions in the country in the years leading to the 1920s (Gelb 1984; Breckenridge 1995). Similarly, scholars working on other parts of the African continent implore us to rethink earlier characterizations (Bohannan 1959; Hopkins 1966) of the impact of colonial currencies as a sweeping revolution from the outside precisely because, there, the adoption of certain colonial currencies was not only gradual and its impact measured, it was equally influenced by local conditions (Guyer 1995). In parts of West Africa, for example, commodity currency predating the arrival of colonial coins continued to circulate alongside the new money brought by colonial rulers (Ekejiuba 1995). In some cases, as in the East African case that Pallaver (2019) so eloquently discusses, African protests drove colonial officials to rethink the introduction of certain denominations.

This chapter adds to this growing literature on the politics of currency by looking at one particular region: Southern Africa. It particularly explores currency politics from the mid-seventeenth century to the early twentieth century in the area that now constitutes South Africa, Lesotho, Eswatini, Botswana, Zimbabwe and, to some extent, Mozambique. There, the essay suggests, the currencies in circulation between the establishment of white settlement at the Cape in 1652 and 1920 reflected the contingent calculations of multiple actors. These include the region's imperial and colonial governments as well as its white settlers. From the late nineteenth century, the currencies in circulation in Southern Africa reflected the integration of the region's political economy. They also reflected the initiatives of a mobile African workforce that was not only paid using these currencies, but also carried them across colonial borders. There, they used them to pay taxes, purchase goods and undertake social transactions including the payment of bridewealth. The currency in circulation in colonial Southern Africa, then, equally reflected the varied adaptations of African social institutions as Africans came to terms with the new conditions of accumulation and social transaction created by a regional colonial capitalist economy.

White Settlement and Colonial Currency Questions in Southern Africa's Coastal Enclaves to the Mid-Nineteenth Century

When representatives of the South African territories gathered to consider the question of a uniform currency in Pretoria in 1893, they were responding to the new conditions that emerged in the wake of the mineral revolution—the social, economic and political changes that followed the discovery of diamonds and gold in the 1860s and 1870s. These changes, as we now know, included, among other things, the rise of a large-scale capitalist mining industry with a voracious appetite for cheap, unskilled, labour, the emergence of a region-wide system of migrant labour as well as the extension of European rule and, with it, new, competing colonial/settler jurisdictions in the region. While currency questions had exercised the minds of the rulers of settler enclaves such as the Cape Colony and, from the mid-nineteenth century, the Orange Free State and the South African Republic/Transvaal for some time, for most of the interior of Southern Africa, the conditions that necessitated this discussion also marked a departure from the ways in which locals had previously completed their economic and social transactions. For centuries, if not millennia, the Bantu and Khoe Khoe speaking inhabitants of this region had long participated in both local and global exchanges (Pikirayi 2017; Chirikure 2014). However, before the nineteenth century, the bulk of their exchanges did not involve the medium of a metallic currency. The extensive trade between the Portuguese and the Africans from both the coastal and the interior of Southern Africa, for example, involved, for the most part, the exchange of cloth in return for gold, ivory and copper among other commodities (Bhila 1982; Mudenge 1988; Correa 1898).

To be sure, items that elsewhere served as currency were found in the interior of Southern Africa, but these seem to have been valued as ornamental items rather than mediums of exchange. These include cowrie shells (*ndoro*) which the ruling elites and commoners alike appropriated as items of adornment (Pikirayi 2017; Chirikure 2014).

Meanwhile, the Europeans who, from the early sixteenth century, maintained a presence at coastal enclaves around Southern and Southeastern Africa, brought with them some currencies which they used in international trade and in settling intra-settler transactions. For example, in 1507, the Portuguese Captain at Mozambique Island paid his counterparts a *cruzado* a month for their labour in the construction of a hospital (Correa 1898, p. 44). In what became the Cape Colony, the story of a colonial currency can be traced back to the arrival of Jan Van Riebeeck and his party in 1652. In the years that followed, "the greater portion of trade was carried on in hard cash... [,] the earliest currency being reals of eight struck at the Mints of Middelburg and Dordrecht for the Dutch East India Company" (*The Star* 1928). However, in their accounting the early Dutch settlers at the Cape assigned this currency a value that was different from the one obtaining in Holland. According to Arndt (1928, p. 4), "in accounts which were kept [in Holland] in rixdollars and stivers after 1738, the rixdollar was considered equivalent to 2 ½ Dutch gulden of 20 stivers each. At the Cape and India, however, a fictitious gulden, of which there was no metallic representation had come to use". The local officials who benefited from manipulating the value of the fictitious gulden in relation to the physical currency instigated this shift. As Arndt (1928, p. 4) observes, "in receiving money for taxes or goods, three of these [fictitious gulden] were considered the equivalent of a rixdollar. But, when money was paid out, *e.g.*, in payment of grain to farmers, the fictitious gulden was reckoned at 16 stivers, thus giving the officer in charge of the granaries a perquisite of 4 per cent".

The gold (gulden) and copper (stivers) coins remained the key currency at the Cape until 1782, when van Plettenberg, the Colony's governor introduced new notes. By 1825, "notes to the amount of 3, 100 000 (three million one hundred thousand) rix-dollar had been issued" (*The Star* 1928). The note introduction was in response to the conditions created by Britain's declaration of war on Holland earlier in 1781. Cut from the metropole by the war, the Cape faced financial problems to which the governor responded by borrowing locally. When local borrowing failed to alleviate the problem, the Governor issued paper money (Arndt 1928, p. 5). This marked the beginning of government note issues in Southern Africa. Following the British annexation of the Cape in 1806, the paper money remained in circulation while, by a proclamation of the same year, the new regime moved quickly to prohibit "the export of gold or silver currency" (Arndt 1928, p. 23).

The ban on the export of coins was meant to prevent the haemorrhaging of metallic money from the colony and the turn by the colonial government towards the issuing of local notes. The Cape settlers and policymakers understood that local note issues undermined one important facet of a currency—store of value. Local note issues injected more money into circulation and undermined the currency's value. This problem worsened as years turned into decades. Valued at 4 s. in 1806, the rixdollar circulating in the Cape Colony had depreciated to 1 s. 6d. by 1825 (*The Star* 1928). Authorities attributed this depreciation to "an excess of a colonial currency" (*The Star* 1928). By this they meant the influx of locally issued paper money or, as one petitioner in the British House of commons put it bluntly in 1826, "the extensive issues of paper money" (Hansard 1826).

For the settler residents of the Cape Colony the implications of this depreciation were not lost. As early as 1783, the Dutch East India Company (VOC) administration at the Cape received frequent complaints "regarding discrimination between coin and paper money" (Ardnt 1928, p. 7). Those who held gold, silver and copper coins charged a premium in return for notes. This premium made the metallic money dear and could, over time potentially necessitate the printing of more money for the purchase of the coins. This created inflationary pressure which alarmed the Cape's settlers. Years after the introduction of the first note issues, Lieut. Col. Bird, whose petition was presented to the British House of Commons by a Mr. Baring, spoke on behalf of many Cape Settlers when he complained that the power—possessed by colonial governors—to issue paper money "had, however, been exercised in this colony without any responsibility, and to such an extent that if the [British] House [of Commons] did not interfere, the property and even the people themselves must be sacrificed" (Hansard 1826). Notes-issue induced inflation could potentially wipe their savings.

By the time of Bird's petition to the British House of Commons in 1826, currency dynamics in the British colonial world, including in Southern Africa, were taking a different turn. Before 1825, Britain periodically shipped copper coins to the colonies but hardly paid much attention to their currency problems (Arndt 1928, p. 44). Things changed in the 1820s when, for the first time, Britain made a "great attempt to introduce British silver into the colonies" (Arndt 1928, p. 44). The impetus to this was the Latin American wars of independence which undercut the universal circulation of the Spanish dollar (Arndt 1928, p. 44). Added to this were the problems with the colonial currency, a fact of life that settlers at the Cape had come to appreciate. The most challenging of these problems was currency depreciation induced by the influx of local note issues. Moreover, by the 1820s the British understood that if their currency circulated in the colonies, they would benefit from seigniorage. And so, the British brought the Cape into the sphere of the Sterling. Close to a half century later, Britain further crystalized this position when it passed the Imperial Coinage Act (1870).

European Colonial Expansion, Migrant Labour and Currency Questions

Meanwhile, as the nineteenth century progressed, European settlers began to move from the coastal enclaves into the interior of Southern Africa. Currency questions became entangled with this expansion. The Orange Free State, the Boer republic established on the South African highveld in 1854, for example, never passed a law to introduce or regulate its own currency. Consequently, for the duration of its existence, it did not possess a coinage of its own.[2] Yet, in 1866, the Orange Free State issued paper notes to finance the deficits that resulted from its wars of land dispossession against the Sotho kingdom (Arndt 1928, pp. 73–77).

Ironically, this turn to note issue to cover costs of colonial expansion and the dispossession of African lands was fiercely opposed by some of the territory's white settlers. In 1867, the Anti-Blueback Association, an organization formed by settlers from Bloemfontein and its immediate environments "pledged to do everything in its power constitutionally to oppose any further issues of notes by the government" (*The Star* 1928). The Anti-Blueback association went on to offer a £15 prize to any author who could write "the best essay in pamphlet form of not more than 20 pages on the injurious effect of the issue of Government legal

[2] Officer in Charge, Department of Finance, Bloemfontein to Acting Secretary for Finance, Pretoria, 7 September 1910, National Archives and Records Services of South Africa [Pretoria] (NARSSA), GG 1468/48/48.

tender notes and the great danger of further issues" (*The Star* 1928). The settlers who opposed the issuing of government notes knew fully well where the danger lay. The notes were inconvertible and the Free State's merchants routinely complained that they were not accepted by businesses in the Cape where they obtained commodities as basic as sugar (Arndt 1928, p. 74). Moreover, the note issues increased money supply, creating inflationary pressures within their territory. When the notes were issued for the first time in 1865, their value stood at 15 shillings (s.) and for a moment went up to 17 s. and 18 s. However, "with the increased amount" issued in 1866 to cover the costs incurred in the Boer republic's attempts to conquer Moshoeshoe's kingdom, "the notes came down in some instances to 12 s. and 11 s" (Arndt 1928, p. 77). Cognizance of these facts, opponents of government issued notes protested against their further injection into the economy. They, instead, argued that rather than issue notes, the government should sell land conquered in the war to close the deficit (Arndt 1928, p. 75).

Unlike the Orange Free State which never possessed its own coinage (though the government issued paper money), in 1874, the South African Republic (the Transvaal) introduced its own coinage. There, the development of the gold mining industry made this possible. By 1874, one observer (Anonymous 1900, p. 253) noted, "the mining camp of Pilgrims' Rest became established... and got fairly under weigh". Thomas Burgers, the Transvaal's president, "thought that the production of gold in the country afforded an opportunity to impress the Volksraad[3] with the importance of its wealth and capabilities, by having some of it coined into real money—an article very much in demand at the time" (Anonymous 1900, p. 253). Burgers "persuaded the Volksraad to allow him to have some of the rough gold of the Transvaal coined into money" (Anonymous 1900, p. 253). And so, in 1874, the territory's first coins, a gold sovereign pound (known as the Burgers pond because it bore the image of the president) were minted in Birmingham, United Kingdom. The move towards a Transvaal coinage was as much about addressing the need as it was about political tokenism. "Burgers", writes Arndt (1928, p. 133), "presented every member of the Volksraad with a specimen and by such sensational deeds succeeded in acquiring a certain amount of popularity".

[3] The Parliament.

Throughout the 1880s, the South African Republic sought to establish its own mint. Arguments for and against the mint reflected the disparate interests among the Transvaal's settlers. Burgers had initiated the process when he tried to import a mint machine in 1874. Shipped to Delagoa Bay, the mint never reached the Transvaal and so the issue went into abeyance. Moreover, the enthusiasm of the South African Republic's settlers towards their own currency was dampened when they found that "it cost 26.*s*. to coin a pound worth 20.*s*.—and the coins of Mr. Burgers were current at 20.*s*., being equal in weight and propotion of pure gold and alloy to British sovereigns" (Anonymous 1900). This reluctance to produce an expensive coin relative to its face value meant that the British gold sovereign remained legal tender in the South African Republic alongside this new coinage (Becklake 1934). It was not until 1882 that the Republic's Auditor General again resurrected the issue of a state mint. Nothing, however, seems to have come out of the Auditor General's suggestion that the South African Republic should establish a mint. When this issue was again raised in the Volksraad in 1884, some of its members argued that this question was to be shelved pending the opinion of experts. However, others "maintained that it was the Christian duty of the Raad to give the people their own mint since they had gold in the country" (Arndt 1928, p. 135). Proponents of the mint insisted that the Republic's settlers "wanted a State Mint and not one in the hands of strangers" (Arndt 1928, p. 135). The republic's new President, Paul Kruger, pointed to the scarcity of money in the neighbouring Free State—without a mint or a currency of its own—as an example of the problems that could befall them if they did not mint their own coins. Pointing out that the Free State administrators were again speaking of issuing notes, Kruger expressed fears that "the Transvaal might have to do likewise" (Arndt 1928, p. 135).

Proponents of the mint further argued that it made economic sense to mint the gold into coins in the Transvaal for this could cut the costs incurred in shipping it to England before it was shipped back as minted coins (Arndt 1928, p. 135). In the end, the South African Republic left the task of establishing a mint in the hands of private actors who, in some sort of compromise, had to collaborate with the state. In 1890, following years of offers and counter offers, the Transvaal government granted Labouchere Oyens & Co. a concession for a mint "in conjunction with the National Bank concession" (Ardnt 1928, p. 140). Under the terms of the Concession, the National Bank was to establish the mint at its own expense "within twelve months of the passing of the law regulating the Mint. Upon its completion however, it was to be transferred to the Government, with everything belonging thereto. The Mint would thereupon be leased to the National Bank for twenty-five years at £500 per annum" among other conditions (Arndt 1928, p. 140).

The gold mining industry—which expanded rapidly after 1886—underlined the economic basis for the development of both the coinage and the mint in the Transvaal. As decades of scholarship (Crush et al. 1991; Harries 1994; Paton 1995; Van Onselen 2019) have shown, the same gold mining industry also drew labour from various parts of Southern Africa. These workers enabled the broad circulation of this and other currencies across Southern Africa, often in contrast to what the legal pronouncements dictated. For example, the Transvaal coinage was not legal tender in the British Empire in Southern Africa. Brought in by mobile African workers returning from work at the Witwatersrand mines, it nonetheless circulated in many parts of Britain's Southern African territories. This was in spite of the fact that British colonial administrators in Southern Africa had declared the British and Cape coinage as legal tender in their territories in line with the Imperial Coinage Act (1870). In Basutoland, which was part of his majesty's dominions, for example, the extension of this Act had been "done by means of a King's proclamation".[4] In the two protectorates of Bechuanaland and Swaziland, the British imperial government effectuated the Imperial Coinage Act (1870) through Orders-in-Council (Stanely 1922). In Southern and Northern Rhodesia, the British South Africa Company (BSAC) declared the coins in circulation at the Cape of Good Hope to be legal tender in the new colonies (Mseba 2005). By design, these legal pronouncements tied the currencies circulating in the various British colonies to the sterling.

Beyond the pronouncements of imperial and colonial officials, however, the circulation of the currency was itself informed by many other forces. It especially reflected the changes that accompanied the emergence of a regional political economy anchored on mining, settler plantation agriculture and black migrant labour. British imperial and colonial legal pronouncements excluded coins from the South African Republic from being legal tender in Britain's Southern African colonies, but as the

[4] H. J. Stanley to Farrer, 15 August 1922, The National Archives of the United Kingdom (TNA), T 160/153.

Resident Commissioner for Basutoland conceded in 1910, in his territory, "this coinage ha[d] always been accepted by the Bank, Traders and Government, and natives returning to their homes after work on the Witwatersrand ha[d] no difficulty in passing it".[5]

The Basutoland Resident Commissioner spoke for many of his counterparts in the South African mines' labour reserves. These coins also circulated in Swaziland and Bechuanaland. The same official also acknowledged a point that his counterparts in Portuguese East Africa had long understood. Way before the regime in Lourenço Marques officially recognized them as legal tender in Portuguese East Africa in 1899, British and South African Republic sovereigns were already accepted as a form of payment among Africans from the Delagoa Bay hinterland. This reflected both the mobility of African workers and the adjustments that Southern Africans made to the cultural meaning they assigned to commodities as they came to terms with these changes and the varied impacts of the cattle epizootics of the 1860s (Breckenridge 1995, p. 281). Patrick Harries (1983, 1994) has shown how this happened. Following the cattle epizootics of the 1860s, Harries (1983, p. 297) points out, Africans in the hinterland of Delagoa Bay increasingly turned to *Beja* hoes as items of bride price and "under no circumstances could they be used for agricultural purposes". The hoes, Harris (1983, pp. 297–298) notes, "rapidly lost their special-purpose value, and despite the opposition of chiefs, bride prices spiraled from 5 to 10 hoes in the 1840s to well over 50 in the late 1870s. This bride price inflation was fanned by migrants who returned from the plantations and mines of South Africa with wages which they used to procure hoes". By 1881, "only money" was used for bride price and hoes were "only used for agriculture" (Director of Lourenco Marques Customs, quoted in Patrick Harries 1983, p. 298).The money was British Sterling gold sovereigns that the migrant workers brought home from the plantations and mines of South Africa. This increased as South Africa's mining industry expanded, drawing more and more of the region's Africans into the gold mines of the Witwatersrand to extract the precious metal from the earth's belly. By 1919, an average of 40,000 Mozambican migrants working at the Rand mines returned to the Portuguese territory each carrying an average of £12 in South African gold sovereigns (Breckenridge 1995, p. 278).

[5] Resident Commissioner, Maseru to British High Commissioner to South Africa, 14 July 1910, NARSSA, GG 1468/48/26.

Enabled as it was by African migrant workers, among others, the circulation of a multiplicity of currency—the British sterling, the South African Republic's gold sovereign as well as Cape coinage—in many parts of Southern Africa, posed a challenge that, beginning, as we saw, with the Mint Conference of 1893, the region's colonial rulers sought to address. However, this failed, but not for the reasons that one might suspect, that is, the reluctance by Britain to allow its colonies to possess their own currencies (Nyamunda 2017a, p. 752). Delegates to the Mint conference rejected the Transvaal government's proposals because their "states would have nothing to gain from them" (Arndt 1928, p. 147). In other words, local colonial administrators were willing to entertain the question of an interstate mint and a uniform currency if they could improve their own states' coffers. Representatives of the Cape, Natal and the Orange Free State objected to the Transvaal's proposal because it required their territories to adopt its coinage as their legal tender. Alternatively, the Transvaal delegates proposed that its Mint would mint coinage for each of the four territories and this would be recognized as legal tender across each of the territories' borders. In contrast, the Cape representative insisted that the Transvaal Mint should be reconstituted as an inter-territorial mint that would not issue a purely local Transvaal coinage, but "genuine South African coins" (Arndt 1928, p. 147). Delegates from Natal and the Orange Free State supported the Cape colony representative's proposal. However, the Transvaal government could not agree to it because, as Arndt puts it, "the existing law was an obstacle" (Arndt 1928, p. 147). This law, in accordance to the Mint Concession had left the mint in the hands of private capital. Therefore, for close to a decade, the matter went into abeyance.

The question of a uniform currency returned to the fore in the wake of the South African War (also referred to as the Anglo-Boer War, 1899–1902). As the war drew to a close, the British imperial government entered negotiations with the Transvaal government "with a view to the withdrawal and demonetisations of this coinage from circulation".[6] However, these negotiations failed because "the Government of the Transvaal were [sic] in favour of its proclamation as legal tender

[6] L. M. Botha to (Details missing), 5 July 1910, NARSSA, GG 1468/48/26.

throughout South Africa".[7] To this, the Cape Colony objected. But why would the Transvaal insist on retaining its own coinage even as the territory became a British colony? By the same token, why did the Cape colony object to the declaration of the South African Republic coinage as legal tender throughout South Africa? It is quite tempting to view this through the lens of white settler ethnic loyalties and to suggest that the Transvaal government interpreted the calls for the demonetisation of its coinage as an attempt by their new English-speaking colonial overlords to destroy their own institutions and heritage. After all, the Transvaal gold sovereign carried the face and the name of the republic's president, Paul Kruger. Equally, one may be forgiven for thinking that, as a British colony, the Cape objected to the circulation of the South African Republic coins in its own territory in deference to imperial authority and to the stranglehold of the Sterling.

Yet, it appears that, again, the key deciding factor in the decision on what to do with the currency of the late South African Republic was economic and not the result of cultural or imperial politics. In 1902, members of the Transvaal Concession Committee raised their objection to the 1890 National Bank Concession upon which the Bank, the Mint, the coinage and the bank notes circulating in the Transvaal was based. "The grant to this Company of the exclusive (as against other Banks) right to issue Legal Tender notes," they reasoned, "was made for inadequate consideration and the important advantage that might have been secured to the Revenue has been lost..." (Transvaal Concessions Commission 1901, p. 98). Two of the three other principal advantages of maintaining the concession—the National Bank's right to issue its own notes, "the keeping without security and without payment of interest thereon of the Government balance... and, the prestige attaching to the position of the Government's Banker,"—the commissioners further argued, were not maintainable under the concession, "while the value of the first would be much impaired should the government decide to have its own notes" (Transvaal Concessions Commission 1901, p. 98). Consequently, the Commissioner recommended, the circumstances appeared to them "to be such as would provide a favourable opportunity for discussion and compromise, should it be decided by his Majesty's government

[7] L. M. Botha to (Details missing), 5 July 1910, NARSSA, GG 1468/48/26.

that the concession cannot be in its present form continued" (Transvaal Concessions Commission 1901, p. 98). Whatever else went on, plans for subsequent negotiations were shelved owing, as one official put it, "to the movement connected to the Union".[8]

The Union of South Africa, the Shift from the Gold Standard and the Problems of Specie

The consummation of the Union of South Africa in 1910 provided the opportunity for the reopening of the old question of what to do with the coinage of the South African Republic and the challenges brought by the circulation, in the region, of a multiplicity of currency. By this time, this question had undergone a slight transformation. When, in late 1910, the new South African government reopened the question of what to do with the coins of the late-South African Republic, the option to demonetise them was taken off the table. Instead, South Africa's new regime proposed that the coinage of the former Transvaal should be made legal tender both in the Union and in Britain's Southern African colonies.

The subsequent responses to this request by the representatives of governments in Southern Rhodesia, Northeast Rhodesia, Northwest Rhodesia, Bechuanaland, Swaziland and Basutoland are quite revealing. F. W. Panzera, Bechuanaland's resident commissioner, first expressed reservations about the introduction of a second currency to circulate in the colony alongside the South African currency but, he eventually consented provided it was also legal tender in the Union of South Africa.[9] His counterparts in Swaziland and Basutoland similarly assented to the idea that the coinage of the South African Republic could be legal tender in their territories, provided it was also legal tender in the Union.[10]

In contrast, H.W. Milton, the administrator for Southern Rhodesia, stating the position of his own colony and on behalf of the administrations

[8] L. M. Botha to (Details missing), 5 July 1910, NARSSA, GG 1468/48/26.

[9] F. W. Panzera to British High Commissioner, Johannesburg, 14 July 1910, NARSSA, GG 1468/48/26.

[10] Acting Resident Commissioner, Mbabane, to British High Commissioner to South Africa, 23 July 1910, NARSSA, GG 1468/48/26; Resident Commissioner, Maseru to British High Commissioner to South Africa, 14 July 1910, NARSSA, GG 1468/48/26.

of Northwest and Northeastern Rhodesia, dissented, placing the conditionality that they would only accede to the request if the currency of the former South African Republic was made legal tender in the *whole* British Empire.[11] Milton consulted the London Board of the British South Africa Company, the chartered company that not only administered Southern and Northwest Rhodesia, but had interests in the affairs of Northeastern Rhodesia, before responding to the Union of South Africa's request to make the coinage of the former South African Republic legal tender throughout the British controlled territories of Southern Africa. "The Company," Milton later told the British High Commissioner to South Africa, "considers the adoption of the proposal would be a retrograde step, since the coinage current in Rhodesia is uniform with that in use throughout the United Kingdom and in many parts of the Empire, and on these grounds, they [Company directors in London] are not prepared to assent to the acceptance in Rhodesia".[12] The Company's reasoning, Milton elaborated, was that it did not believe that members of the Legislative Council and the people of Southern Rhodesia were "in favour of the introduction into this Territory of a coinage which differs from that which is now recognized by the whole white and native population as the only legal currency of the country".[13] Further, Milton added rather dubiously, "the natives throughout Rhodesia have long been familiar with a coinage bearing the effigy of the Imperial Sovereign to whom they owe allegiance. The Company would view with regret the introduction into Rhodesia as legal tender of a coinage bearing any other symbol of authority as they fear that such an innovation might tend to confuse the mind of the native and to depreciate in his view the power and influence of the Imperial authority".[14]

Milton's (1910) claim was rather dubious, if revealing of the racial prejudices that underpinned settler colonialism in Southern Africa, because many of the African residents of Southern, Northeast and Northwest

[11] Milton to British High Commissioner in Cape Town, 29 December 1910, NARSSA, GG 1469/48/93.

[12] Milton to British High Commissioner in Cape Town, 29 December 1910, NARSSA, GG 1469/48/93.

[13] Milton to British High Commissioner in Cape Town, 29 December 1910, NARSSA, GG 1469/48/93.

[14] Milton to British High Commissioner in Cape Town, 29 December 1910, NARSSA, GG 1469/48/93.

Rhodesia certainly encountered the South African Republic's coinage from their experiences as labour migrants. The Witwatersrand mines, the largest employer of migrant labour and, since the late nineteenth century, the major hub of economic activity in Southern Africa, was in the South African Republic. As the resident commissioner for Basutoland explained, those who worked at the Rand mines were not only paid in the said currency; upon the end of their contracts, they also carried it home where they used it to purchase goods and pay government taxes.[15]

The objections from the Rhodesias, then, could not have been about the challenges that the circulation of this currency posed to Africans' recognition of the money and the Crown. In fact, the logic of these contrasting responses of the Rhodesias and the High Commission territories was economic and aimed at supporting the availability of labour in their territories. The Rhodesias' administrators understood the significance of Africans' disaffection on labour recruitment. However, in this case, such a dissatisfaction especially worked to the advantage of Southern Rhodesia whose economy could not compete with the comparatively higher wages paid by the South African mines and bitterly resented the latter's hemorrhaging of labour from territories north of the Limpopo River. Consequently, anything that could hinder this was welcome. It was in this context that colonial administrators in the Rhodesias imposed the conditions that they would only assent to the proposal if the currency of the former South African Republic was made legal tender in the whole British empire. It is difficult to see how Britain would have entertained such a proposal and so it was impossible for this condition to be met. The South African government officials understood this to be the case and so never pursued this option.

By contrast, the administrators in the High Commission territories understood the futility of objecting to the circulation of the currency of the former South African Republic as legal tender in their territories. By 1910, they, unlike Southern Rhodesia, did not have emerging mining industries of their own and were firmly integrated into the Southern African capitalist economy as labour reservoirs for the Rand mines. Each year, thousands of their subjects trekked to the Rand where they were paid in this currency. They also carried it back home. Any measures that would pose difficulties to those in possession of the former South African

[15] Resident Commissioner, Maseru to British High Commissioner to South Africa, 14 July 1910, NARSSA, GG 1468/48/26.

Republic money could potentially cause disaffection among Africans with concomitant repercussions on both labour supply and remittances. Consequently, they agreed to its circulation in their territories. Subsequently, the Union's Governor General recommended that the currency of the former South African Republic be made legal tender in Bechuanaland, Swaziland and Basutoland.[16] This recommendation carried the day (Arndt 1928, pp. 122–123).

Milton, then, deployed a cultural meaning of money that, if misleadingly, was supposedly anchored upon Africans' understanding of the iconography of colonial coins to simultaneously underscore the significance of currency to the imperial project and to contest a regional struggle for labour. He was not alone. A few years later, Rand minelords and South African Native Department administrators similarly deployed African customary uses of money to contest the injection of paper money into the South African economy (Gelb 1984; Breckenridge 1995, p. 276). The larger context for this was the currency problems that accompanied the outbreak of the First World War in 1914 and the subsequent formal abandoning of the gold standard in 1919. "After 1915" Keith Breckenridge (1995, p. 276) tells us, "the British government bought sterling in order to hold the market price of the currency at rough parity with the dollar. In March 1919 the purchase stopped, and sterling dropped precipitously against the dollar". The decline in the value of the sterling further meant the depreciation of South African and colonial currencies which were pegged to it at par. It also "meant that the sale of gold could earn a 25 per cent premium on the face value of the currency" (Breckenridge 1995, p. 276).

The South African gold mining industry stood to benefit from the gold premium, but the premium itself contributed to a different set of problems. "In broad strokes," writes, Breckenridge (1995, pp. 277–278), "the problem was that the South African Treasury and the commercial banks faced was that gold paid out in wages at the Witwatersrand was being exported from Delagoa to the Indian gold markets where it could be sold at a premium". The problem of gold leakage was not restricted to South Africa. The leakage of gold was, equally, a problem in Southern Rhodesia. Consequently, in May 1920 the colony's administrator published regulations banning the export of gold or silver coins exceeding £5 per person

[16] Gladstone to The Earl of Crew, 19 September 1910, NARSSA, GG 1468/48/48.

(Southern Rhodesia Government 1920). At about this same time, in July 1920, the South African parliament passed an Act imposing an embargo on the export of specie. Moreover, the gold mines went on to replace the gold coins that had constituted the form of payment for their workers with paper money (Breckenridge 1995, p. 278).

The rationale for and the responses to these measures reflected the interests of various economic groups and their standing in the South African body politic. The embargo on specie hurt the pockets of migrant workers. Yet, it was meant to protect the interests of South Africa's white farmers. "The most important consequence of this exceptional leakage of specie, which has rendered it almost impossible for the Banks to maintain adequate reserves", noted the Select committee of the South African parliament (1920), "has been the restriction of the necessary facilities for financing the export business of the country, involving in the case of wool, the missing of a favorable market, and as a result serious losses to the wool producers and dealers of South Africa". It was the interests of these wool farmers that the South African state was protecting by imposing an embargo on the export of gold specie.

Unsurprisingly, immigrant labourers were the key opponents of the embargo and the replacement of gold sovereigns with paper money. Leading the crusades against the payment of wages in paper money were immigrant mine workers from Portuguese East Africa who, as we saw, had long appropriated the gold sovereigns for the purposes of social transactions such as bridewealth (Breckenridge 1995, pp. 278–280; Harries 1983, pp. 297–298). Ironically, in their opposition to the introduction of paper money in preference for continued payment in gold sovereigns, the African migrant workers were supported by the very people who stood to benefit from the move off the international gold standard: the minelords of the Witwatersrand. This, Breckenridge (1995, p. 272) suggests, "was motivated by the shared idea that gold was a touchstone of value", but might have as well been based on a consideration on the part of mining capital of the implications of African discontent on labour recruitment.

There were many others who opposed the shift from gold sovereigns to paper money, but not for the same reasons as the migrant labourers and the minelords. Members of the select committee that investigated the question of the embargo on specie in 1920 were one such group. "It is clear that the severance of our connection with the gold basis brought about by the embargo on the export of gold coin has led to inflation, and to the real value and purchasing power of money in the hands of the people being divorced from reference to any concrete value in commodities", they argued. "The removal of the natural restraint on the Banks imposed by adherence to an effective gold basis", they added, "has resulted in an excessive increase of paper issues and other forms of commercial currency beyond the legitimate requirements of commerce, thereby creating an excess of money in circulation and an undue increase of the money prices of the necessaries of life" (Select Committee on Embargo on Export of Specie 1920, p. xxxvii).It is important to note that the reasoning of the committee mirrored the then dominant argument for the maintenance of the gold standard among economists. As Breckenridge (1995, p. 274) puts it, "the intellectual model offered by the gold standard wielded uncontested sway over the field of international finance before 1933". Though not realized in practice, the thinking behind this was "that the gold standard placed severe constraints on the state's ability to manipulate the value of currency" (Breckenridge 1995, p. 274).

Conclusion

The politics that informed attitudes towards paper money and the embargos on gold specie in the 1920s were understandably different form the issues that had informed currency questions in the earlier years. Yet, something remained consistent. Over the years, currency questions were informed by a multiplicity of actors. It was not just the interests of imperial and colonial actors which influenced currency questions let alone the scope of circulation of colonial Southern Africa's coins. African migrant workers contributed to this. Occasionally, blocs with disparate interests bended together to challenge the trajectory that currency matters took. This was the case when both migrant workers and the Witwatersrand's minelords opposed the replacement of gold coins by paper money in 1920. All this is to suggest the need to think about the multiplicity of forces that contingently shaped currency questions even in colonial, racially structured, capitalist systems of Southern Africa.

References

Anonymous. 1900. "The Coinage of the South African Republic," *The Numismatic Chronicle and Journal of the Numismatic Society* 20: 252–263.

Arndt, Ernst H. D. 1928. *Banking and Currency Development in South Africa, 1652–1927*. Cape Town and Johannesburg: Juta and Company.

Becklake, J. T. 1934. "Notes on the Coinage of the South African Republic." *The Numismatic Chronicle and Journal of the Numismatic Society* 14 (55): 183–215.

Bhila, Hoyini H. K. 1982. *Trade and Politics in a Shona Kingdom: The Manyika and their Portuguese and African Neighbour, 1575–1902.* Essex: Longman.

Bohannan, Paul. 1959, "The Impact of Money on an African Subsistence Economy." *The Journal of Economic History*, 19 (4): 491–503.

Breckenridge, Keith. 1995. "Money with Dignity: Migrants, Minelords and the Cultural Politics of South African Gold Standard Crises, 1920-1933." *Journal of African History* 36 (2): 271–304.

Chirikure, Shadreck. 2014. "Land and Sea Links: 1500 Years of Connectivity Between Southern Africa and the Indian Ocean Rim Regions, AD 700 to 1700." *African Archaeological Review*, 31 (4): 705–724.

Correa, Gaspar. 1898. "Lendas Da India." In *Records of South Eastern Africa. Volume 2*, compiled by George M. Theal. London: William Clowes and Sons, 1898.

Crush, Jonathan, Alan Jeeves, and David Yudelman. 1991. *South Africa's Labor Empire: A History of Black Migrancy to the Gold Mines*. Boulder: Westview Press.

Ekejiuba, Felicia. 1995. "Currency Instability and Social Payments Among the Igbo of Eastern Nigeria, 1890–1990," In *Money Matters: Instability, Values and Social Payments in the Modern History of West African Communities*, edited by Jane I. Guyer, 133–161. Portsmouth, NH: Heinemann.

Gelb, Steve. 1984. "The Origins of the South African Reserve Bank." African Studies Seminar Paper No. 157, Institute of African Studies, University of the Witwatersrand.

Guyer, Jane I. 1995. "Introduction: The Currency Interface and Its Dynamics," In *Money Matters: Instability, Values and Social Payments in the Modern History of West African Communities*, edited by Jane I. Guyer, 1–33. Portsmouth, NH: Heinemann.

Hansard, British Parliament, 19 May 1826.

Harries, Patrick. 1994. *Work, Culture, and Identity: Migrant Laborers in Mozambique and South Africa, c. 1860–1910*. Portsmouth, NH: Heinemann.

Hazelwood, Arthur. 1952. "Sterling Balances and the Colonial Currency System." *Economic Journal* 64: 942–945.

Hinds, A. 2001. *Britain's Sterling Colonial Policy and Decolonization, 1939–1958*. London: Greenwood Press.

Hopkins, Antony G. 1966. "The Currency Revolution in South-West Nigeria in the Late Nineteenth Century." *Journal of the Historical Society of Nigeria* 3 (3): 471–483.

Krozewski, Gerold. 2001. *Money and the End of Empire: British International Economic Policy and the Colonies, 1947–1958*. Houndmills: Palgrave.

Mseba, Admire. 2005. "The Establishment and Operations of the Southern Rhodesia Currency Board: A Study of Monetary Dependency in Southern Rhodesia, 1938–1956", BA dissertation, University of Zimbabwe.

Mudenge, Stanislus I.G. 1988. *A Political History of Munhumutapa, c.1400–1902*. Harare: Zimbabwe Publishing House.

Narsey, Wadan. 2016. *British Imperialism and the Making of Colonial Currency Systems*. New York: Palgrave Macmillan.

Newlyn, Walter T. and David C. Rowan. 1954. *Money and Banking in British Colonial Africa: A Study of Monetary and Banking Systems of Eight British African Territories*. Oxford: Clarendon Press.

Nyamunda, Tinashe. 2015. "Financing Rebellion: The Rhodesian State, Financial Policy and Exchange Control, 1962–1979." Ph.D. Thesis, University of the Free State.

Nyamunda, Tinashe. 2017a. "Money, Banking and Rhodesia's Unilateral Declaration of Independence," *The Journal of Imperial and Commonwealth History* 45 (5): 746–776.

Nyamunda, Tinashe. 2017b. "British Imperialism. Settler Colonialism and the Political Economy of Money and Finance in Southern Rhodesia, 1945 to 1963." *African Economic History* 45 (1): 77–109.

Pallaver, Karin. 2019. "A Currency Muddle: Resistance, Materialities and the Local Use of Money during the East African Rupee Crisis (1919–1923)." *Journal of Eastern African Studies* 13 (3): 546–564.

Paton, Bill. 1995. *Labour Export Policy in the Development of Southern Africa*. London: MacMillan Press.

Pikirayi, Innocent. 2017. "Trade, Globalisation and the Archaic State in Southern Africa." *Journal of Southern African Studies* 43 (5): 879–893.

Schenk, Catherine R. 2010. *The Decline of Sterling: Managing the Retreat of an International Currency, 1945–1992*. Cambridge: Cambridge University Press.

Select Committee. 1920. "Report of the on Embargo on Export of Specie", House of Assembly, Cape Town.

The Star. 1928. "Finance in History: Study of Currency and Banking in South Africa. Development over 275 Years." June 19, 1928.

Sutton, Alex. 2015. *The Political Economy of Imperial Relations: Britain, The Sterling Area and Malaya*. New York: Palgrave Macmillan.

Transvaal Concessions Commission. 1901. *Report of the Transvaal Concessions Commission*, London: Wyman and Sons.

Van Onselen, Charles. 2019. *The Night Trains: Moving Mozambican Miners to and from South Africa, circa; 1902–1955*. Johannesburg and Cape Town: Jonathan Ball.

CHAPTER 7

Poverty and the Transition to Instability: The Italian Lira in Eritrean History

Steven Serels

The outbreak of the First World War ushered in a monetary crisis in Italy. The remittances that had countered Italy's negative trade balance stopped coming because many Italians working in North America or elsewhere in Europe lost their jobs. At the same time, disruptions to global supply chains increased the price of the imported raw materials used by Italian factories. In addition, the Italian government was forced to take on ever-increasing amounts of foreign-denominated debt because it could not secure loans otherwise. These factors pushed the lira into a vicious cycle of depreciation. Though the lira regained some of its value after the 1918 armistice, the underlying fiscal situation in Italy did not improve. As a result, the lira began losing value in 1919 when the post-war economic boom ended. Further monetary instability over the next few years deepened existing political fissures, opening the way for the rise of Fascism.

S. Serels (✉)
Leibniz-Zentrum Moderner Orient, Berlin, Germany
e-mail: Steven.Serels@zmo.de

K. Pallaver (ed.), *Monetary Transitions*,
Palgrave Studies in Economic History,
https://doi.org/10.1007/978-3-030-83461-6_7

When Benito Mussolini came to power in October 1922, it was with a pledge to strengthen the lira (Fratianni and Spinelli 1997, pp. 114–154).

This currency crisis was also an African story because Eritrea, Somalia, and Libya were all Italian colonies at the time, and the lira was their official currency. There was no difference between the lire that circulated in the colonies and in the imperial metropole. The two were physically identical. The paper notes and metal coins were made of the same material, had the same dimensions, and were stamped with the same designs. They were issued by the same authorities with the same backing, and they had the same status as legal tender. They were the same. There was only one lira and it had an imperial reach. As a result, the lira crisis that began during the First World War necessarily reverberated across imperial lines into the colonies. The Italian lira's African history was in some ways unique. Other European powers created new currencies for their colonies, often after some time of experimenting with utilizing already circulating local currencies or attempting to introduce the metropolitan currency. For example, British officials established the East African Shilling in 1921 to circulate in Kenya, Tanganyika, and Uganda after decades of using the rupee locally. Portuguese officials replaced the metropolitan escudo with the angolar in 1928, only to reverse course thirty years later and unify the metropolitan and colonial currency system. In 1948, French officials created the *Franc de l'Afrique-Occidentale française* after having used the metropolitan franc, cowry shells, and other local media of exchange for over a century. Nonetheless, these new colonial currencies had a fixed exchange rate with their metropolitan counterparts and therefore the former can be considered a subsidiary of the latter. As a result, the currency policy pursued by British, French, and Portuguese officials did not differ substantially from that pursued by their Italian counterparts.

There was another important commonality across these four empires. The British pound, French franc, Portuguese escudo, and Italian lira repeatedly proved to be structurally weak during the twentieth century. Each of these imperial currencies entered at least one period of uncontrolled depreciation so rapid and deep that it threatened the metropolitan political order. Nonetheless, scholars of African history largely ignore these currency crises. The few notable exceptions include the studies of the East African Rupee Crisis by Karin Pallaver (2019) and Wambui Mwangi (2001), as well as Ayodeji Olukoju's study of the 1916–1920 Nigerian currency crisis (1997). Despite these accounts, scholars of

African history conventionally characterize imperial currencies as inherently strong colonial institutions that unproblematically functioned as units of account, media of exchange, and stores of value. This characterization reflects the general acceptance in African Studies of a schematized chartalist theory of money. Echoing George Knapp (1924), and Alfred Mitchell-Innes (1914) writings from a century ago, these scholars explain the circulation of imperial currencies in terms of taxes. They assert that the requirement to pay taxes in imperial currencies forced Africans to seek out these currencies, which in turn pushed them into an imperial-currency-based cash economy that came to permeate their lives (some notable examples include: Rodney 1974, pp. 147–154; Iliffe 2007, p. 209; Reid 2009, p. 181). Despite its prevalence, this theory about the nature of colonial currency systems is a radical chartalist vision with which few outside of the field of African Studies would agree. Even contemporary proponents of chartalism, many of them champions of Modern Monetary Theory, accept that governments must coordinate adjustments in both taxes ***and*** spending in order to ensure that currencies circulate and retain their value.[1]

This chapter uses a study of the lira in colonial Eritrea to propose an alternate understanding of the monetary history of Africa that acknowledges that imperial currencies were weak institutions. It begins from the position that levying taxes in a specific currency alone is not enough to ensure the functioning of a currency system. As even scholars sympathetic to Modern Monetary Theory acknowledge, currencies require a more elaborate infrastructure. While libertarian-minded economists often locate this infrastructure in the private sphere, Christine Desan (2016) has convincingly argued that much of it must be created and maintained by the state. Desan has shown that money is a legal institution and as such requires a legal infrastructure that: (1) defines credit, sale, contract, and property, as well as a number of other related concepts; (2) outlines the rights and obligations associated with these concepts; and (3) contains a mechanism for protecting and enforcing these rights and obligations. This legal infrastructure is independent from the minting of currencies. In fact, many states and state-like entities in Africa and the Indian Ocean World before the twentieth century provided this infrastructure without creating their own currencies or forcing market actors to use ones of their choosing

[1] For a concise lay summary of Modern Monetary Theory and its critiques, see Matthews (2019).

(Serels 2019). Imperial currencies needed the support of a new colonial legal infrastructure that, in the Eritrean case, was only ever partially developed. Italian officials in Eritrea refused to make the investment of time, effort, and capital that building this infrastructure required. Instead, they granted local political elites a large measure of control over the colonial legal system through a system of indirect rule similar to that implemented elsewhere in Africa by other European empires.

Underinvestment in the colonial state allowed African communities to retain a significant level of control over the infrastructure that undergirded their currency system. In the first half of the twentieth century, these communities used this control to selectively engage with imperial currencies and to develop new modes of utilizing traditional ones. This reorganization of systems of value and patterns of exchange has been termed "Africa's monetary transition" by Jane Guyer and Karin Pallaver (2018) and Natalie Swanepoel (2015). According to these scholars, Africans selectively engaged with imperial currencies in ways that ultimately limited their functionality and rendered them special purpose money. While this literature emphasizes African agency and resistance, this was a collaborative effort. In order for currencies to circulate, diverse groups across relatively large territories had to work together to sustain the currency system. In the case of Eritrea, this required the collaboration of not only members of the country's various ethnic, linguistic, and religious communities, but also the Arab, Greek, and Indian merchants that dominated foreign trade well into the twentieth century. Their collaboration created and maintained the colonial currency system.

Colonial underinvestment and private sector collaboration only partially explain "Africa's monetary transition." These two factors do not explain why imperial currencies took on larger and larger roles within colonial currency systems at the precise moment when these very currencies were faltering. One would expect private sector actors to use their control over this system to shield themselves from the negative consequences of uncontrolled devaluations of imperial currencies. However, this did not happen. As the literature on "Africa's monetary transition" shows, African communities began using imperial currencies more intensely after the First World War, after these currencies had already revealed themselves to be untrustworthy stores of value and unsteady units of account. As the history of the lira in Eritrea shows, there were limits to African agency. Many communities in Africa became trapped in a cycle of poverty and food insecurity that limited their choices. By the interwar period, they could no longer depend on traditional economic activities to survive. They needed a supplemental cash income and, often, the only employer was the colonial state. Where they could, these communities hedged their exposure to risky imperial currencies as much as possible by continuing to use other local ones.

The Lira as a Failed State Institution

Italy occupied Massawa in February 1885 as Egypt withdrew from its African colonial empire. This was the second Italian attempt to establish a colony on the African Red Sea littoral. The first had been short-lived. In 1869, a representative of the *Società di Navigazione Rubattino*, a Genovese shipping company purchased land from local *shaykhs* near the port of Assab with the intention of establishing a coaling station and trading settlement. However, the company was unable to derive a profit from its new possession and quickly abandoned it. The second attempt proved to be longer-lasting. The Italian government used its new base at Massawa to penetrate the interior, progressively expanding its colonial possession via treaty and conquest over the next decade. In 1890, the government consolidated these territories into the colony of Eritrea. The drive further inland continued until 1896, ending only with a resounding defeat by Ethiopian forces under the command of Menelik II at the Battle of Adwa (Mesghenna 1988, pp. 67–71).

Simultaneous with this campaign of conquest, Italian officials began the process of building the colonial state. This process was helped by a recognition that Massawa and its coastal hinterland was not *terra nullius*. In taking over this port city, Italian officials retained many of the previous Egyptian government's institutions. Most importantly for the monetary history of Eritrea, the new Italian administration held over the schedule of fees, fines, taxes, tribute payments, and customs duties imposed by the previous colonial rulers. But they made one key modification; amounts previously calculated in Egyptian pounds were now entered into official ledgers in Italian lira. Despite the change in the unit of account, the colonial government did not try at first to implement a lira-only currency policy. Instead, Italian officials sought to encourage the use of the lira by undermining the Egyptian pound while continuing to support the circulation of other currencies.

On 19 February 1885, the Italian *Ministero delle Finanze* issued a decree allowing the new administration of Massawa to accept British pounds and Maria Theresa thalers at a fixed lira exchange rate.[2] The Maria Theresa thaler was a high-value silver coin that had been used as a medium of exchange in settling the import/export trade in the Red Sea for over a century (Kuroda 2007). The British pound, on the other hand, was not a widely circulating currency in the Red Sea at the time. However, the British were important regional players and Italian officials were seeking to gain British support for their expansionist plans. By refusing to accept Egyptian pounds, Italian officials were trying to create an opening for the lira to settle low-value transactions and to serve as small change in transactions that utilize Maria Theresa thalers.[3] This plan did not succeed. In the months after issuing the 1885 decree, officials in Massawa discovered that they could not insist on payment in lira instead of Egyptian pounds because there was not enough in circulation. After a year of having to turn away people offering to pay in small denominations of Egyptian pounds, the colonial government had to change course. In May 1886, officials began accepting Egyptian piaster coins at a newly set official exchange rate.[4]

Efforts to encourage the use of the lira were further undermined by the system of indirect rule that Italian officials relied upon from the outset. S*haykhs*, sultans, *diglals*, *naibs*, *kantibais*, etc. were brought into the state structure as their territory was incorporated into the colony. These local political elites were given salaries and tasked with ensuring that their communities complied with government directives, including the payment of taxes. They also were tasked with adjudicating civil and, to a lesser extent, criminal cases involving their followers. At the start of colonial rule, these local political elites were powerful enough to dictate the terms of their incorporation into the state. They used this power in ways that blocked the spread of the lira. Rather than accept salaries in lire, they demanded payment in Maria Theresa thalers. For example, at the turn of the twentieth century, the colonial government paid the Sultan of Rahayta 50 thalers and his *wazir* 30 thalers each month.[5] These salaries were a substantial part of the state's expenditures; accounting for over

[2] "Decreto Ministeriale 19 febbraio 1885," in Mori (1914, p. 72).

[3] Gené to the Ministro delle Finanze, 11 February 1886, Archivio Storico Diplomatico del Ministero degli Affari Esteri, Rome (ASDMAE), Archivio Eritrea (AE) Pacco 31.

[4] Ministero delle Finanze. *Decreto*. 13 May 1886, ASDMAE, AE Pacco 31.

[5] Cattoi. *Raheita*. 9 March 1897, ASDMAE, Archivio Storico del Ministero dell'Africa Italiana (ASMAI) I, Posizione 6/1.

80 percent of the budget of some districts in the early twentieth century (Negash 1987, p. 103). Large salaries did not ensure compliance with government directives. Significantly, local political elites often did not collect taxes or tribute in lira. Instead, they insisted on paying in kind, turning over grain, live animals, and other goods to the state. Rather than push back against their local political allies, officials amended their regulations in 1891 to formally authorize this practice.[6] The extent to which taxes were paid in kind has been partially obscured by government bookkeeping practice. Though the business of government was being conducted in lira, Maria Theresa thalers, bushels of wheat, heads of cattle, etc., government ledgers recorded revenues and expenditures exclusively in lira.

Government bookkeeping practices further hid the real costs of this multi-currency system. Since the colonial state was too politically and economically weak to unilaterally impose a lira-only policy, officials had to import Maria Theresa thalers in large quantities to make payments. These thalers were purchased from the Austrian mint and then shipped to Eritrea. In the 1880s, this cost the government 4.20 lire per thaler.[7] The August 1886 decree allowing the government to accept payment in thalers fixed the exchange rate at 3.75 lire per thaler, representing a loss of 0.55 lire per imported thaler.[8] In December of that year, the government raised the exchange rate to 4 lire per thaler.[9] Officials did not raise the exchange rate further likely out of a fear of creating an arbitrage opportunity. Already in 1887, there were rumors circulating in Massawa that local merchants were profiting from the difference between the thaler/lira exchange rate in Eritrea and Aden.[10] As a result, the state continued to lose money on every Maria Theresa thaler it put into circulation.

[6] Agenzia delle tribù to Governo Civile e Militare, 12 October 1891, ASDMAE, AE Pacco 1036.

[7] Ministero del Tesoro to Ministero Affari Esteri, 14 December 1886, ASDMAE, AE Pacco 60.

[8] Comando Superiore in Africa to Segretario per gli affari indigeni, 1 July 1886, ASDMAE, AE Pacco 31.

[9] Ministero del Tesoro to Ministero Affari Esteri, 14 December 1886, ASDMAE, AE Pacco 60.

[10] "Courrier du soir: Nouvelles de Massaouah." *L'Italie,* 2 September 1887, ASDMAE, AE Pacco 27.

To stem this loss, the colonial government launched a two-front campaign against the Maria Theresa thaler in 1890. First, officials sought to limit the currency's usefulness. In August of that year, officials again announced that they would no longer accept Maria Theresa thalers as payment.[11] Second, officials created what they believed would be a viable competitor to the Maria Theresa thaler. The *tallero eritreo* was an Italian-minted silver coin that mimicked the dimensions of its Austrian counterpart—both weighed approximately 28 g and had a diameter of 40 mm. To encourage the adoption of the new thaler, the state minted fractional coins of 1/10, 2/10, and 4/10 in silver, and of 1/100 and 2/100 in bronze. The two bronze coins were never put into circulation. This new thaler was a truly colonial currency. It was given legal tender status only in Eritrea. Outside of Eritrea it would be worth no more than its constituent silver. Inside the colony, it was given an official face value of 5 lire. By giving it a fixed lira valuation, officials believed that the circulation of the *tallero eritreo* would pave the way for the further circulation of the lira.[12]

Officials were wrong. They fundamentally misunderstood the nature of the Eritrean currency system and, as a result, created a new currency that no one wanted. Officials believed that the local population did not understand the difference between the physical dimensions of a coin, the intrinsic value of its constituent precious metal and its value. This mistaken belief stemmed from a misinterpretation of the common Eritrean practice of treating the Maria Theresa thaler as a basic unit of weight. The main wholesale and retail units of measurement, respectively the *qintar* and the *rotl*, were multiples of the weight of a thaler. A *qintar* was made of 100 *rotl*, which, in turn, was equal to the weight of 16 Maria Theresa thalers (Checchi 1910, pp. 3–5). So the Italian government created a coin that weighed the same as a Maria Theresa thaler. But, the new thaler differed from the old one in a key respect—it contained approximately 3.96% less silver. This difference led the local population to refuse to accept the *tallero eritreo* at face value. Officials, in turn, refused to offer the coin at the demanded discount. As a result few of the 10 million lire's worth of *tallero eritreo* imported between 1891 and 1896

[11] Governo Civile e militare della Colonia Eritrea. *Talleri di Maria Teresa*. 5 August 1890, ASDMAE, AE Pacco 98.

[12] Il Governatore Civile e militare della Colonia Eritrea. *Ordina*. 24 September 1890, ASDMAE. AE Pacco 98.

went into circulation (Carboneri 1912, p. 6). Over this period, the colonial government continued to import Maria Theresa thalers and put them into circulation, as it was the only way that they could pay for goods and services provided to the state.[13]

In 1896, officials gave up; the minting of the *Tallero Eritreo* was abandoned, as was the campaign against the Maria Theresa thaler (Carboneri 1912, p. 6). The colonial state was forced to accept a new status quo. The lira was the official currency but, in this capacity, it served almost exclusively as a unit of account. Though officials may have wanted to deal only in lire, they could not. Local political elites continued to demand payment in thalers. In addition, these elites collected taxes and tribute in whichever form was expedient for them. For nearly two decades, the government accepted that the costs of colonial rule included the cost of purchasing and importing Maria Theresa thalers and the transaction costs associated with exchanging lire.

The economic contraction in Italy during the First World War and attended lira crisis made these costs too expensive and rendered the status quo unsustainable. In 1916, officials convened a commission to address the effects of the lira crisis on Eritrea and to make recommendations for transforming the colonial currency system. Following the commission's recommendation to mandate the use of the lira, the colonial government issued a decree on 1 July 1916 outlawing the use of the Maria Theresa thaler and requiring all cash transactions, both private and public, to be settled in lira.[14] To facilitate this transition, the colonial government required all holders of Maria Theresa thalers to exchange them at their neighboring administrative office (Santagata 1935, p. 190). Like the similar policy two decades earlier, this too was a resolute failure. Those who came in to exchange their thalers refused to accept the paper money they were offered, perhaps having expected to receive an alternate silver coin instead. As a result, the exchange of thalers for lire did not take place. At the same time, trade seized up because people were afraid to publicly use their thalers.[15] Whatever market activity continued

[13] Governo Civile e militare della Colonia Eritrea. *Talleri di Maria Teresa*. 5 August 1890, ASDMAE, AE Pacco 98.

[14] Direttore Affari Civili to Commissari regionali, 1 July 1916, ASDMAE, AE Pacco 51.

[15] Commissariato Regionale Del Barca. *Relazione del mese di Dicembre 1916*, ASDMAE, AE Pacco 828.

was furtively conducted in thalers, even if prices were publicly quoted in lira.[16] By the end of 1916, officials had accepted defeat. They resumed making payments in Maria Theresa thalers and the mandate to use lire became a dead letter.[17]

Having accepted a limited role for the lira, officials turned their attention to capturing the seigniorage earned by the Austrian mint on Maria Theresa thalers. In 1918 the Italian government created a new currency, the *tallero d'Italia*, for use in Eritrea. Like the *tallero eritreo*, this new silver coin purposefully mimicked the dimensions of its Austrian counterpart, both weighing 28 g and measuring roughly 40 mm in diameter. The *tallero d'Italia* went even further. While the *tallero eritreo* had a bust of King Umberto I on its face, the *tallero d'Italia* had the bust of an allegorical female personification of Italy styled to resemble that of Maria Theresa. To further encourage their circulation, Italian officials mandated that the *tallero d'Italia* have a slightly higher silver content than its Austrian counterpart (0.835 instead of 0.833). This choice proved to be the plans undoing. The few *talleri d'Italia* that were introduced quickly fell out of circulation owing to hoarding. After just one year, the Italian mint stopped issuing the new thalers. Without any other viable options, colonial officials again accepted a limited role for the lira.

The Role of the Private Sector

The colonial government's lira-only policy failed over and over again because officials could not get sufficient private sector collaboration. Despite government efforts, retail and wholesale trade continued to be conducted primarily in Maria Theresa thalers well into the twentieth century. Trade remained in the hands of Arab, Greek, and Indian merchants, many of whom were members of families that had been operating in the Red Sea prior to Italian colonial rule. Generally, these families had regional bases in Aden and networks that extended to other part of the Arabian Peninsula, the Ottoman Mediterranean, or the Indian subcontinent. These merchants either sold wholesale in Eritrea to local

[16] Commissario regionale della Dancalia to Governo, 1 September 1916, ASDMAE, AE Pacco 51.

[17] Commissariato Regionale Del Barca. *Relazione del mese di Dicembre 1916*, ASDMAE, AE Pacco 828.

Jeberti pedlars or retail directly to end consumers (Miran 2009, pp. 69–88). Since they were firmly situated within the silver-based economy of the Indian Ocean World and eastern Mediterranean, Arab, Greek, and Indian merchants sought to secure profits in silver currencies that could be easily exported from Eritrea to their primary fields of operations. The lira did not meet this criterion, but the Maria Theresa thaler did.

Italian-owned merchant firms may have preferred dealing in lire, as doing so would have lessened the transaction costs associated with currency exchanges. However, they failed to capture a significant share of the market. Though several such firms began operating in Eritrea under Italian rule, nearly all closed within a few years. They simply could not compete against well established Arab, Greek, and Indian merchants. The few Italian firms that succeeded did not directly trade with the local population. Instead, they sold imported Italian manufactures wholesale to Indian, and to a lesser extent Greek and Arab merchants, who then sold them on (Boselli 1910, p. 9). Those that chose not to trade through these intermediaries often did so indirectly, through multiparty transactions. To gain access to sufficient silver currencies to operate in Eritrea, these Italian firms typically contracted with London merchants who in turn contracted with Bombay-based Indian merchant houses to open a line of credit that could be used to pay merchants in the Red Sea region. This was a common practice up until the outbreak of the Second World War, after which such transactions became impossible (Santagata 1935, p. 190).

Like the merchants that dominated Eritrea's international trade, Eritrean producers continued to demand payment in Maria Theresa thalers well into the twentieth century. In 1923, Addison E. Southard, the United States' Consul at Aden, wrote when reporting on conditions in Eritrea: "The Red Sea native much prefers the Austrian dollar to any other coin, and often he refuses to sell his coffee, skins, hides, and other products for other coins." (Southard 1923, p. 32) Though Southard thought this preference significant enough to warn American merchants about it, the colonial state's accounting practices tended to hide it. Officials almost always reported market prices in lire because this was the official unit of account and not because it reflected prevailing local practices. As a result, the local preference for thalers has been partially occluded by the archival record. Occasionally, officials would note prices in Maria Theresa thalers. For example, the *Commissariato Regionale* of Akele-Guzai wrote in 1915 that the price of a head of cattle ranged from 25 and 30 Maria Theresa thalers.[18] Similarly, a report from 1925 mentions in passing that prices in the Assab grain market were denominated exclusively in thalers.[19] Since officials had no reason to convert lire into thalers for accounting reasons, this further indicates the continued use of thalers in marketing Eritrean produce.

Foreign merchants and local producers did not completely shun the lira. Rather, they initially incorporated it selectively into their thaler-based currency system. The Maria Theresa thaler was too valuable to be useful for small market transactions. It also had no fractional coins. To overcome this hindrance to trade, market actors began using bronze lira pieces and 1 or 2 lira paper notes as fractional denominations of the thaler. Larger denominations were not used because they were not needed; the Maria Theresa thaler could serve this function. As a result, they were not accepted and did not circulate. Exactly when the practice of using small lira denominations took off cannot be derived from the historical record. However, it was well established before the time Southard wrote his report (Southard 1923, p. 32).

The use of lire as fractional denominations of the thaler was also likely a minor practice because retail traders tried to avoid using cash where possible. There was a natural seasonal cycle to the velocity of money in Eritrea. Most of the population of colonial Eritrea cultivated land. As a result, their access to cash was seasonal, i.e., the sale of crops for cash could only take place after the harvest. To overcome this, traders offered lines of credit in the form of crop futures contracts. During the growing season, traders agreed to purchase a fixed quantity of crops at harvest in exchange for a line of credit that the cultivator could draw upon in the meantime to make purchases. Cash exchanged hands only after the harvest, and then only to settle the difference between the price paid and the debt owed.[20] Retail traders would only need to insist on cash payment in cases where extending credit was not possible.

[18] Commissariato Regionale dell'Acchelè Guzai. *Relazione sulla fornitura dei buoi allo Stabilimento del Sembel da parte del Commissariato Regionale dell'Acchelè Guzai*, 19 August 1915, ASDMAE, AE Pacco 804.

[19] Annaratone to Governo. 19 July 1925, ASDMAE, AE Pacco 955.

[20] Commissariato Regionale del Serae to Direzione Affari Civili, 1 September 1919, ASDMAE, AE Pacco 859. This was also a common practice in neighboring Sudan, see Serels (2013).

There was just one economic constituency that preferred lira over thalers—the white settler population. Though their opinions on the matter have generally not been recorded in the colonial archive, Europeans in Eritrea were accustomed to using lire or similar money forms. Nearly all were immigrants and almost all were Italian. Having largely grown up with the lira, they likely used it unreflexively as a unit of account. They understood prices, wages, and wealth in its terms. Though Italian imperial planners at the end of the nineteenth century had envisioned a white settler colony of small holder planters scattered across the Eritrean countryside, this never came to pass. The few white farms that were established at the turn of the twentieth century failed within their first two years. Officials interpreted these failures as a sign that the farms had been too small and too undercapitalized to be successful. So, in the first decades of the twentieth century they granted larger parcels of land to better funded settlers. By 1921, the colonial government had awarded 138 land concessions to Italian settlers or Italian-owned companies. The median concession was approximately 20 hectares, though the largest was a 16,000-hectare concession at Tessenei run by the *Società Imprese Africane*.[21] European-owned plantations similarly tended to fail. By 1930 nearly all had ceased operations (Istituto Agricolo Coloniale Italiano 1932, pp. 8–9). As a result, few settlers stayed for very long, with most re-emigrating after just a couple of years. Out migration canceled out the effect of immigration until the 1930s. For the first fifty years of Italian colonial rule, the European population fluctuated between 2000 and 4000 people (Istituto Agricolo Coloniale Italiano 1932, pp. 43–44). Though these settlers may have wanted to use lire, they were too few to meaningfully impact the colonial currency system.

The Emergence of a Lira Economy

The lira only began to circulate widely in Eritrea in the 1930s. This can only partially be explained by the sudden rapid growth of the Italian settler population. Over the course of the decade, the European population in Eritrea increased starkly, driven first by the contraction of the Italian economy during the Great Depression and then by the Fascist government's renewed support for immigration to the colonies. By 1940,

[21] Guido Mangano, *La Cotonicoltura e le Iniziative Cotoniere nell'Eritrea,* Istituto Agronomico per l'Oltremare, Florence (IAO), FASC2435.

there were over 71,000 Italians in Eritrea, accounting for slightly less than 10 percent of the total population. Nearly all of these new immigrants settled in Asmara.[22] The population of that city swelled rapidly from 4600 inhabitants in 1934 to 75,000 in 1939, making it by far the largest city in Eritrea (Volterra 2005, p. 172). These new immigrants commanded a disproportionate share of the circulating lira. A survey conducted by British authorities after they conquered Eritrea in 1941 found that Italians owned 100 million of the 260 million lire in circulation in the colony.[23]

Eritreans earned only a small fraction of their 160 million lire directly from Italian settlers. In 1940, less than 3 percent of Eritreans lived in cities and few settlers lived in the countryside. Some city-dwelling Eritreans worked as laborers. However, they generally had poorly paid menial jobs, and as a result, could have earned only a small fraction of the circulating lire (Volterra 2005, p. 172). In the countryside, some Eritreans worked for the few successful Italian-owned plantations. Generally, these plantations hired indigenous men as either permanent or seasonal laborers.[24] Though the wage arrangements at the start of the twentieth century remain unclear from the archival records, by the 1930s agricultural laborers were paid in lire.[25] However, this practice had a limited impact because few men worked in this capacity. A survey of the labor market conducted by the British Military Administration in 1943 found that there were only 850 indigenous Eritrean men working as agricultural or pastoralist wage laborers.[26] Here too these laborers were poorly paid and therefore could have amassed only a few lire.

Eritreans did earn their lire from working, though not in the private sector. They worked for the government, primarily as *ascari* (soldiers enlisted in African regiments). This work was not open to all, as only

[22] Direzione Generale degli Affari Politici. Ministero dell'Africa Italiana. *L'Italia e le sue colonie prefasciste*. 1947, IAO, FASC113.

[23] *Notes by Controller of Finance on Currency Situation in Eritrea*, 13 April 1941, National Archive, London (NA), WO 230/32.

[24] Comando del III Battaglione indigeni to Comando del R. Corpo di Truppe Coloniali dell'Eritrea, 24 August 1916, ASDMAE, AE Pacco 51.

[25] Guido Mangano. *La Cotonicoltura e le iniziative cotoniere nell'eritrea*. 1945, IAO, FASC2435.

[26] British Military Administration. Eritrea. *Annual Report by the Chief Administrator on the British Administration of Eritrea, Report V, for Period 1 January to 31 December 1943*, p. 39.

men physically capable of soldiering were enlisted. However, that did not mean that soldiering was a minor economic activity. When Britain finally conquered Eritrea in 1941, nearly half of all Eritrean men were serving in the army (Volterra 2005, p. 111). In exchange, they received a salary. Most received 90 lire per month, though some with specialized training and higher rank received more (Volterra 2005, pp. 174–175). The 160 million lire held by Eritreans in 1941 was less than a year's total salary for all Eritrean men serving in the colonial army. As a result, understanding the spread of the lira requires understanding the dynamics of military service in colonial Eritrea.

The practice of recruiting soldiers locally predates Italian rule. The Egyptian officials who governed parts of Eritrea's Red Sea littoral in the nineteenth century also engaged in this practice. When these officials handed Massawa over to an Italian military force in 1885, they left behind their local soldiers. The new Italian rulers reenlisted these men, forming the first nucleus of Italy's colonial armed force (Chelati Dirar 2004, p. 545). From just a few hundred men, Italian colonial officials expanded their native regiment in fits and starts to approximately 5000 men in 1896, 10,000 in 1916, and then 20,000 in 1920 (Connell and Killion 2011, pp. 84–85; Bellucci and Zaccaria 2014, p. 95; Volterra 2005, pp. 32–33). After a retrenchment in the 1920s that saw the number of *ascari* reduced to 10,000, Italian imperial planners mandated a rapid increase in the indigenous force in the 1930s. The expanded force was needed because there was a new military goal—to conquer and hold Ethiopia. To ensure sufficient numbers, service was made mandatory for all fit men in Eritrea. The number of enlisted men increased to 60,000 in 1934 and topped out at 150,000 on the eve of the 1941 British conquest of the colony (Volterra 2005, pp. 86, 111).

Though service was mandatory, Eritrean men generally wanted to serve. Interviews with veterans conducted in the 1990s by Alessandro Volterra revealed that many took pride in their service, seeing it as honorable work that paid at a time when many needed money (Volterra 2005, p. 61). Structural poverty had set in Eritrea because traditional economic strategies were no longer viable. As I have shown elsewhere, these strategies had been based on patterns of human–environment interaction that had been disrupted by the introduction of rinderpest in 1887. Rinderpest is a highly contagious cattle disease with a case fatality rate of 90 percent in virgin herds as had been the case in Eritrea. This viral disease was likely brought to the country in the bodies of live cows imported to provision the Italian military based at Massawa. The disease quickly spread along overland trade routes in 1888 and 1889, with devastating consequences. Hundreds of thousands of cattle got sick and died. Cultivation was disrupted in the grain-producing highlands because there were not enough survivors to pull the plows. Yields shrunk, food became scarce and trade collapsed. As the epizootic spread, a deadly famine set in. So many people died that in some areas the population shrunk by as much as two-thirds by the time the famine finally abated in 1892 (Pankhurst 1964; Serels 2018a, pp. 90–99). In the 1930s, almost four decades after the famine, Eritrean communities were still struggling to recover what they had lost.

In the intervening years, efforts to rebuild were repeatedly disrupted by outside forces, including the Italian campaign to conquer Ethiopia in the 1890s, the First World War and then the Great Depression (Serels 2018b). Since the recovery had only been partial, Eritrean pastoralists and cultivators did not regain the ability to weather the country's normal environmental variability. Subsistence in Eritrea has always required the production of surpluses in good years that could be carried over into bad ones. Following the rinderpest epizootic and the devastating famine, this stopped being possible. Many pastoralists and cultivators barely made it through good years. Bad years became deadly and survival was only possible with outside assistance. This new dynamic was especially pronounced in the years before the mass mobilization of the mid-1930s. Drought in southern Eritrea in 1927 resulted in such poor pastures that 60 percent of local herds died. To forestall a looming famine among pastoralists, the colonial government had to distribute grain and offer loans to the poor in the region (Bolsi 1936, pp. 2–3). Two years later, locusts and drought devastated the Eritrean highlands. Almost the entirety of the grain harvest was destroyed. Cultivators lost so much that they did not have enough to both feed themselves and invest in preparing the ground for cultivation at the start of the 1930 planting season. Again, the government had to intervene by offering grants and loans.[27] This highland drought, and with it the government assistance, continued for the next two years.[28]

[27] *Attività Agricola durante il mese di luglio 1930.* July 1930. IAO, FASC1224.

[28] Luigi Massa to il Direttore Ufficio Agrario della Colonia Eritrea, 17 January 1934, IAO, FASC852.

From the mid-1930s on, the income that *ascari* received from their service allowed them and their dependents to survive a series of ecological catastrophes. In 1934, the spring rains failed, reducing yields throughout the country. In 1937, there were regional droughts in the eastern lowlands and the southern highlands, the effects of which were compounded by grain-damaging parasites. The following year, locusts destroyed crops in the highlands and western lowlands.[29] Drought returned in 1939, causing extremely poor yields and a sharp reduction in pastures.[30] At the same time, an epizootic of contagious bovine pleuropneumonia killed some cattle and forced the government to restrict the movement of herds.[31] Despite these hardships, there were no reports of famine in the country in the 1930s. Eritrean cultivators and pastoralists did not have to turn to the government for supplemental help. They did not struggle in these hard times because they had the money that they earned through soldiering.

Soldiering was not a lucrative profession in the 1930s and *ascari* generally did not become rich. This had not always been the case. As mentioned above, the Italian colonial state had inherited the practice of recruiting soldiers locally from their Egyptian counterparts. Initially the new Italian colonial rulers followed their Egyptian predecessors in paying their soldiers as much as 4 Maria Theresa thalers per year (Martini 1896, p. 116). Shortly after taking over command of Massawa in 1885, the new Italian rulers changed the wage for the *ascari* to 1.6 lire per day (Scardigli 1996, p. 46). This new salary was significantly higher than the old rate at the then prevalent exchange rate and as a result was likely welcomed by the *ascari*. However, the impact of the change likely had little impact on the overall Eritrean economy. During the first fifty years of Italian rule, a sizable percentage of *ascari* were not Eritrean and most *ascari* were stationed outside of the colony. From the outset, Italian officials enlisted any willing fit man regardless of origin. As a result, men who crossed the border from Sudan and Ethiopia, including many runaway slaves, served as *ascari*. In 1920, at least one out of every four *ascari* were not

[29] Verdecchia. *Notizie generali sulla cerealicoltura Eritrea dall'anno 1933 all'anno 1938.* IAO, FASC851.

[30] Ufficio Agrario, Governo d'Eritrea. *Relazione Annuale Sull'Agricultura e Pastorizia in Eritrea nel 1939.* 2. IAO, FASC638.

[31] Ufficio Agrario, Governo d'Eritrea. *Relazione Annuale Sull'Agricultura e Pastorizia in Eritrea nel 1939.* 17. IAO, FASC638.

Eritrean (Volterra 2005, pp. 32–33). The *ascari* generally served outside of Eritrea, initially deployed to conquer and hold Somalia and Libya. As a result, three out of every four *ascari* were stationed abroad prior to the 1930s. This may explain why *ascari* initially accepted payment in lira—they lived and worked in a trans-local imperial space in which the lira was the only common currency (Zaccaria 2019).

The practice of paying *ascari* in lira became extremely relevant after the outbreak of the First World War. The ensuing uncontrolled devaluation of the lira meant that *ascari* salaries were worth less and less. In 1909, a Maria Theresa thaler was worth 2.28 lire in Asmara (Paoli 1913, p. 47). By 1925, the exchange rate had declined so much so that one thaler was worth 20 lire.[32] Though the colonial government nearly doubled the *ascari* basic wage, this made up a small fraction of the difference. In 1920s, this wage was worth just 20 percent of the pre-war wage when exchanged into thalers. Though the value of the lira relative to the thaler continued to drop in the 1930s, *ascari* did not complain about their wages and few deserted. They had to continue serving because no one else was hiring (Bellucci and Zaccaria 2014, p. 95). Survival without a regular wage was impossible. They needed lira at any price.

Acquiring lire would have been meaningless to *ascari* and their dependents if they could not spend them. This required merchants to accept lire in payment, which they began to do without objection in the 1930s. Instability in the lira exchange rates opened arbitrage opportunities that Greek and Arab merchants seized upon. In the 1930s, these merchants discovered that they could supplement their profits from trading in Eritrea with currency exchange gains by acquiring lire locally and exchanging them for their gold backing or for other hard currencies in Italy. Italian colonial officials first became aware of this trading strategy in 1938, when they broke up a ring of fifteen primarily Greek merchants who were exporting lira from Eritrea to Europe via Asmara, Kassala (Sudan), Alexandria, and Greece. In October of that year, Italian officials accused these merchants of exporting over 7.5 million lire, as well as 4575 British pounds and 63,000 Greek drachmae from Eritrea.[33] The following year, officials uncovered another currency exporting ring run by Yemeni

[32] Gasparini. *Telegram*. 19 May 1925, ASDMAE, AE Pacco 51.

[33] Governo dell'Eritrea to Ministero Africa Italiana 26 October 1938, ASDMAE, ASDMAI Posizione 180/41; Doadiace to Ministero dell'Africa Italiana, 18 October 1938, ASDMAE, ASDMAI Posizione 180/41.

merchants.[34] By 1940, Italian officials had come to understand that the exporting of lira was widespread. Small and large merchants alike exported lire and various precious metal coins to Sudan, Djibouti, and Aden via steamer, dhow, railroad, and camel.[35] These merchants willingly accepted the lire earned by the ascaris because their export had become very profitable.

Conclusion

The lira proved to be a poor store of value. When British forces conquered Italy's East African Empire in 1941, the local value of the lira collapsed. Lire ceased to circulate because merchants again refused to accept them. They had resumed insisting on payment in Maria Theresa thalers because another arbitrage opportunity had opened up. The new British rulers of Eritrea established a fixed exchange rate between the East African shillings they preferred to use and the Maria Theresa thaler. This rate was fifty percent above the market rate, ensuring a significant currency exchange profit for all merchants who could export thalers and import shillings.[36] Since merchants refused payment in lira, the lira/thaler exchange rate dropped precipitously. By the end of 1943, a single Maria Theresa thaler was worth 2016 lire.[37] Lire had become effectively worthless in Eritrea even though they remained legal tender. Out of expediency, the new British rulers of Eritrea had declared that all circulating currencies were legal tender in 1941.[38] Until the British authorities turned Eritrea over to Ethiopia in 1951, Eritreans could continue to pay government fees in lira. But this did not make lira circulate.

The collapse of the value of the lira did not turn Eritreans off from using imperial currencies. Throughout the 1940s, they sought out ways

[34] Ministero dell'Africa Italiana. *Promemoria*. 25 September 1939, ASDMAE, ASDMAI Posizione 180/41.

[35] Stato Maggiore, Ufficio Informazioni Militari. *Contrabbando* 22 April 1940, ASDMAE, ASDMAI Posizione 180/41.

[36] Corps Commander in the Middle East to War Office, 15 March 1942, British Library, London (BL), IOR/F/7/527.

[37] British Military Administration. Eritrea, *Annual Report by the Chief Administrator on the British Administration of Eritrea, Report V, for Period 1 January to 31 December 1943*, 10.

[38] Lewin to Lynch 3 January 1952, NA, FO371/96766.

of earning East African shillings, a subsidiary currency of the British pound. Many had no choice in the matter. The underlying structural economic problems that had pushed Eritreans into the lira economy in the 1930s persisted. Structural poverty did not end with the British conquest. In fact, economic conditions for many deteriorated in the wake of this conquest. The new British government dissolved the Eritrean army in 1941. Most former soldiers went back to their farms and pastures where they struggled. But this was not a viable option for many. Over 50,000 Eritrean men did not return home. Instead, they migrated to cities where economic opportunities were limited. Under 11,000 of these men found employment in the private sector. An additional 13,500 were hired by the administration, most as skilled and unskilled labour in the workshops set up to support the Allied war effort. More than 25,000 could not find jobs but remained in the city because they could not survive elsewhere.[39] Poverty limited their choices.

The impoverishment of Eritrea was the backdrop for the country's monetary transition. The spread of imperial currencies, the transformation of traditional livelihoods, the setting in of structural poverty, and the migration from the countryside to cities were all intertwined. Eritreans sought out imperial currencies not because they needed to pay taxes but because they needed them to buy food and other necessities. Poverty had made it impossible to survive without lire. But the lira proved to be a faulty tool because its value was unstable. Unfortunately, this was the only option available to Eritreans at the time. In this, Eritrea was not alone. While the specifics may be different, many parts of Africa experienced a decline in rural livelihoods under colonial rule. Other communities elsewhere also coped with the faltering of traditional economic practices by seeking out wage labor paid in imperial currencies. Other communities saw these currencies loose value and still sought to earn them because they had no choice. There were no other options. Poverty compelled them to earn weak imperial currencies that could not retain their value.

Acknowledgements Researching and writing this chapter was supported by grants from the Gerda Henkel Foundation and the Deutsche Forschungsgemeinschaft.

39 British Military Administration. Eritrea. *Annual Report by the Chief Administrator on the British Administration of Eritrea, Report V, for Period 1 January to 31 December 1943*. IAO, M-255-21.

References

Bellucci, Stefano, and Massimo Zaccaria. 2014. "Wage Labour and Mobility in Colonial Eritrea, 1880s to 1920s." *International Labor and Working-Class History* 86: 89–106.

Bolsi, Ugo. 1936. "Note economiche su la Dancalia Italiana Settentrionale." *Rassegna delle Colonie* 14 (1–2): 2–3.

Boselli, G. E. 1910. *Nota sul commercio della colonia Eritrea*. Rome: Istituto coloniale italiano.

Carboneri, Giovani. 1912. *Il tallero di Maria Teresa e la questione monetaria della Colonia Eritrea*. Rome: Tipografia Nazionale di G. Bertero.

Checchi, Michele. 1910. *Pesi e misure in uso nella Colonia Eritrea*. Rome: Istituto Coloniale Italiano.

Chelati Dirar, Uoldelul. 2004. "From Warriors to Urban Dwellers: Ascari and the Military Factor in the Urban Development of Colonial Eritrea." *Cahiers d'études africaines* 175: 533–574.

Connell, Dan, and Tom Killion. 2011. "Ascari." In *Historical Dictionary of Eritrea*, 84–85. 2nd edition. Lanham, MD: Scarecrow Press.

Desan, Christine. 2016. "Money as a Legal Institution." In *Money in the Western Legal Tradition: Middle Ages to Bretton Woods*, edited by David Fox and Wolfgang Ernst, 18–35. Oxford: Oxford University Press.

Fratianni, Michele, and Franco Spinelli. 1997. *A Monetary History of Italy*. Cambridge: Cambridge University Press.

Guyer, Jane I., and Karin Pallaver. 2018. "Money and Currency in African History." In *Oxford Research Encyclopedia of African History*. Oxford: Oxford University Press.

Iliffe, John. 2007. *African: The History of a Continent*. 2nd edition. Cambridge: Cambridge University Press.

Istituto Agricolo Coloniale Italiano. 1932. *L'economia Eritrea: nel cinquantennio dell'occupazione di Assab (1882–1932)*. Florence: Istituto agricolo coloniale Italiano.

Knapp, George. 1924. *The State Theory of Money*. London: Macmillan and Co.

Kuroda, Akinobu. 2007. "The Maria Theresa Dollar in the Early-Twentieth Century Red Sea Region: A Complementary Interface between Multiple Markets." *Financial History Review* 14 (1): 89–110.

Martini, Ferdinando. 1896. *Nell'Africa Italiana*. Milan: F.lli Treves.

Matthews, Dylan. 2019. "Modern Monetary Theory, Explained," *Vox*. Accessed April 7, 2021. https://www.vox.com/future-perfect/2019/4/16/18251646/modern-monetary-theory-new-moment-explained.

Mesghenna, Yemane. 1988. "Italian Colonialism: A Case Study of Eritrea, 1896–1934: Motive, Praxis and Result." PhD diss., Tycho Brahsev.

Miran, Jonathan. 2009. *Red Sea Citizens: Cosmopolitan Society and Cultural Change in Massawa*. Bloomington and Indianapolis: Indiana University Press.

Mitchell-Innes, Alfred. 1914. "The Credit Theory of Money." *The Banking Law Journal* 31: 151–168.

Mori, Angiolo. 1914. *Manuale di legislazione della colonia Eritrea*. Vol. 1. Rome: L'Universelle.

Mwangi, Wambui. 2001. "Of Coins and Conquest: The East African Currency Board, the Rupee Crisis, and the Problem of Colonialism in the East African Protectorate." *Comparative Studies in Society and History* 43 (4): 763–787.

Negash, Tekeste. 1987. "Italian Colonialism in Eritrea, 1882–1941: Policies, Praxis and Impact." PhD diss., Uppsala University.

Olukoju, Ayodeji. 1997. "Nigeria's Colonial Government, Commercial Banks and the Currency Crisis of 1916-1920." *The International Journal of African Historical Studies* 30 (2): 277–298.

Pallaver, Karin. 2019. "A Currency Muddle: Resistance, Materialities and the Local Use of Money during the East African Rupee Crisis (1919-1923)." *Journal of Eastern African Studies* 13 (3): 546–564.

Pankhurst, Richard. 1964. *The Great Ethiopian Famine of 1888–1892: A New Assessment*. Addis Ababa: Haile Sellassie I University.

Paoli, Renato. 1913. *Le Condizioni commerciali dell'Eritrea*. Novara: Istituto Geografico De Agostini.

Reid, Richard. 2009. *A History of Modern Africa: 1800 to the Present*. Oxford: Wiley-Blackwell.

Rodney, Walter. 1974. *How Europe Underdeveloped* Africa. Washington, DC: Howard University Press.

Santagata, Fernando. 1935. *La Colonia Eritrea nel Mar Rosso davanti all'Abissinia*. Naples: Libreria Internazionale Treves di Leo Lupi.

Scardigli, Marco. 1996. *Il braccio indigeno: Ascari, irregolari e bande nella conquista dell'Eritrea 1885–1911*. Milan: Franco Angeli.

Serels, Steven. 2013. *Starvation and the State: Famine, Slavery and Power in Sudan, 1883–1945*. New York: Palgrave Macmillan.

———. 2018a. *The Impoverishment of the African Red Sea Littoral, 1640–1945*. New York: Palgrave Macmillan.

———. 2018b. "Starving for Someone Else's Fight: The First World War and Food Insecurity in the African Red Sea Region." In *Environmental Histories of the First World War*, edited by Richard P. Tucker, Tait Keller, J. R. McNeill, and Martin Schmid, 208–230. Cambridge: Cambridge University Press.

———. 2019. "Introduction: The Indian Ocean World Currency System." In *Currencies of the Indian Ocean World*, edited by Steven Serels and Gwyn Campbell, 1–16. New York: Palgrave Macmillan.

Southard, Addison E. 1923. *Eritrea: A Red Sea Italian Colony of Increasing Interest to American Commerce*. Washington DC: United States Bureau of Foreign and Domestic Commerce.

Swanepoel, Natalie. 2015. "Small Change: Cowries, Coins, and the Currency Transition in the Northern Territories of Ghana." In *Materializing Colonial Encounters: Archaeologies of African Experience*, edited by François G. Richard, 41–69. New York: Springer.

Volterra, Alessandro. 2005. *Sudditi coloniali: Ascari Eritrei 1935–1941*. Milan: Franco Angeli.

Zaccaria, Massimo. 2019. "Italian Colonialism in Africa as a Connected System: Institutions, Men and Colonial Troops," *The Journal of Imperial and Commonwealth History* 47 (4): 718–741.

CHAPTER 8

“We Had to Feed the People”: The Italian Lira and the Political Economy of Currency in British Eritrea, 1941–1950

Luca Puddu

Introduction

In April 1941, following the defeat of Italian troops, Eritrea was placed under British military occupation. Soon after, a new set of currencies was introduced in parallel with the lira, the currency introduced in Eritrea by the Italians. One year later, in May 1942, the Occupied Enemy Territory Administration (OETA) in Eritrea established the East African shilling (EAS) as legal tender. The main purpose of this currency reform was the enforcement of a sterling-based monetary system. In spite of this, however, the Italian lira remained in circulation until the end of British rule, when it disappeared owing to a combination of financial and demographic factors.[1] The resilience of the lire confirms that the introduction

[1]Tel 602/3, 3 January 1952, The National Archives (TNA) FO 371/96766.

L. Puddu (✉)
Scuola Superiore Meridionale, University of Naples Federico II, Napoli, Italy

K. Pallaver (ed.), *Monetary Transitions*,
Palgrave Studies in Economic History,
https://doi.org/10.1007/978-3-030-83461-6_8

of European currencies in colonial Africa did not translate into a top-down revolution of the existing monetary framework (Bohannan 1959; Hopkins 1966). Rather, the British administration in Eritrea tolerated the coexistence of a complementary currency system in response to overlapping pressures from both higher metropolitan authorities and the colonial subjects (Şaul 2004; Pallaver 2015; Swanepoel 2015; Guyer and Pallaver 2018).

The British political economy of currency towards Eritrea should be understood within the framework of the broader re-organisation of the sterling area in the 1940s. Policy-makers in the United Kingdom came to the conclusion that a closer integration of African colonial trade within the sphere of influence of the pound was critical to financing the war effort and, at the end of the hostilities, to ensure the enduring centrality of London as a global financial hub (Cain and Hopkins 1993; Krozewski 1993). After having been a marginal part of the Empire for decades, African dependencies were now set to become a buffer against the decline of the sterling and the emerging hegemony of the American dollar (Cooper 2011, p. 199). The case of Eritrea made no exception. The monetary policy elaborated by higher authorities in London was primarily aimed at maximising the economic benefits for the central government's coffers, with lesser consideration to the social consequences on the ground.

The British administration in Asmara, on the other hand, framed the new currency regime as a technology of rule aimed at territorialising state authority in the Eritrean space. The OETA's primary concern was the relationship with local subjects, whose support or benevolent neutrality was worth a challenge to monetary orthodoxy. British authorities ruled over a 58,000-strong Italian community that controlled the key sectors of the local economy and also ensured the regular functioning of the bureaucratic machine. For Italian settlers, the lira was the main venue for wage earning and capital accumulation. Small denomination lire were also entrenched in African economic networks, providing a complementary device to the more popular Maria Theresa thaler (MTT) (Kuroda 2007). The trajectory of the Italian currency, in this respect, was linked to the renegotiation of the economic status of the Italian and Eritrean population, whose collaboration was essential for the control of the territory (Makki 2011, p. 430; Longrigg 1945, p. 150; Lucchetti 2012).

The purpose of this chapter is to investigate the underlying factors of the British political economy of currency in Eritrea during the occupation. The posture of the United Kingdom's different layers of government towards the circulation of the lire is a useful lens to unpack the multiplicity of interests that shaped the British policy towards former Italian colonies. The case study also offers a new perspective on the unfolding of state-society relations in Eritrea after the demise of Italian rule. The assignment of legal status and fixed exchange rate to certain denominations of lire notes and coins played a critical role in the process of spatial enforcement of British sovereignty, redrawing racial hierarchies between Africans and Italian settlers.

A Monetary Policy for British Eritrea

When Eritrea was placed under military occupation in the spring of 1941, there was no predetermined strategy for the government of the territory, nor sufficient staff to run the administration (Trevaskis 1960, pp. 19–22). Central authorities in London also had fluctuating ideas on what to do with Italian colonies in the aftermath of occupation. Eritrea, for instance, changed administrative affiliation three times throughout the decade. From 1941 to 1943, it was subject to the OETA; from 1943 to 1949 it became a British Military Administration (BMA), before finally transitioning under the authority of the Foreign Office from 1949 to 1952. The same uncertainty surrounded the hierarchical relationship of Asmara with higher administrative centres of power. At the onset of occupation, the territory was placed under the command of the Headquarters for the Middle East in Cairo, which had jurisdiction over North and East Africa. In February 1942, the two areas were separated and assigned to different regional offices, Eritrea falling under the authority of the Chief Political Office (CPO) for East Africa stationed in Nairobi (Boobbyer 2018). The Eritrean military administration was headed by a brigadier general, who was in turn supported by a number of civilian officers. The departments dealing with financial matters were directly responsible to the Controller of Finance and Accounts (CFA) in Nairobi and, ultimately, to the War Department in London, which were in turn expected to implement general guidelines drawn up by the Bank of England and the Treasury.[2] British rule in Eritrea was also mediated by non-state actors. The unavailability of British personnel and the presence of a large Italian community encouraged the OETA to come to terms with pre-existing ruling structures, keeping in place most of the original Italian civil administration (Lucchetti 2012).

The different articulations of the metropolitan government in London—including financial institutions that lay beyond the realm of the state narrowly defined, but were directly involved in the management of overseas dependencies, such as the Bank of England (Stockwell 2019)—held opposing views on the relevance of Eritrea within the wider framework of imperial politics. The Bank of England and the Treasury looked at Asmara as a marginal appendix of the empire, if not just as a temporary burden. The Eritrean policy of these institutions was dominated by economic concerns and somewhat detached from the local context, being primarily aimed at minimising the financial burden of local administration (Louis 1984). Not incidentally, the Treasury advocated a strategy of de-industrialisation and dismantling of the existing infrastructural network, which was then transferred to other British possessions in Asia and Africa. The rationale behind this policy was to obtain some sort of compensation for the chronic deficit of the Eritrean budget, even at the cost of additional strains on local rates of employment and the cost of living (Makki 2011, p. 429). The Foreign Office, on the contrary, looked at Eritrea as a bargaining card in the re-organisation of the British empire in East Africa and the Middle East. Until the rejection of the Bevin-Sforza Plan in 1949 by the General Assembly of the United Nations, the British diplomacy insisted on the partition of the former Italian colony between Sudan and Ethiopia with the twofold objective of securing control of western Eritrea's riverine system and, at the same time, satisfying Ethiopian pledges for a direct access to the sea.[3] In turn, the concession to Addis Ababa was supposed to be exchanged for

[2] Tel from CFA Nairobi to Major Logie, 3 June 1941, TNA, WO 230/32.

[3] The Bevin-Sforza plan was an agreement reached by the ministers of foreign affairs of the United Kingdom and the Italian Republic on the future of the Italian colonies. According to the plan, Italy should have received the trusteeship of Tripolitania and Somalia, while Eritrea should have been partitioned between Ethiopia and the Anglo-Egyptian Sudan. The plan was rejected by the General Assembly of the United Nations in May 1949 (Morone 2018).

territorial adjustments in favour of British Somali subjects in the north-eastern section of the Ethiopian empire (Kibreab 2005). It was indeed for the purpose of avoiding any misunderstandings with Emperor Haile Selassie that, until 1949, Eritrea was assigned to the authority of the War Office, rather than to the jurisdiction of the Colonial and Foreign Office (Boobbyer 2018, p. 308). British military officials, in turn, had their own plan for the territory, which was considered a strategic outpost for the defence of British positions in the Red Sea. Though the OETA was supposed to only take care of the daily administration, local authorities manoeuvred to put the basis for the preservation of a sphere of influence in the area for the years to come. Not incidentally, in 1948 the Chief of Staff of the Italian Army noted that "the official government policy is paralleled by a more subtle one, whose proponents pursue an imperialist strategy without the knowledge of higher authorities."[4]

The monetary policy was one of the subtle arenas of confrontation between these conflicting views. A transitional currency regime was set up in Eritrea in the early summer of 1941 under instructions from the Bank of England, which had envisaged the same solution for all Italian possessions in Africa. The new monetary architecture was based on the experience in the former Ottoman territories in Palestine and Mesopotamia, which had fallen under British occupation during the First World War. In that case, London did not issue a new currency, but let the existing local one circulate freely in parallel with the coins and notes introduced by British troops. The Ottoman currency apparently disappeared naturally, through the payment of wages and services by the armed forces stationed in the area.[5] In Eritrea, the British authorities followed a similar path and introduced a mixed set of currencies on which the United Kingdom had power of issue: the EAS, the Indian rupee, the Egyptian piastre and the MTT.[6] The lire, however, were not withdrawn

[4] Appunto per S.E. il Sottosegretario di Stato, Archivio Storico Diplomatico del Ministero degli Affari Esteri (ASDMAE), II Direzione per l'Africa Orientale, 1943–1950, F. 1.

[5] Meeting of Hornsby committee at the Treasury, Notes on currency in Italian East Africa, 31 October 1941, Archives of the Bank of England (ABE), OV 36/28, p. 1.

[6] The United Kingdom had begun to mint MTT in India a few years earlier. At the end of 1941, the monthly production amounted to 2 million MTT. Meeting of Hornsby committee at the Treasury, Notes on currency in Italian East Africa, 31 October 1941, ABE, OV 36/28, p. 15.

overnight: they could be used in private transactions, while lower denomination notes and coins up to lire 10 were temporarily accepted also for the payment of fiscal obligations to the administration.[7]

Apparently, the debate on what currency should be finally adopted in Eritrea was driven by immediate technical and financial concerns. The adoption of rupees and MTT was based on their widespread use in local and regional trading networks (Mauri 2009). The choice of piastres and shillings, on the other hand, was due to their availability in the hands of invading British troops stationed in Sudan and Kenya.[8] Soon, however, it became clear that rupees found little acceptance beyond the port of Assab, while the hypothesis of confirming the legal status of the MTT was discarded "having regarded the cost of this currency due to its high silver content."[9] As a consequence, the final choice was between the piastre and the EAS, provided that the emission of special notes for Italian East Africa was not found acceptable in London.[10] At a closer look, the competition for becoming Eritrea's legal tender was also nurtured by the overlapping geo-political ambitions of the different articulations of the British empire in north-east Africa. For the Middle East Command in Cairo, the piastre was a tool to build a potential sphere of Egyptian economic influence in the area. This was something that could have been useful on the negotiating table with the Egyptian government for the control of the Suez Canal and associated army installations (Kelly 2000). The superior suitability of the EAS to the Eritrean economy, on the other hand, was supported by the Chief of Finance and Account (CFA) in Nairobi,[11] who was the link between East Africa and the East African Currency Board in London.

At the end of 1941, Nairobi finally had the upper hand, and the British government opted for the withdrawal from the circulation of piastres, rupees, and MTT. The motivation was that the piastre could not serve the purpose of being a general currency, since the scarcity of its small

[7] Banco di Roma, Asmara, 6 April 1941, TNA, WO 230/32.

[8] Tel 223 from Khartoum, 7 April 1941, TNA, WO 230/32. p. 2.

[9] Meeting of Hornsby committee, ABE, OV 36/28, p. 19.

[10] Ibid.

[11] Ibid.

denominations made it unsuited to the needs of African commerce.[12] The EAS, on the contrary, was supposed to fit better with the monetary needs of the African population, in light of the large availability of its small denomination coins, the East African cents. Moreover, the proximity of Asmara to Nairobi facilitated the transportation of EAS coins.[13] A Monetary Proclamation was therefore issued in May 1942 that sanctioned the EAS as legal tender in the former Italian colony.[14] However, the lira was not ousted from circulation. On the contrary, besides 10 lire notes, also 50 lire notes could be used in the transactions with the administration such as the payment of taxes and fees. This decision was the outcome of a harsh debate that had taken place throughout the second half of 1941 and the first months of 1942 among the different layers of the British administration involved in the elaboration and implementation of the monetary policy for Eritrea.

Orthodoxy Against Flexibility: The Debate on the Lira

The British government's initial decision, at the onset of occupation, to allow the use of smaller denomination lire for payments to the administration—as well as of higher denomination lire for private transactions—was, to a large extent, the result of an adaptation to the monetary situation on the ground. According to concerned British officials, the Italian currency had become a local tender in Eritrean markets, where it was completely independent from the fluctuations of the metropolitan currency in Rome.[15] The large amounts of lire in circulation were due to a specific action of the Italian government. In previous years, the *Banca d'Italia* had injected almost 8 billion lire in the territory in preparation for the 1935–1936 war with Ethiopia. British Authorities estimated that approximately 350 million lire still circulated in local markets.[16] In addition, the Italian government had distributed payments worth five

[12] Tel from Assistant Controller of Banks, 31 May 1941, TNA, WO 230/133; Tel from Troopers to Nairobi, 3 June 1941, TNA, WO 230/133.

[13] Tel from GOC East Africa to War Office, 6 December 1941, ABE, OV 36/28.

[14] East African Currency Circulating in Eritrea, Annexure 21, TNA, T 236/3179.

[15] Memorandum: valorising the Lira, 27 September 1941, TNA, WO 230/133, p. 5.

[16] Note on the Financial Policy in Eritrea, 17 February 1942, TNA, WO 230/133.

months of salary to public officials just a few days before the evacuation of Asmara. The purpose of this measure was to reduce the amount of money in local banks that would become war booty for the British, while also keeping the allegiance of Italian settlers before the envisaged Italian re-conquest of the colony.[17] Another factor behind the popularity of the lire, and in particular of the 10 lire notes, could be found in the functioning of the market itself. As Akinobu Kuroda points out, "the reason was simply that a currency valued at a quarter or a sixth of the (Maria Theresa) dollar was required in local transactions" (Kuroda 2007, p. 103). The circulation of the lire was so widespread that Barclays itself created two parallel accounting systems—one in pounds and one in lire—"because the majority of the currency in circulation was made up of small denominations lire."[18]

For higher authorities in London, this decision had a temporary nature and was mostly dictated by concerns for cost-maximisation and financial stability, rather than by the desire to nurturing an amicable relationship with the new Eritrean and Italian subjects. The lira was expected to disappear gradually "without having recourse to exchange of currencies," thereby serving His Majesty's government desire not to "valorise Italian currency in occupied territories in any form that could possibly be avoided."[19] For the British Treasury, the temporal maintenance of some sort of lira's purchasing power "was calculated to obviate having to make early cash relief payments."[20] The Bank of England shared the same opinion. That metropolitan concerns dominated over other calculations emerged clearly at the onset of the occupation, when the Bank of England was called to fix an official exchange rate for the lire. The Italian currency was set at 480/1 against the pound, 24/1 against the EAS, and 492/1 against the Egyptian sterling, with a five-fold devaluation compared to pre-war exchange rates.[21] This measure was supposed to be applied to all former Italian possessions, without taking into account

[17] Letter from Legal Adviser to CPO, 29 April 1941, TNA, WO 230/32.

[18] Banking in Eritrea, Barclays Historical Archives, 1784/0002, p. 5.

[19] Meeting of Hornsby committee, ABE, OV 36/28, p. 15.

[20] Meeting of Hornsby committee, ABE, OV 36/28, p. 17.

[21] Tel from Political Branch, Asmara, TNA, WO 230/133, p. 10. In 1936, the exchange rate was fixed at 62\1. Bank of Ethiopia, Dire-Dawa branch, 12 June 1936, National Archives of Ethiopia, 1.2. 76.04.

the peculiarities of specific territories. The rationale behind this policy was clearly of an economic nature. In this manner, British authorities hoped to shift the financial burden of the occupation onto the Italian community through the sudden reduction of the cost of wages and services. In addition, a lower exchange rate would prevent a rush to sell lire in return for British currency, thereby protecting the stability of the pound in a time of distress.[22]

Cost maximisation had its drawbacks, however. Wages in the private sector of the former Italian colonies rose rapidly, while food prices increased immediately five-fold in comparison to the preoccupation period.[23] The reaction of Italian residents varied according to the actual gap between the new exchange rate and the prevailing black market's exchange rate. On the one hand, British authorities did not record any major grievance in Ethiopia. In Somalia and Eritrea, on the other hand, the new monetary policy was welcomed as a measure "that will lead to widespread price increases and chaos."[24] Inflation was so high that the British government in London acknowledged that devaluation had been "perhaps excessive compared to what was desirable or perhaps necessary."[25] The sudden depreciation of the Italian currency had significant consequences on the ability of the new military authorities to mobilise manpower for public works associated to the needs of the war effort. The problem emerged more clearly in those sectors that were more integrated with the colonial monetary system. At the port of Mogadishu, for instance, British authorities found themselves unable to recruit labour for the expansion of the harbour, because Somali workers did not accept any currency other than the lira.[26] The same problem occurred in Eritrea, where the OETA had the mandate to make purchases only in Egyptian piastres. At the port of Massawa, the English company tasked with renovation works was stigmatised for the decision to provide a daily wage of 15

[22] Report on currency and Exchange Part II, ABE, OV 36/28, p. 8.

[23] Tel from Political Branch, Asmara, TNA, WO 230/133. p. 11.

[24] Meeting of Hornsby committee at the Treasury, Section II, Part II, Exchange, ABE, OV 36/28, p. 22; Extract from Letter to the Permanent Undersecretary of State, War Office, 14 April 1941, TNA, WO 230/32.

[25] Meeting of Hornsby committee at the Treasury, Notes on currency in Italian East Africa, 31 October 1941, p. 17, ABE, OV 36\28.

[26] Extract from Letter to the Permanent Under Secretary of State, War Office, 14 April 1941, TNA, WO 230/32.

piastres, in line with the standards in force in neighbouring Sudan. This wage rate was deemed to be too high by the OETA Eritrea, which argued that, according to pre-occupation standards, the maximum daily wage should not exceed 5 piastres (Puddu 2021). The idea of contracting an Italian company with greater knowledge of the Massawa labour market, was however discarded because of the contradiction with the objective of driving the Italian currency out of the territory. The Italian firm, in fact, might "feed you up with a cock and bully story that the labour will not accept anything except Italian lire so as to force you to buy up Italian notes which someone is sure to have handy at the very moment."[27]

The OETA Eritrea had a radically different view of what priorities should be pursued through the new monetary policy. The armed forces were more inclined to find a modus vivendi with the local population and satisfying the basic needs of the occupation, rather than being preoccupied with enforcing the financial orthodoxy of the City. British soldiers, for instance, did not hesitate to exchange their piastres and pounds with lire to buy goods on the local market, adapting to the local merchants' reluctance to accept the new coinage.[28] The OETA itself informally accepted any kind of Italian currency for the payment of goods and services to the administration, in open defiance to the ban introduced on notes higher than 10-lire. The line of conduct of the OETA Eritrea was shaped by the objective of securing support from the new subjects. British authorities did not want to worsen the already difficult situation faced by the Italian community, from which they depended for the daily business of the administration. The chaotic monetary framework and the constraints of war had triggered an impressive inflationary spiral, with dramatic consequences on settlers' living conditions (Almedom 2006; Makki 2011). The urgency of the situation was such that the OETA was forced to set fixed prices for the sale of basic foodstuff, which appeared to be the only counter-measure to large-scale riots.[29] The operation could be conducted only by accepting payments in all lire denominations, since this was the only currency available to Italian residents.[30]

[27] Tel 223 from Khartoum, 7 April 1941, TNA, WO 230/32, p. 1.

[28] Ibid., p. 2.

[29] Banca d'Italia, Archivio Storico Banca d'Italia (ASBI), Segreteria Particolare, pratt. n. 10, fasc. 43, p. 5.

[30] Meeting of Hornsby committee at the Treasury, Section IV, Trade and Economics, ABE, OV 36/28, p. 43.

The second preoccupation of the OETA was the African population in the colony. After British occupation, the Eritreans had suffered the sudden contraction of working opportunities in the colonial military apparatus, which had offered employment to 55,000–60,000 individuals at the onset of the war with Ethiopia in 1935 (Zaccaria 2019, p. 732). The acceptance of the circulation of the lira can be also explained with the intention to avoid riots while also enforcing British fiscal sovereignty in a quick and cost-effective way. Indeed, the enforcement of a 10-lire threshold in transactions with the administration had created a two-track currency system, whereby higher denomination lire were available in Eritrean bazaars at an exchange rate of 1000 against 600 of lower denomination notes and coins.[31] The OETA, on its part, agreed to collect cattle tax owed by Beni Amer chiefs in the western lowlands in banknotes worth 100 lire or higher, regardless of the fact that this currency was in theory banned from use.[32] In this manner, Eritrean subjects were able to pledge their allegiance to the new rulers while also enjoying a sharp reduction of the actual fiscal burden. The acceptance of this medium of exchange in fulfilment of fiscal obligations, in fact, allowed Eritrean taxpayers—at least those better positioned to get access to informal currency markets—to obtain a significant discount of their duties.

The OETA exploited the loopholes in the legislation to bring forward its own policy objectives without waiting for authorization from the higher spheres in London, Cairo, and Nairobi. This erratic behaviour was nonetheless justified by the OETA on moral grounds, since it was deemed to be the only means to secure the legitimacy of British rule in enemy territory. The tension between orthodoxy and flexibility emerges clearly from the harsh discussion involving Francis Rennell of Rodd—the CFA in Nairobi with supervisory role over Eritrea's economic affairs—and the Chief of the Eritrean administration, William Platt, once the latter proposed a radical revision of monetary policies in August 1941. Platt argued that the intention to ban the lire was too drastic and against the interests of the Eritrean population, which would have suddenly lost its main medium of exchange. He pointed out that the original 492:1 exchange rate set by the Bank of England between the lira and the

[31] Tel 454 from BMA Asmara, 10 October 1941, TNA, WO 230/35.

[32] Meeting of Hornsby committee at the Treasury, Notes on currency in Italian East Africa, 31 October 1941, ABE, OV 36/28, p. 15; Legal Tender Status of Italian Currency, 17 November 1942, ABE, OV 36/29.

piastre had made the Egyptian currency useless for low value transactions among Africans.[33] The OETA was of the opinion that a smooth transition towards a sterling-based currency could be achieved through the free conversion of all types of lire banknotes at the official exchange rate, in parallel with the communication to the population of the colony that the Italian currency would be deprived of its legal value soon thereafter.[34] The proposal sanctioned a net departure from the strategy followed so far, because it devised the creation of specific guidelines for each territory according to local economic conditions. However, the CFA declined the proposal, arguing that it would have represented an indirect valorisation of the lira.[35] Moreover, Rennell accused the OETA of insubordination, pointing the finger against the habit to accept payments in higher denomination lire. The OETA reacted to the accusations with an outer defence of the strategy adopted so far. According to Platt, the monetary proclamation issued in the summer of 1941 was dictated by financial considerations, but had not taken into due account the social consequences for ordinary people on the ground. For the OETA, what Nairobi termed "insubordination" was necessary to ensure public order, since "the administration would be faced with far more serious social and economic disruption, were the local currency experience a complete loss of value within a short period of time... than any ***unpleasant developments*** [*sic*] that can fairly be attributed to ***valorising*** [*sic*] the lira."[36] The letter continued with a detailed dismantlement of the arguments advanced by the CFA, which were dismissed as "an academic exercise."[37] In contrast, the OETA defended its behaviour as being dictated by exceptional circumstances that legitimised the circumvention of general norms. The acceptance of higher denomination lire was not a matter of policy. According to them, it was an imperative necessity imposed by higher humanitarian principles, because "we had to feed the people [*sic*]."[38]

[33] Tel from Deputy Chief Political Office, Asmara, 26 August 1941, TNA, WO 230/133.

[34] Tel from Political Branch, Asmara, TNA, WO 230/133, pp. 12–14.

[35] Tel from CFA, Nairobi, 29 August 1941, TNA, WO 230/133.

[36] Tel from OETA, Asmara, a CFA, Nairobi, October 1941, TNA, WO 230/133, p. 1.

[37] Tel from OETA, Asmara, a CFA, Nairobi, October 1941, TNA, WO 230/133, p. 2.

[38] Tel from OETA, Asmara, a CFA, Nairobi, October 1941, TNA, WO 230/133, p. 4.

The Hornsby Committee

The confrontation between the supporters of orthodoxy and the proponents of flexibility resurfaced again in October 1941, when a meeting was convened in London to deliberate on the monetary policy to be followed in Eritrea and the former Italian East African Empire. The Hornsby Committee—from the name of its chair, the former governor of the National Bank of Egypt Sir Bertram Hornsby (Jones 1993, p. 231)—included representatives from the Treasury, the Bank of England, the Foreign Office, the War Office, the Colonial Office and the India Office. The purpose of the meeting was to elaborate a strategy for the enforcement of a currency system anchored to the pound, which in the case of Eritrea would take the form of the introduction of the EAS.[39] On the table there were originally two proposals, which in turn reflected two radically different rationalities of rule. The first solution was a tribute to financial orthodoxy and profit-maximisation, since it prescribed the sudden loss of the lira's legal status and its exclusion from any kind of transaction. It found the enthusiastic support of the Treasury and the Bank of England, attracted by a solution that would shield government coffers from an additional financial burden.[40] The second proposal reflected the point of view of the OETA, since it suggested the withdrawal of all lire in circulation through their conversion against EAS at the official exchange rate of 480. The supporters of this option concurred that it would protect occupying authorities form the threat of social disturbance, but at an estimated cost of 4 million pound for the government of the United Kingdom and without any immediate economic return.[41]

The CFA in Nairobi, on his part, advanced a potential compromise between the two extremes. Rennell argued that convertibility should be limited to banknotes worth lire 10 and lire 50, while higher denomination banknotes could have been gradually eliminated by encouraging their outflow to Italy through financial remittances. At the same time, he suggested that all coins worth lire 5 and below should become legal tender along with the EAS. This would have ensured a significant saving

[39] Meeting of Hornsby committee at the Treasury, Notes on currency in Italian East Africa, 31 October 1941, ABE, OV 36/28, p. 3.

[40] Meeting of Hornsby committee at the Treasury, Notes on currency in Italian East Africa, 31 October 1941, ABE, OV 36/28, p. 1.

[41] Meeting of Hornsby committee at the Treasury, Draft Attached, ABE, OV 36/28.

for the government, the overall cost of the operation being around £1 million. In addition, the solution relieved the administration from the burden of issuing East African cents, while also shielding the armed forces from the danger of widespread social unrest.[42] Rennell's proposal was in line with the OETA's concerns for the relationship with the African population, who made ample use of Italian coins and small banknotes as an auxiliary medium of exchange along with the MTT.[43] According to the CFA, "the natives may consider the maintenance of the value of small change as a British pledge," while on the contrary "British prestige might suffer if we were to say, whenever it suits our convenience, that henceforth lire will have no value."[44] In other words, the EAS was supposed to remain the official currency in the interactions between the British government and the Italian community, while lower denomination lire were expected to serve the needs of African trade on a complementary basis with East African cents, which the administration described as "essential for the small trader."[45] To ensure the suitability of British currency to Eritrean business, Rennell also advanced the proposal to modify the exchange rate between the lira and the shilling from 24 to 25. This adjustment would diminish the economic burden of currency exchange for 10 and 50 lire banknotes while also eliminating inconsistencies at a decimal level between the two currencies, as shown in Table 8.1.

The set of proposals made by Rennell generated mixed reactions in London. The policy guidelines elaborated by the Hornsby Committee remained anchored to the principle of cost maximisation advocated by the Bank of England and the Treasury. As a result, the hypothesis of free convertibility of banknotes worth lire 10 and 50 against EAS was rejected on the ground of the financial sustainability of the operation, as well as the possible repercussions on the stability of the pound.[46] The Committee, however, also took into account the concerns for the Eritrean

[42] Meeting of Hornsby committee at the Treasury, Draft Attached, ABE, OV 36/28, p. 1.

[43] Tel to Troopers from Nairobi, 3 June 1941, TNA, WO 230/133.

[44] Meeting of Hornsby committee at the Treasury, Notes on currency in Italian East Africa, 31 October 1941, p. 4, ABE, OV 36/28.

[45] Tel from Asmara to CFA, 28 June 1943, TNA, WO 230/133.

[46] Meeting of Hornsby committee at the Treasury, Draft Attached, ABE, OV 36/28.

Table 8.1 Lire/EAS exchange rate according to Rennell's proposal

Lire	*EAS*
5	20 cents
2	8 cents
1	4 cents
50 cents	2 cents

Source Meeting of Hornsby committee at the Treasury, Notes on currency in Italian East Africa, 31 October 1941, ABE, OV 36/28, p. 5

population and opted for assigning the status of legal tender to Italian banknotes until the threshold of lire 50, while limiting the use of higher denomination notes to private transactions or debt repayments indexed in Italian currency.[47] In this manner, Africans would retain a set of currencies better suited to the needs of local trade, pending the shipping of additional shilling small denomination coins to Asmara.[48]

The 1942 Monetary Proclamation and Its Implementation

The decisions taken in London should have paved the way to the transition from the mixed currency system based on the coexistence of five different tenders, to a semi-homogenous one based on EAS banknotes and coins plus smaller denomination lire. The new monetary system elaborated by the Hornsby Committee, however, did not put an end to sky-rocketing inflation, food scarcity, and the associated threat of social unrest. The drawbacks of the situation pushed the OETA to advance again the proposal of the recognition of all lire coins and banknotes, without discrimination between smaller and higher denomination notes. The hope was to change the posture of the central government before the official adoption of the new monetary legislation.

According to the OETA, the ban on higher denomination lire could concretely lead to mass starvation. Even though the population remained dependent on government-controlled food supplies at a fixed price, only

[47] Meeting of Hornsby committee at the Treasury, Notes on currency in Italian East Africa, 31 October 1941, ABE, OV 36/28, p. 16.

[48] Tel from Asmara to CFA, 28 June 1943, TNA, WO 230/133.

50 per cent of the Italian community and less than 1 per cent of the African community had alternative currencies other than the lira at their disposal.[49] The only remedy was the full recognition of the lire without restriction. The request was also grounded on financial reasons. The OETA was struggling to find new sources of finance to make ends meet. In this manner, the military authorities could make use of the 28 million lire accumulated until that moment, thereby expanding their capacity to pay for wages and services to the public. To make the point stronger, the administration stressed that this change of policy was in the interests of the United Kingdom as well, because it would terminate currency speculation by Italian capitalists who were enriching themselves at the expense of British taxpayers.[50] The argument did not succeed in changing the position of higher authorities, however. For the CFA in Nairobi, the elimination of the lire and the incorporation of the Eritrean territory within the sterling area had now become a matter of prestige: the dual currency system adopted by the Hornsby Committee was the only possible derogation to the rule. Nairobi did not discard the tremendous social pressure that the OETA was facing on the ground, but deliberated a diametrically alternative solution. Rennell ordered prices of consumer goods to be indexed in EAS and, at the same time, invited the OETA to let circulate the rumour that the lira was going to be outlawed by a new Proclamation. To make matters clearer, the CFA pointed out that the monetary policy had been decided in advance in London and was not subject to negotiation by lower authorities.[51]

The Monetary Proclamation of May 1942 confirmed the structure outlined by the Hornsby Committee, though maintaining the existing exchange rate of 480/1 between the lira and the shilling. The objective was the gradual elimination of higher denomination lire from circulation, with the exception of those banknotes and coins better suited to the needs of intra-African trade.[52]

In spite of the new law, the OETA Eritrea continued to lobby for its partial amendment, fearing unpredictable effects on social peace in

[49] Note on the Financial Policy in Eritrea, 14 February 1942, TNA, WO 230/133, p. 2.

[50] Ibid.

[51] Tel from CFA to Military Administrator, 4 March 1942, TNA, WO 230/133.

[52] Proclamation 19, 1942, TNA, WO 230/133.

the colony. The discrimination between smaller denomination and higher denomination lire, in particular, was deemed to be morally unacceptable and "contrary to the standards of justice that foreigners normally accord us,"[53] since it was likely to encourage speculation at the expense of wage labourers and the lower strata of society. To avoid this, the OETA advanced again the proposal of the free convertibility of higher denomination lire, though at a significant discount that would lower the financial burden for the coffers of the United Kingdom. Lire banknotes could have been exchanged against shillings at a value corresponding to 20% of the official exchange rate, with the commitment to return the money at the same price to the seller in case of repatriation to Italy.[54] The OETA was clearly lobbying on behalf of the Italian community, which detained the lion's share of higher denominations notes and whose collaboration remained critical for the daily running of the administration.

The debate resurfaced two months later, when the combined effect of the Axis military victories in North Africa and the Bank of England's authorization to remittances in lire to Italy pushed the informal exchange rate between the Italian currency and the pound at 370, that was well below the standard rate of 480.[55] The recognition of all lira notes as legal tender, the OETA argued, could bring the actual value of Italian currency at parity with the official exchange rate, encouraging the conversion against EAS and, consequently, the elimination of the lire from the territory.[56] The argument found this time a ready audience in Nairobi, where Rennell was coming to the conclusion that a more structural collaboration with the Italian community was necessary for an effective administration of the Eritrean territory.[57] The alignment between Asmara and Nairobi was not however enough to change the posture of the guardians of financial orthodoxy in London. The Bank of England rejected any attempt to recognise the lira as legal tender and insisted that the monetary policy's ultimate goal was the ban of all lire without exception: the dual currency

[53] Tel from OETA to CFA, TNA, WO 230/133, p. 2.

[54] Tel 537\166, 7 May 1942, TNA, WO 230/133.

[55] Tel 11,370/160, 13 August 1942, TNA, WO 230/133, p. 3.

[56] Draft 11,043, Tel from Deputy CFA Asmara to CFA Cairo, TNA, WO 230/133.

[57] In his memories, Rennell underscored the importance of the Italian community in the government of the highlands and the coastal city of Massawa as well (Rennell 1948).

system based on lower denomination lire was the only exception that could be accepted for the sake of social order.[58]

The 1942 Monetary Proclamation gradually achieved its original purpose. The actual value of the lire on the black market and in private transactions entered into a downward spiral in the years to come, with only one minor exception for a short period in the summer of 1943.[59] This negative trajectory was also favoured by the evolution of the war in favour of the Allied forces and the rumours that Italy was going to have no role in Eritrea after the end of the conflict. Italian residents were those who suffered the most from devaluation, since their wages were usually indexed in lire. That depreciation was hindering the purchasing power of Italian settlers is indirectly confirmed by the correspondence between the Italian banks' branches in Eritrea and the metropolitan headquarters. At the end of 1943, the former requested authorization to increase the salary of local staff, since the existing level had become totally outdated by devaluation.[60] At the end of 1944, Italian higher denomination notes were exchanged against pounds at 800:1, making them almost useless outside of debt repayments indexed in the same currency.[61]

In spite of the inability to impose its own point of view on monetary affairs at government level, the OETA continued to exploit every margin of bureaucratic autonomy for the purpose of advancing a currency policy that would better serve its own needs in the relationship with the local population. One of the main problems of the new monetary framework was the lack of decimal units of exchange, in spite of the growing quantity of East African cents that had been injected by the East African Currency Board. The first container of EAS coins worth £ 850,000 had arrived at the end of 1941 to fill the gap left by the withdrawal of the Egyptian piastre, but the injection of small change continued in the years to come.[62] In May 1943, total shipments amounted to 10,920 coins worth 10 cents, 7920 coins worth 5 cents, and 1670 one cent coins.[63] According to the OETA, however, a large part of these coins was hoarded

[58] Tel from Bank of England to Rowe-Dutton, 1 April 1942, ABE, OV 36/28.

[59] Tel from CFA Cairo to Asmara, 19 March 1943, TNA, WO 230/133.

[60] Tel from Nairobi to War Office, 18 December 1943, TNA, WO 230/35.

[61] Tel 454 from BMA Asmara, 10 October 1944, TNA, WO 230/35.

[62] Tel from GOC East Africa to War Office, 6 December 1941, ABE, OV 36/28.

[63] Tel from Asmara to CFA, 28 June 1943, TNA, WO 230/133.

by speculators or exported abroad through smuggling channels, with the administration unable to put a halt to the outflow of money.[64] It seems plausible that British authorities in Asmara were facing the same problem experienced in other colonial territories, where copper coins were in high demand and thereby barely available outside of African economic networks. The scarcity of small change was such a concern that, in 1944, British authorities were forced to take counter-measures to stop "the depletion of coin reserves."[65] Eritrea was included in the list of countries of election for banknotes worth one shilling, which were supposed to solve the problem. The OETA had no control over the supply of shillings from Nairobi, but could nonetheless affect the availability of small denomination lire in other ways.

One of the solutions envisaged by the administration consisted in making pressure to put into circulation the lire that were still in the coffers of Italian banks in Eritrea. In 1948, Italian institutes held assets for a total amount of 80 million lire, most of which were probably composed of smaller denomination banknotes and coins.[66] This is suggested by the fact that, since the authorization to financial remittances in 1942, there had been a rush to sell small change lire against higher denomination banknotes, which were then remitted to Italy in order to recover part of the value stored in that currency.[67] A controversy took place in 1948 between the OETA and Italian banks. The latter complained for the bureaucratic obstacles imposed by the Economic Department in Asmara on the expatriation of lire, arguing that authorizations were subject to multiple conditions not directly sanctioned by law.[68] The reason for this could probably be found in the OETA's reluctance to let small denomination lire flow out of circulation, in light of their importance for the legitimacy of British rule in the eyes of the African population. It should be actually noted that, at the end of the 1940s, Africans were indeed the main users of lire, which were widely used as means of payment in

[64] Note on the Financial Policy in Eritrea, 14 February 1942, TNA, WO 230/133.

[65] Tel from CFA to Asmara, Mogadishu, Hargheisa, 25 June 1944, TNA, WO 230/133.

[66] Reopening of Italian Banks in Occupied Territories, Annexure A, ABE, OV 77/2, 3, p. 1.

[67] Tel 11,370/160, 13 August 1942, TNA, WO 230/133.

[68] Reopening of Italian Banks in Occupied Territories, Annexure A, ABE, OV 77/2, 3, p. 1.

minor transactions with the administration.[69] This solution brought some evident benefits to the Eritrean population: small denomination lire were accepted by the OETA at the official rate of 480:1, but in 1948 their actual value on the black market was close to 1800:1.[70] In other words, the persistence of Italian currency as a medium of exchange between British rulers and African subjects authorised the OETA to provide an informal subsidy to Eritrean taxpayers, whose revenues were indexed in undervalued British currency.

The financial burden of this fiscal incentive was supported by the banking system. Not incidentally, Italian banks were the most vocal critics and pushed for the alignment of the official exchange rate with the one prevailing on the black market. They argued that they were forced to operate currency conversion and accept debt repayment on mature loans at the official exchange rate, thereby bearing the loss resulting from the gap with the actual price of the EAS.[71] The position of Italian banks was shared by the Bank of England, which was concerned for the stability of Eritrea's financial system. But this time it was the OETA to have the upper hand in collaboration with the Foreign Office. The official exchange rate between small denomination lire and pound was maintained at 480:1, on the basis that any revision could be detrimental to the relationship with the Eritrean community.[72] Local support to British rule was particularly important in the eyes of the Foreign Office, which was in the meantime negotiating in international *fora* the future political destination of the territory.

Conclusions

The British political economy of currency in Eritrea is a useful lens to appreciate the multiplicity of interests pursued by the different articulations of the British state in the decade of the occupation. Central institutions acted for the protection of financial orthodoxy and imperial stability. The monetary policy envisaged by the Bank of England

[69] Tel from Asmara to CFA, 28 June 1943, TNA, WO 230/133.

[70] Reopening of Italian Banks in Occupied Territories, Annexure A, ABE, OV 77/2, 3, p. 3.

[71] Banca d'Italia, Vigilanza sulle Aziende di credito, ASBI, pratt. n. 9946, fasc. 4, p. 35.

[72] Minutes of the meeting held on 8th September at the Treasury to discuss the reopening of Italian banks in the ex-Italian colonies, ABE, OV 77/2, 3.

was primarily aimed at stabilising the new currency issued by the United Kingdom, thereby creating "a singular, bounded homogenised place with London as a primary economic and political referent" (Mwangi 2001, p. 784). The possibility of social upheavals was certainly contemplated, but tolerated in the name of the overall interests of the sterling. Local administrators in Asmara, on the other hand, were more prone to meet local demands and adapt general rules to the specific conditions of Eritrea. This approach was not driven simply by philanthropic reasons. Rather, it reflected the desire to promote the territorialisation of British rule. The acceptance of the lire as a medium for the payment of taxes was instrumental in ensuring recognition of the new hierarchy between rulers and subjects, while also nurturing political networks that could be spent at a later date to preserve British influence in the area.

The trajectory of the lira in British Eritrea confirms the assumption that currency revolutions in colonial Africa were not as revolutionary as originally assumed, but rather consisted in "nuanced and prolonged transitions, whose effects were negotiated and absorbed over time" (Pallaver 2015, p. 206). Not differently from what happened in other African possessions of the British empire, pre-existing mediums of exchange did not disappear overnight. The Italian currency remained in circulation throughout the decade in spite of repeated attempts to enforce a homogenous monetary system anchored to the sterling.

The case study also highlights the importance of local practices and hidden forms of negotiations in shaping colonial monetary policies imposed from above. Currency and exchange rate regimes were technologies of rule devised to favour or discriminate different interest groups. The replacement of the Italian currency and the establishment of the 480:1 exchange rate with the pound were originally conceived to discharge the cost of occupation from the British government onto the Italian community. Soon, however, the OETA was forced to come to terms with pressures from Italian settlers, from which it depended for the daily management of the administration. With the depreciation of the lira on informal markets, the maintenance of currency convertibility lost its original logics and acquired new ones. Though more research is needed, especially on primary sources in Eritrea, the archival material analysed here suggests the importance of local agency in affecting the British administration's attitude on currency matters. It was African pressure for the preservation of what was actually an indirect subsidy that changed the meaning of the official exchange rate, turning it into a tool to mediate the relationship between the administration and selected categories of subjects.

References

Almedom, Astier. 2006. "Re-Reading the Short and Long-Rigged History of Eritrea 1941–1952: Back to the Future?" *Nordic Journal of African Studies* 15 (2): 103–142.

Bohannan, Paul. 1959. "The Impact of Money on African Subsistence Economy." *Journal of Economic History* 19 (4): 491–503.

Boobbyer, Philipp. 2018. "Lord Rennell, Chief of Amgot: A Study of His Approach to Politics and Military Government." *War in History* 25 (3): 304–327.

Cain, Peter and Antony G. Hopkins. 1993. *British Imperialism II, Crisis and Deconstruction, 1914–1990*, London: Longman.

Cooper, Frederick. 2011. "Reconstructing Empire in British and French Africa". *Past and Present* 6: 196–210.

Guyer, Jane and Karin Pallaver. 2018. "*Money and Currency in African History.*" In *The Oxford Research Encyclopaedia of African History*, edited by Thomas Spear, New York: Oxford University Press.

Hopkins, Antony G. 1966. "The Currency Revolution in South-West Nigeria in the Late Nineteenth Century." *Journal of the Historical Society of Nigeria* 3 (3): 471–483.

Jones, Geoffrey. 1993. *British Multinational Banking, 1830–1990.* Oxford: Oxford University Press.

Kelly, Saul. 2000. "Britain, the United States and the End of the Italian Empire in Africa, 1940–1952." *The Journal of Imperial and Commonwealth History* 28 (3): 51–70.

Kibreab, Gaim. 2005. "Ethnicity, Religion, and the British Disposal of Eritrea, 1941–1952." *Africa: Rivista Trimestrale di Studi e Ricerche* 60 (2): 159–200.

Krozewski, Gerold. 1993. "Sterling, the Minor Territories, and the End of Formal Empire." *The Economic History Review* 46 (2): 239–265.

Kuroda, Akinobu. 2007. "The Maria Theresa Dollar in the Early Twentieth Century Red Sea Region: A Complementary Interface Between Multiple Markets." *Financial History Review* 14 (1): 89–110.

Longrigg, Henry. 1945. *A Short History of Eritrea.* New York: Oxford University Press.

Louis, Roger. 1984. *The British Empire in the Middle East, 1945–1951: Arab nationalism, the United States, and Post-War Imperialism.* Oxford: Clarendon Press.

Lucchetti, Nicholas. 2012. *Italiani d'Eritrea: 1941–1951, una storia politica*. Roma: Aracne.

Makki, Fouad. 2011. "Culture and Agency in a Colonial Public Sphere: Religion and the Anti-Colonial Imagination in 1940s Eritrea." *Social History* 36 (4): 418–442.

Mauri, Arnaldo. 2009. "The Re-Establishment of the Ethiopian National Monetary and Banking System." *The South African Journal of Economic History* 24 (2): 82–130.

Morone, Antonio M. 2018. "Introduzione: quando è finito il colonialismo italiano?" in *La fine del colonialismo italiano*, edited by Antonio M. Morone, Roma: Carocci.

Mwangi, Wambui. 2001. "Of Coins and Conquest: The East African Currency Board, the Rupee Crisis, and the Problem of Colonialism in the East African Protectorate." *Comparative Studies in Society and History* 43 (4): 763–787.

Pallaver, Karin. 2015. "The African Native Has No Pockets:" Monetary Practices and Currency Transitions in Early Colonial Uganda." *International Journal of African Historical Studies* 48 (3): 471–99.

Puddu, Luca. 2021. "Ragion di stato e ragioni del capitale: il lungo crepuscolo della lira nell'Eritrea britannica." In *Una moneta per l'impero: pratiche monetarie, economia e società nell'Africa orientale italiana*, edited by Karin Pallaver and Gianluca Podestà, Milano: Franco Angeli.

Rennell Rodd, Francis. 1948. *British Military Administration of Occupied Territories in Africa, 1941–1947*. London: HMSO.

Şaul, Mahir. 2004. "Money in Colonial Transition: Cowries and Francs in West Africa." *American Anthropologist* 106 (1): 71–84.

Stockwell, Sarah. 2019. *The British End of the British Empire*. Cambridge: Cambridge University Press.

Swanepoel, Nichole. 2015. "Small Change: Cowries, Coins, and the Currency Transition in the Northern Territories of Ghana." In *Materializing Colonial Encounters. Archaeologies of African Experience*, edited by Francois Richard, New York: Springer.

Trevaskis, Gerald K. N. 1960. *Eritrea, a Colony in Transition*. Oxford: Oxford University Press.

Zaccaria, Massimo. 2019. "Italian Colonialism in Africa as a Connected System: Institutions, Men, and Colonial Troops." *The Journal of Imperial and Commonwealth History* 47 (4): 718–741.

PART III

Global and Transnational Dimensions of African Monetary Transitions

CHAPTER 9

How and Why Did the Rupee Become the Currency of Zanzibar and East Africa?

Catherine Eagleton

Introduction

The island of Zanzibar, now a place whose name is familiar to more people as a tourist destination than can pinpoint its location in the Western Indian Ocean, was, in the nineteenth century, a wealthy and important place. Connected to Eastern Africa, the Gulf and India by Indian Ocean trade routes, its economy grew rapidly in the first half of the nineteenth century. Recognising the growing importance of the island, its ruler, Said bin Sultan Al-Busaidi, Sultan of Oman, moved his capital to Zanzibar in 1840, around the same time as European and American consuls established consulates on the island to look after their citizens' and merchants' interests (Sheriff 1987). Sultan Said's daughter, Princess Salme, wrote that his wealth was stored as property, houses, slaves, cattle, jewellery and also in cash—the latter two kept in the house in a special

C. Eagleton (✉)
University of St Andrews, St Andrews, Scotland
e-mail: cte1@st-andrews.ac.uk

K. Pallaver (ed.), *Monetary Transitions*, Palgrave Studies in Economic History,
https://doi.org/10.1007/978-3-030-83461-6_9

chest with drawers in it. Treasuries in each of his residences were "full of Spanish gold coins, English guineas, and French louis [gold coins]" and the Sultan's personal wealth was inseparable from the state finances, a situation common to other Muslim rulers in Africa (Hunwick 1999). In general, gold coins were kept as stores of wealth, while silver coins tended to be used in transactions, as well as in annual gifts made by the Sultan to his wives and children along with cloth, perfume and other luxury commodities (Reute 2009, pp. 15, 28, 96, 172). By around 1900, however, a very different political situation prevailed, in which European rather than Omani rule dominated, and the currency on the Eastern African coast had become the Indian rupee. Indeed, this coin was made legal tender in British East Africa in 1898, providing legal backing to the currency that had by then been the only silver coin in use on much of the coast for some time.

This seems at first glance to be unsurprising, given the ocean trade routes, and processes of globalisation that brought Zanzibar into closer contact with other parts of the world during the nineteenth century (e.g., Prestholdt 2008, 2012; Metcalf 2008). Erik Gilbert argues that Zanzibar had a crucial role in an Indian Ocean "shaped by British India" (Gilbert 2013). In this context, the reasons for the rupee becoming the currency of Zanzibar and of Eastern Africa, replacing European and American gold and silver coins, seem to be simple. Given the importance of links to Western India, so the commonly accepted argument goes, merchants brought with them the coin that most easily facilitated trade with ports in India, and the rupee entered circulation gradually and naturally. To give just two examples, numismatist Shailendra Bhandare characterises the rupee's use on the African coast as "the fallout of the trade and political links the region had with Oman"—and economic historian Ed Ferguson explains that the rupee became currency in Zanzibar "because of the close commercial ties with that mighty British colony and the powerful role of its merchants in the Zanzibar economy" (Bhandare 2007). This chapter, however, argues that these assumptions, although apparently logical, are incorrect.

This chapter begins by describing the multiple currencies in use at Zanzibar in the mid-nineteenth century, before considering several attempts to fix the values of coins. Looking in detail the 1860s, I will show that it is possible not only to determine exactly when the rupee began to be used in Zanzibar, but also to identify that it was the economic and trade impact of the American Civil War that precipitated a currency change in Eastern Africa. The picture that emerges is one that shows that the rupee did not come into circulation in Zanzibar (and from there in Eastern Africa) as a natural result of Indian Ocean trade links, but in spite of them.

This chapter also sheds light more broadly on the processes of globalisation. Classic studies of these have discussed price convergences in commodity trade, with Kevin O'Rourke and Jeffrey Williamson arguing this to be a key measure of globalisation (O'Rourke and Williamson 2002a, b, p. 26). Looking in particular at the Atlantic, they argue that a dramatic reduction in transport costs, and price convergence, indicates that globalisation began in the nineteenth century rather than earlier. In this context of increased global trade, there were advantages in reducing transactions costs, which Eric Helleiner argues was one of the key factors in the development of colonial currency policies (Helleiner 2003). This case study, however, shows that communities did not necessarily push their national currencies unless it was in their interest to do so, and they also had the practical ability to do so. Nor was this a case where currencies competed in a sort of "Darwinian struggle" to find the most advantageous (Cohen 2000, p. 96). In Zanzibar, the balance of local and global interests was complex, and the island was simultaneously linked to the Atlantic and Indian Ocean trade networks. Although they tried to exert their influence, there were clear limits on the bargaining power of European and American consuls and merchants in Zanzibar. When the balance of merchants' interests changed, in this case suddenly and in response to trade disruption resulting from the American Civil War, it was not always possible to revert to the situation that had prevailed before. The introduction of the rupee into circulation in Zanzibar was intended as temporary expediency, but ended up becoming rather more long-lived.

Multiple Currencies and Fluctuating Values

Explorer Richard Burton wrote an account of his visit to Zanzibar in 1857, including a detailed description of currency there. References to the "dollar," he explained, always referred to the Maria Theresa thaler (MTT), and merchants kept their accounts in dollars and cents. The thaler was also a standard of weight used in the bazaars in Zanzibar, called *wakia*, and used for weighing expensive commodities like gold, silver and perfumes, as well as the unit in which goods were priced, with varying quantities of foodstuffs and other commodities sold for a dollar (Steere and Madan 1884, p. 456).[1] The thaler was not the only coin in circulation, and there were also silver dollars (8-reales coins) from Spain and South America, silver 5-franc coins imported by French merchants (which circulated only at an 8–10% discount), as well as Spanish and English gold coins brought from Mozambique (Rigby 1862, p. 248). Burton reported that the value of silver dollars, or pillar dollars, was subject to "incessant fluctuations," from which moneychangers made significant profit (Burton 1860, p. 529; 1872, p. 405). Other writers around the same time give similar descriptions, and make clear that any coin other than the Maria Theresa thaler circulated with difficulty or at variable values. American Consul Charles Ward wrote in January 1851 that "the only coin that has a fixed & reliable value is the German Crown [the Maria Theresa thaler]," and six years later his successor Danile Mansfield wrote that pillar dollars "do not circulate freely" and that merchandise was "bought and sold for dollars [thalers] and cents" (Bennett and Brooks 1965, pp. 473–474, 500).

Writing in 1859, newly arrived British Consul Christopher P. Rigby reported on trade in Zanzibar, and the commodities imported into and exported. However, he noted that since no duty was charged on exports, and no manifest required from departing ships, his figures for exports were unreliable as he had compiled the report based on information from the Customs Master and European and American merchants in Zanzibar. Nonetheless, the tables in the report clearly show the scale and value of the entrepôt trade in Zanzibar, and the types of goods involved (See Tables 9.1 and 9.2).

Much of the bullion imported and exported would have been coins of various types, and it is also notable that some of the most important commodities listed—including cotton cloth, beads and brass wire—were used as currencies in Eastern Africa (Pallaver 2019, pp. 71–92; Prestholdt 2008, p. 7). However, on the island, these non-coin currencies were not used as money, but were usually exchanged between merchants as bundles of goods. Larger transactions in Zanzibar could be arranged by exchanging goods, based on credit, or settled through money transfers organised by merchants based there. Whether for trade with mainland Africa, or to equip and supply explorers like Burton, Zanzibar merchants

[1] C. P. Rigby, "Currency," 1859, report enclosed with dispatches to London, Zanzibar National Archives (ZNA) AA 2 4.

Table 9.1 Total values of imports and exports at Zanzibar, 1859

(Values in Maria Theresa thalers)	*Imported from*	*Exported to*
Arabia	$79,231 (1.9%)	$105,200 (3.1%)
British India	$448,230 (11.0%)	$467,500 (13.8%)
Cutch	$260,424 (6.4%)	$313,400 (9.2%)
East Coast of Africa	$1,636,500 (40.0%)	$1,233,900 (36.4%)
France	$516,451 (12.6%)	$247,500 (7.3%)
Great Britain	–	$25,050 (0.7%)
Hamburg	$455,701 (11.1%)	$161,000 (4.7%)
Madagascar	$89,000 (2.2%)	$73,800 (2.2%)
Singapore	$35,523 (0.9%)	–
United States	$568,795 (13.9%)	$534,100 (15.5%)
West Coast of Africa	–	$230,000 (6.8%)
TOTAL	$4,089,855	$3,391,500

Source C. P. Rigby, "Shipping 1859," 1859 reports enclosed with dispatches to London, ZNA AA 2 4

would typically advance money and merchandise, for repayment either on their return, or through money transfers (Loarer 1851, p. 294; Sheriff 1987, pp. 126–127). Money was usually advanced at 8–12% interest, although this might sometimes be indirectly rather than directly charged, and 100 thalers in Zanzibar was worth between 213 and 220 rupees in Bombay.[2] Rigby's report estimated that "nearly the whole of the foreign trade" passed through the hands of the 5000 British Indian subjects resident in Zanzibar, and that they had also bought or obtained possession

[2] C. P. Rigby, "Currency," 1859, report enclosed with despatches to London, ZNA AA 2 4.

Table 9.2 The top 20 articles imported and top 20 exported in Zanzibar, by value, 1859

(Values rounded to nearest £ sterling)	*Imported*	*Exported*
Brass wires	£7556	£8444
Bullion	£166,667	£82,222
Cloves	–	£55,667
Coconut oil	–	£4067
Coconuts	–	£2711
Copra	–	£13,333
Cottons—American	£93,744	£103,890
Cottons—English	£37,711	£35,895
Cottons—Indian	£53,777	£50,089
Cowries	£33,333	£51,444
Ghee	£7778	£2667
Gum copal	£33,333	£37,167
Gunpowder	£8875	£11,667
Hides	£17,778	£25,556
Ivory	£195,556	£146,667
Jowar wheat and c	£7022	£156
Mangrove poles	–	£1250
Muskets and fowling pieces	£18,840	£15,111
Red pepper	–	£1422
Rice	£38,445	£1445
Salt fish	£8889	–
Sandalwood	£7778	£667
Sesame seed	£5333	£20,800
Silk—Muscat lunghis	£11,889	£10,000
Slaves	£57,778	–
Venetian beads	£21,880	£25,556

Source C. P. Rigby, "Principal Articles of Import at Zanzibar" and "Principal Articles of Export at Zanzibar", 1859, reports enclosed with dispatches to London ZNA AA 2 4

by mortgage of a number of estates on the island (Sheriff 1987, pp. 108–109).[3] So, it is perhaps surprising that the rupee was neither in circulation there, nor used as a money of account. Even the British Consul, who was the representative of the Indian government in Zanzibar, kept records of amounts payable in Zanzibar in thalers, while recording amounts payable

[3] C. P. Rigby, "Shipping,"1859, report enclosed with dispatches to London, ZNA AA 2 4.

in Bombay in rupees, and deposited the balance in thalers with Customs Master Damji.[4]

Moving from large transactions to smaller purchases in the bazaar, a problem with the currency in Zanzibar was that there had been a "dearth of small change on the island" until the 1840s. Small change had been given as packets of *mtama* (millet) or corn, both in Zanzibar and on the East African coast, at "exceedingly variable measures to the dollar" (Steere 1870, p. 397; Burton 1872, pp. 405–406). As trade increased, so too did the demand for small change. Soon after moving his capital there, the Sultan had taken action to rectify this situation, by importing (with the assistance of the British Consul) MTT 5000-worth of copper pice coins from Bombay, to become the circulating small change at Zanzibar either in 1840 (Burton 1872, pp. 405–406) or 1845 (Steere 1870, p. 103). This move initially seems to have met with some opposition from Indian merchants, and Richard Burton noted "Kojas and Banyans offered the ruler... a considerable annual sum if he would retain the primitive [millet or corn] currency" (Burton 1872, p. 405). The pice initially circulated at 132 to the thaler, but moneychangers bought them up and raised their value to 98 to the thaler. The rate later stabilised, but fluctuations in the value of the pice continued to cause problems locally. Despite attempts by Sultan Majid to fix the pice at 128 to the thaler in the late 1850s, there were usually between 110 and 130 pice to the thaler in the 1860s. In addition to these fluctuations in value, there was an enduring shortage of small change as the copper coins began to circulate along the East African coast, creating shortages of coin in Zanzibar during a period of economic growth—importing copper pice had not fully solved the problem it had been intended to.[5]

Europeans in Zanzibar regularly discussed (usually complaining about) these shortages and fluctuations in the values of coins on the island, but their focus was almost always on silver and gold coins rather than on small change.[6] Beyond trade records and merchants' complaints, the coins in

[4] "Government Balance held by Luddah Damba at Zanzibar," Maharashtra State Archives, Mumbai, Political 1858, vol. 148, pp. 111–130; and "Accounts 1858 to 1891," ZNA AA 9 1.

[5] C. P. Rigby, "Currency," 1859, report enclosed with dispatches to London, ZNA AA 2 4.

[6] This perhaps indicates that there was a separation between small change for local use and small purchases, and the larger denominations used for trade and larger transactions.

Table 9.3 Coins listed in Steere's dictionary

reale ya mazinga (cannon dollar)	Silver pillar dollar of Spain and South America
reale ya sham (Syrian dollar)	Silver Maria Theresa thaler
reale ya kifaransa (French dollar)	French silver 5-franc coin
reale ya thahabu (gold dollar)	American gold 20-dollar coin
robo ingrezi (English quarter)	British gold sovereign (which was worth around a quarter of the gold $20 coin)

Source Steere (1870), pp. 39, 61, 66, 70

circulation—and in some cases the places from which they came—also left their traces in the Swahili language. In his handbook of Kiswahili, written in the first half of the 1860s using sources including lists of vocabulary compiled by representatives of the German trading firm of O'Swald & Co. in Zanzibar, and information given by Zanzibari contacts, the English bishop and scholar Edward Steere recorded the names of the gold and silver coins in circulation (See Table 9.3).

Steere's dictionary records information about the smaller denominations of coin used in Zanzibar, too, describing them as fractions of a thaler, down to sixteenths known as *nuss ya themuni* (half an eighth; Steere 1870, p. 92). Indeed, Steere notes that these subdivisions to describe coins were "the only fractions in common use." It is unclear exactly what form the circulating coins for these smaller denominations took—they seem not to be copper pice. There were some 1/2-*real* (1/16 dollar) coins minted which may have circulated at Zanzibar along with 1-*real*, 2-*reales* and 4-*reales* coins, although perhaps infrequently since contemporary records usually note the main subdivisions of the dollar in circulation as quarter and eighth-dollar coins (Mansfield 1857, p. 367; Burton 1860, p. 529).[7] It is also possible that these fractions refer to cut coins, similar to the cut fractions of silver dollars that were used in Madagascar (Bennett and Brooks 1965, p. 242; Osgood 1854, pp. 9–10; Campbell 2005, pp. 287, 300). It may even be that there was a combination, with a *nuss ya themuni* referring to a 1-real (or 1/8 dollar) coin that had been cut in half. As a companion to his dictionary, Bishop Steere published a book of *Swahili Tales*, and in one of these stories, a beggar, scratching in a dust heap looking for millet grains to eat, finds an eighth

[7] Rev. Dr. L Krapf, "The island of Zanzibar or Ongodja," 1844, Church Missionary Society archives, C A5 016.

of a pillar dollar (*themuni ya mzinga*; Steere 1870, pp. 50–51). Whether this is a silver 1-*real* coin, or a cut part of a thaler coin, it is clear that the *themuni* was a physical coin that could be found in a dust heap and not only a unit used in account books. Whatever its form, its purchasing power was decreasing, and fairly rapidly. The beggar in the story thinks himself rich (and buys a gazelle with his found coin), but by the 1860s a *themuni* would buy only 12–15 eggs, about 3 lb. of first-quality rice, or 1.5 lb. of beef—prices that were more than double what they had been a few years earlier.[8]

Changes in demand sometimes created shortages in the availability of coin in Zanzibar, and concern for merchants there. In 1851 the American Consul reported that Sultan Said had raised a MTT 500,000 advance from the Zanzibar Customs Master to pay for a military campaign in Muscat," "draining Zanzibar of black dollars [Maria Theresa thalers]" (Bennet and Brooks 1965, p. 488; Allen 1982, pp. 117–127). Although large, this payment was not the only large shipment of coin to Muscat from Zanzibar. When after the death of Sultan Said in 1856, the Sultanate was split into two parts, each ruled by one of his sons, the Sultan of Zanzibar had to pay the Sultan of Muscat a subsidy of MTT 40,000 a year, which had to be in thaler coins.[9]

In addition to these exceptional and large payments in coin, there was also seasonal demand connected with trade and the monsoon winds, which also caused fluctuations in value of coins and shortages of preferred types of coin. Much of the wealth accumulated in Zanzibar was remitted to the Middle East or India, and at the beginning of the southwest monsoon merchants in Zanzibar bought large quantities of Spanish and Mexican silver dollars at a premium of around 2–3%, to be shipped to Bombay, where they could be sold at a premium of 6–8% for export to

[8] C. P. Rigby, "Currency," 1859, report enclosed with dispatches to London, ZNA AA 2 4., p. 139.

[9] A report on the financial condition of Zanzibar in 1862, outlines the serious difficulties in obtaining enough coin to pay the subsidy and two years' arrears in coin: "Financial Condition of Zanzibar," Maharashtra State Archives, Mumbai, Political 1862, Vol. 23, pp. 227–304. The potential problems with the payment of such large sums in cash were made clear in 1864, when one of the Sultan of Muscat's ministers disappeared "under mysterious circumstances" with $35,000 of the subsidy payment: "Secret: Hajee Ahmed Minister of H H the Sultan, departure of __ from Muscat under mysterious circumstances with thirty five thousand dollars...," Maharashtra State Archives, Mumbai, Political 1864 vol. 33, pp. 129–142.

China (Mansfield 1857, p. 367; Burton 1860, p. 529). At this time of year, the usually-less-popular Mexican dollars sold at par, and if there were shortages of coin even the unpopular and heavily discounted French silver 5-franc coin and English gold sovereign would sell for close to their par values to merchants preparing to send money and cargoes northwards (Bennett and Brooks 1965, pp. 473–474, 486). For those who could afford to hold stocks of coin, seasonal fluctuations made it profitable to import and exchange coin in Zanzibar—specie did not attract the flat 5% levied on all other commodities imported, so as long as a merchant could import or buy coins when they were at a discount, and hold them for sale at close to par when monsoon-season remittances began, there was profit to be made. As a result, powerful merchants and moneylenders in Zanzibar had little motivation for changing the system and adopting a single circulating currency.

Fixing the Value of Coins in Circulation

There was competition between European and American merchants in Zanzibar, and each country had its own treaty with the Sultan of Zanzibar, and a resident Consul in Zanzibar pursuing the greatest possible advantage for their interests. Merchants, attempting to secure the largest possible share of the Zanzibar market but also influenced by demand, tended to bring particular imports in order to purchase merchandise and produce for export. Ships from Hamburg often imported beads and brass wire, while American and Indian vessels brought cotton cloth, all of which were important commodities because of their use as currencies on the mainland. French merchants struggled to compete, and when they did import textiles they sometimes found that they were perceived by Zanzibar merchants to be inferior to American cottons, and rejected (Grandidier 1868, pp. 29–30). So, coins tended to be imported from France, to pay for merchandise for export, but this trade was dismissed as "trifling" by Rigby, who thought it would soon cease (Sheriff 1987, p. 99).[10] Because of this, French merchants were the most vulnerable to fluctuations in value of 5-franc coins in Zanzibar, and were the first to make efforts to fix their value there.

[10] C. P. Rigby, "Currency," 1859, report enclosed with dispatches to London, ZNA AA 2 4., p. 135.

During treaty negotiations in the early 1840s, the French Consul attempted to secure the right for French merchants to trade directly on the mainland coast, so that they could bypass the powerful Zanzibar middlemen, but Sultan Said resisted, to the Consul's disappointment (Bennet 1969, pp. 154–164). When the treaty was ratified in 1846, there was another unsuccessful attempt made to secure a concession relating to the value of the 5-franc coin—the coin was not much in demand in Zanzibar, and French merchants could make little profit on importing them (Bennet 1973, p. 606). Moreover, French merchants were keen to secure easy trading links (and to reduce exchange losses) between Zanzibar and the French settlements and colonies at Bourbon, Mayotte and Nosy-Bé, where 5-franc coins circulated at their full value. The Sultan listened cordially to the case made, but declared himself powerless to act without agreement from the merchant community. A meeting was duly convened, and the French negotiator made his case, but was told that they could not hear of fixing the rate. A year later, he tried again to convince the Sultan and merchants to fix the rate, but again failed. As a gesture of goodwill, the Sultan offered to accept the 5-franc coins at a better rate than their market value. The new rate offered by the Sultan, of 110 5-franc coins for 100 thalers was better than the market rate, but had little impact in practice other than reducing the amount French merchants had to pay to the Customs Master, since the Sultan could not compel other merchants to accept the French coin at this rate (Guillain 1856, pp. 43–46, 94–95; Bennet 1973, p. 608). When a new French Consul was appointed in 1849, he tried once again to resolve the currency-exchange question, but got no further than had his predecessors. The American Consul, Richard Waters, explained that the attempt to fix the rate of the French coin had failed in the face of what he described as "steadfast Indian opposition," as the Indian merchants and moneychangers sought to protect the profit they made from the fluctuating and discounted value of the French 5-franc coin compared to the thaler (Bennet 1973, p. 614, p. 614 n22, p. 626). Writing about the situation ten years later, in the late 1850s, Burton described this change in the value of the 5-franc coin as "a somewhat arbitrary process," explaining that 5-franc coins still had no currency, although moneychangers "attempt to pass them off upon strangers at 108 for 100 Maria Theresas," using the agreed rate to profit further from transactions with those who didn't know the current rates (Burton 1860, p. 529; 1872, p. 419).

Once the special rate had been agreed with the Sultan for his acceptance of French 5-franc coins, the American Consul then tried to persuade the Sultan of the benefits to trade of fixing the values of other coins in circulation. He hoped to convince the Sultan that there were benefits to "his own subjects—the Arabs" of fixing the values of circulating coins, and explained that he thought many of the Indian merchants and moneychangers were in favour of fixing the values of silver and gold coins including Spanish-American dollars and French 5-franc coins. However, the merchant community was not in agreement with Consul Ward's plan, and he later complained that one of the Indian merchants who was most strongly opposed to the change convened a meeting at his house to talk other merchants out of accepting the proposal. Their opposition was due to a concern that if silver dollars were introduced into currency in Zanzibar, American merchants would make so much money that they would no longer bring the American cotton (known as *merekani*) cloth with which Indian merchants made substantial profits on the east coast of Africa. In this case, then, the Indian merchants' opposition to the fixing of the values of coins related not only to the money to be made from exchange, but also to their wish to protect profits on other commodities imported for trade with the mainland, particularly American cotton cloth. The principal objector, who had convened the meeting, Ward noted "is the great money broker among the Banyans" who was acting to protect the "great profits he was then making when exchanging the different coins" while Mexican dollars were at 5% discount and 5-franc coins at 12.5% discount (Bennet and Brooks 1965, pp. 473–474). Ward suspected that the proposal to fix the values of coins would have passed had the powerful Customs Master, Jairam Sewji, been in Zanzibar to influence the other Indian merchants, since he and Sewji had a close connection. However, without that influence, there was little Ward could do.[11]

[11] The close connection and commercial partnership between the American merchants and the Customs Master had been noted in the past, including in complaints by English merchant Robert Norsworthy about what he described as a "monopolist ring" in the 1830s. In the early 1840s, another English merchant, Edgar Botsford, complained of the "unwarrantable monopoly" in which the American Consul "is an abetter". See Bennett and Brooks (1963, pp. 238–240). By the later 1840s, however, the relationship between the American merchants and Customs Master Jairam Sewji had become more distant, as the Americans complained about Sewji's efforts to encourage more foreign vessels to come to Zanzibar; see Sheriff (1987, pp. 91, 99).

By the early 1860s, however, a more significant—albeit distant—factor had begun to impact on the trade in Zanzibar: the American Civil War. The immediate impact of the war as far as Zanzibar merchants were concerned was that there was a decline in trade (Sheriff 1987, p. 135, Table 4.6). Specifically, few American ships now visited the island, and those that did no longer imported cotton cloth, but brought specie and other goods instead. Cotton imports from America that had totalled 12,000 bales before the Civil War dwindled to less than 1000 bales—exactly the situation that Indian merchants had been concerned about in the 1850s, even if they could not have foreseen that it would happen not due to fixing exchange rates, but instead due to a war thousands of miles away. To meet the demand for cloth on the East African coast, German merchants began to import English cotton goods instead of silver Maria Theresa thalers, reducing the quantity of coinage arriving in Zanzibar.[12] French merchants continued to import 5-franc coins, so as the thaler became more and more scarce, the market in Zanzibar became flooded with the undesirable French 5-franc coins. Merchants were now losing money, rather than profiting, from the fluctuating values of the circulating coins, and there were shortages of the more desirable types of coin.

Within about six months of the beginning of hostilities in America, the combined impact of the decline in cotton imports and shortages of coin persuaded Zanzibar's merchants of the need to act. They met to discuss the values of coins in circulation, and on 29 Rabi al-awwal 1278 (Friday 4 October 1861) the Sultan issued a notice confirming the outcome of the meeting: rates had been agreed for the coins in circulation, and his proclamation declared them legal tender, with each valued in Maria Theresa thalers[13]:

Gold ounce[14]—MT$15.
Gold sovereign—MT$4.75.
Gold 20-franc coin—MT$3.75.

[12] Norman Robert Bennett, "Americans in Zanzibar: 1845–1865," Tanganyika Notes and Records, 57 (1961), p. 136. See also Bennett and Brooks, New England merchants in Africa, p. 522.

[13] Letter from Sultan to French Consul, 29 Rabi al-awwal 1278, in Archives Diplomatiques, Nantes, 748 PO/A 123.

[14] A Spanish and South American 8-escudo coin, also known as the "doubloon". By the 1860s it was becoming scarcer at Zanzibar: see Bennett and Brooks (1963, pp. 540–541).

Gold 10-franc coin—MT$1 7/8.
Silver 5-franc coin—MT$0.94.

This proclamation immediately seems to have had the desired effect—there was no longer profit to be made on exchange, so more coins stayed in circulation and the currency shortage eased. Moreover, the agreed and now fixed rates encouraged more coin to be imported, and figures obtained from the Customs Master by the French naturalist and explorer Alfred Grandidier showed that imports of coinage had increased in value from MTT 707,500 in 1861, to MTT 1,886,550 in 1862–3. At the same time, exports of coin dropped, from MTT 1,925,000 in 1861–2 to MTT 1,219,000 in 1862–3 (Grandidier 1868, pp. 25–29).

Reactions from the European and American communities in Zanzibar were mixed. Presumably, the French Consul was delighted that the 5-franc coin had, at last, a value in Zanzibar close to its par value. However, the newly appointed British Political Agent, and later Consul in Zanzibar, Robert Lambert Playfair, was concerned that the sovereign was undervalued, and that the exclusion of the rupee from the agreed valuations was "to the great injury of Indian commerce" despite also stating in a later letter that "that coin [the rupee] never had been current at Zanzibar."[15] Playfair, motivated by "the advantage which would accrue to Indian merchants" by encouraging the rupee to come into circulation, spoke to the Sultan, who agreed that the rupee would be added to the list of coins accepted as legal tender, at a rate of half that of the French 5-franc coin, or MTT 0.47 per rupee.[16] Sultan Majid issued the necessary decree on 6 July 1863, and his covering note sent with the decree to Playfair, confirms that there were no rupees circulating in Zanzibar at that time:

> We inform you that we shall order all our subjects in Zanzibar and elsewhere, to receive as current, the Indian rupee, at the rate of half a French

[15] Playfair to Anderson, letter 45, 1 July 1863, ZNA AA 3 21; Playfair to Gonne, letter regarding currency, number 48, 16 March 1865, ZNA AA 3 27.

[16] Playfair to Anderson, letter 45, 1 July 1863, ZNA AA 3 21; see also Playfair (1864, p. 181).

dollar (5-Franc piece) and as soon as Rupees shall arrive (in the Zanzibar market) from that date their value shall be as afore specified.[17]

Playfair reported his success to Bombay, explaining that as rupees were more easily obtained than European coinage, he hoped the rupee would soon become the main currency in Zanzibar.[18] This is the first hint that there may have been political as well as economic factors at play—and if Playfair was also acting out of concern about growing French influence in the region, hoping that the rupee might oust the franc as the currency of parts of the Western Indian Ocean, he did not say so in his despatch.

The American Consul then moved to ensure that American merchants did not lose out, towards the end of 1863 persuaded the Sultan to allow the acceptance of American gold coins at par with the Maria Theresa thaler—effectively a premium of about 2% over their intrinsic value (Sheriff 1987, p. 136; Bennet 1963, p. 137). The necessary proclamation was made on 3 January 1864, and Consul Hines reported that this would "enable American merchants to pay down funds for the purchase of homeward cargoes without much loss" while the Civil War meant that export trade was much larger than the import trade from America (Bennet and Brooks 1965, p. 524).

After these various proclamations had taken effect, the silver and gold coins whose values had been fixed by the proclamations of 1861–1863 circulated at those values, but the Maria Theresa thaler became scarce in circulation. When thalers were needed, for some remittances to the Middle East or for trade on the mainland coast, they could only be purchased in Zanzibar at a premium over the official rate, and although still the unit of account they ceased to be the circulating currency.[19] In 1865, Colonel Playfair reported to Bombay in 1865 that the Sultan "has no interest" in the currency situation, but that the Maria Theresa thaler "is day by day becoming dearer and scarcer, so much so that for years past it has ceased to be the universal circulating medium tho still used as

[17] "Letter from His Highness Seyid Majid bin Said," 1 July 1863, copy enclosed in dispatch 45, ZNA AA 3 21.

[18] Playfair to Anderson, letter 45, 1 July 1863, ZNA AA 3 21.

[19] "Administration Report of Zanzibar (1864)," 1 May 1864, Maharashtra State Archives, Political 1864 vol. 54, pp. 1–43. "Letter of 25 October 1864" in Bennett and Brooks (1963, pp. 534–535).

the standard of accounts." Rupees, on the other hand, had "come down in great quantities and that coin is now abundant in the market."[20]

It is, of course, not clear what might have happened had the American Civil War been averted or avoided, since European influence in the Western Indian Ocean was in any case increasing in the mid-nineteenth century. But it is clear that the conditions caused by the American Civil War and its impact on trade meant that the Indian merchants changed the positions they had firmly held in the 1840s and 1850s, when they opposed the French and American Consuls' attempts to fix values for their countries' coins. In 1861, suffering from losses on exchange, shortages of circulating coin, and a reduction in imports of American cotton cloth, leading to problems with the East African coastal trade, the interests of all the merchant communities in Zanzibar converged and they agreed fixed rates for the circulating coins. Within only a year or two, the circulating currency in Zanzibar had changed dramatically, to American gold coins and Indian rupees, circulating at the rates assigned to each in the proclamations. The rupee had not been in circulation at all in Zanzibar in 1860, but by 1865 it was the main circulating silver coin there. Contrary to what has usually been assumed, it had not come into use gradually, as a natural consequence of Indian merchants and Indian Ocean trade routes, but had instead been introduced through the initiative of the British Consul, and responding to disruptions of trade caused by a war thousands of miles away.

Overvaluation and Undervaluation

In 1864, the American Consul noted with satisfaction that the agreeing of values for the circulating coins had been beneficial, and that business was much improved. Thalers were no longer imported by German and French merchants, and were "now very rarely seen" (Bennet and Brooks 1965, pp. 534–535). American gold coins could now circulate more easily, but merchants (including the American merchants) could now obtain their silver coins in rupees from Bombay.[21] The slight overvaluation of American gold coins meant that some merchants (including the Sultan himself) could profit from importing American currency, although

[20] Playfair to Gonne, letter 48, 15 March 1865, ZNA AA 3 27.

[21] Playfair to Gonne, letter 48, 15 March 1865, ZNA AA 3 27.

Table 9.4 Agreed and assay values of coins in circulation in Zanzibar, from report by Mint Master, Bombay

By whom value was fixed	*Nature of coin*	*Nationality of coins*	*Value of coin*	*Value in German Crowns*	*Assay value*
By a meeting of merchants	Gold	South American	Ounce	15.00	15.13
"	"	English	Pound	4.75	4.77
"	"	French	20 francs	3.75	3.78
"	"	French	10 do	1 7/8	1.89
"	"	French	5 do	15/16	0.94
"	Silver	French	5 do	0.94	0.96
By H. Highness	"	Indian	Rupee	0.47	0.46
"	Gold	American	Double Eagle	20.00	19.60
"	"	"	Single do	10.00	9.80
"	"	"	Half do	5.00	4.90
"	"	"	Qr do	2.50	2.45
"	"	"	Dollar	1.00	0.98
"	Silver	"	Dollar	1.00	1.02
"	"	"	½ dollar	0.50	0.51

Source "Zanzibar to Bombay," dispatch 48, 16 March 1865, ZNA, AA 3 27

the overvaluation was not recognised in Bombay and remittances there could only be made in gold at a loss (Sheriff 1987, p. 136). Some merchants complained about this, and among the most vociferous was a newly founded British company in Zanzibar, H. A. Frazer & Co., whose representative complained of the "injurious effect" this overvaluation of American gold coins had on British interests. In response to their complaints, the British Consul requested a report from the Bombay Mint on the intrinsic value of all the coins in circulation in Zanzibar.[22] The report confirmed what everyone had suspected, which was that the American gold coins were indeed slightly overvalued, and the sovereign undervalued, in relation to their metal content (Table 9.4).

However, in the table, and the letter accompanying it, the Bombay Mint Master quietly pointed out something that had not previously been

[22] Currency, exact value, 21 June 1864 and 20 June 1864, Maharashtra State Archives, Political 1864 vol. 54, pp. 92–108.

discussed: the Indian rupee was also overvalued.[23] Consul Playfair was then conflicted about what to do. The undervaluation of the sovereign compared to the American gold effectively gave 12 cents, or 8%, per dollar disadvantage to merchants importing sovereigns from England, but the rate fixed for the Indian rupee was favourable, and "more than compensates for the undervaluation of the sovereign." Ultimately, he reassured officials in Bombay that it would be more important to secure a high rate for the rupee than for the sovereign, and was also rather unsympathetic to Frazer & Co.'s complaints of making a loss.[24] It seems that Frazer & Co. were not the only business in Zanzibar complaining of losses due to the changes in the values of coins in circulation, and although it is not clear what prompted it, early in 1865 Sultan Majid attempted to revoke the proclamation he had made fixing the rate of American gold coins. The Sultan's revocation of his previous proclamation was, however, widely ignored, indicating that his word alone was not sufficient to create a change in the value of the circulating coins without agreement from the merchant community, and the American gold coins stayed in circulation at the agreed rate (Sheriff 1987, p. 136).

While the American Civil War was ongoing, the effect of the overvaluation of American gold coins was rather limited, since few were in circulation. However, once the Civil War had ended in late 1866 that changed, and Frazer & Co. made fresh complaints that large amounts of American gold coin had been imported, becoming "the only available circulating medium... forced upon merchants as legal currency at considerably above its intrinsic and marketable value." All exchange operations, they reported, were at a loss, and specie remittances were particularly badly affected, with substantial losses not only on money sent to Bombay, but also on money sent to the mainland, which had to be sent in thalers bought at a premium of 4–5%.[25] British officials discussed two main options for how to solve these problems and balance the competing interests: should they raise the value of English and French gold by creating a fictitious Zanzibar dollar as a unit of account, or should they lower the value of American gold and rate all coins at their intrinsic value? Each

[23] "Currency, exact value," 4 August 1864, Maharashtra State Archives, Political 1864 vol. 54, pp. 92–108.

[24] "Playfair to Gonne," letter 48, 15 March 1865, ZNA AA 3 27.

[25] Dr. Seward, "Readjustment of value of currency," 5 November 1866, Maharashtra State Archives, Mumbai, Political 1867 vol. 123, pp. 117–121.

of these options was unacceptable for different groups of merchants at Zanzibar. Raising the value of English and French gold could only be done "in direct opposition to [American merchants'] wishes and interests," while lowering the value of American gold would have no effect on restoring the Maria Theresa thaler to daily circulation.[26] Indian merchants opposed any solution that replaced the Maria Theresa thaler with a Zanzibar dollar as unit of account, since that coin "has been in circulation from the time of our forefathers—it is current along the coast, all our values are rated by it, and it is essentially the Zanzibar dollar."[27] Nor were the Indian merchants in favour of raising the value of British and French gold coins, which would have involved a reduction in the value of the rupee. Whichever remedy was chosen, the Indian merchants asked for a year to prepare for the change.[28] Their views were still the most powerful and listened to—by 1865 it was estimated that only about one-twentieth of the trade in Zanzibar was carried out without their involvement. The Bombay Chamber of Commerce was consulted, and they expressed concern at both proposals, noting that the disappearance of the Maria Theresa thaler from circulation in Zanzibar had been going on for some time, and was "due to other causes than the enhancement of the American Eagle."[29]

In the end, the Accountant-General in Bombay decided that the only option was to persuade the Sultan to reduce the assay value of the American gold coins.[30] The opinion of the Accountant-General, as well as a new report from the Bombay Mint Master, were read to a meeting of the principal merchants of Zanzibar. German merchants at the meeting argued in favour of the thaler, American merchants in favour of the dollar, and British merchants "wavered between the two." Indian merchants

[26] Dr. Seward, "Readjustment of value of currency," 13 November 1866, Maharashtra State Archives, Mumbai, Political 1867 vol. 123, pp. 113–115.

[27] Dr. Seward, "Readjustment of value of currency," 8 June 1867, Maharashtra State Archives, Mumbai, Political 1867 vol. 123, pp. 104–112.

[28] Dr. Seward, "Readjustment of value of currency," 8 June 1867, Maharashtra State Archives, Mumbai, Political 1867 vol. 123, pp. 104–112.

[29] "Trade and prospects of Zanzibar, 1865," Maharashtra State Archives, Mumbai, Political 1865 vol. 52, pp. 121–138; "Views of Bombay Chamber of Commerce," 1 February 1868, Maharashtra State Archives, Mumbai, Political 1868 vol. 136, pp. 111–114.

[30] "Note by Accountant General," 15 August 1867, Maharashtra State Archives, Mumbai, Political 1867 vol. 123, p. 132.

"expressed themselves quite satisfied with the present state of things," despite only a few years earlier having resisted all attempts to fix the values of coins in circulation. Now, it was the European merchants who wanted to see a change, while the American and Indian merchants were content with the agreed fixed values, from which they benefited. Each group tried to persuade Sultan Majid of their point of view, but after 4 hours of discussions there was no decision, and the British Consul suspected that the Sultan had "pledged himself to all."[31] Eventually, the American merchants offered to lower the value of their coin to that of the Maria Theresa thaler. But this then led to the fear that it would lead to "virtual repudiation" of the American merchants' debts to Indian moneylenders, causing a 2% loss and lawsuits in America.[32] A compromise was agreed, and Sultan Majid issued a proclamation in November 1868 confirming that the Maria Theresa thaler would remain "the dollar of Zanzibar and the unit of account," and that from November 1869 all other coins would be left to find their values in the market, giving the merchants the requested year to make the necessary arrangements.[33] The proclamation was announced as usual, by a street crier going around the town, blowing a buffalo horn and calling out the Sultan's orders. The British Consulate published a notice that, from November 1869, it would reckon coin received in payment at the intrinsic values that had been determined by the Bombay Mint, with the thaler would the unit for those calculations.[34] The experiment with fixed rates for the various coins in circulation at Zanzibar had, it seemed, ended.

Things were to change again, in part due to the opening of the Suez Canal in 1869, which changed trade routes in the north-Western Indian Ocean, and made it cheaper and easier to travel between Europe and Zanzibar. In 1870, the British Consul John Kirkreported to Bombay that

[31] "Response by Churchill to reports sent from Bombay," 15 July 1868, Maharashtra State Archives, Mumbai, Political 1868 vol. 136, pp. 119–120.

[32] "Response by Churchill to reports sent from Bombay," 15 July 1868, Maharashtra State Archives, Mumbai, Political 1868 vol. 136, pp. 119–120.

[33] John Kirk, "Settlement of the Currency Question," 4 February 1869, Maharashtra State Archives, Mumbai, Political 1869 vol. 153, pp. 127–132. "Proclamation issued by Sultan Barghash prohibiting British Subjects from carrying out trade beyond the limits of the town of Zanzibar," Maharashtra State Archives, Mumbai, Political 1872 vol. 203, pp. 169–182.

[34] "Proclamations, notices, regulations," 1863–1908, ZNA AA 12 9, number 7a.

British and British Indian trade in Zanzibar was now more than three times greater than the trade of any other nation.[35] American cotton was still in demand for trade on the East African coast, but the influence of American merchants was in decline (Bennett 1963, pp. 49, 57) Despite the proclamation removing the fixed values of the coins in circulation, in 1875 the circulating currency was primarily made up of American gold coins and Indian rupees, and it may even be that the Sultan's proclamation had been widely ignored, since John Kirk reported that American gold and Indian silver coins were "considerably overvalued" and had driven English gold from the market.[36]

The situation was not stable, however, since the value of silver relative to gold fell in the 1870s, significantly impacting the Indian economy and affecting trade and taxation, as well as remittances to the gold-backed economy of Britain (Tomlinson 1996, pp. 14–15; Kumar 1983, vol. 2, chap. IX and XI). Zanzibar merchants traded mostly with the mainland of East Africa, or with the silver-based economies of the Gulf and India, so were little affected by the depreciating silver rupee. Indeed, the drop in the value of silver enabled merchants to make, rather than lose, money—reports from the Colony of Natal complained that every steamer from Zanzibar, India or Mauritius brought rupees which were used to buy gold sovereigns for export, causing the banks there to refuse what they saw as an artificially overvalued rupee.[37] Kirk complained in 1876 that those who had to convert money from sterling to rupees (including British officials like him) were losing around 10% on each transaction, but admitted that as "the mass of British subjects, Indians, [are] making money out of the situation, I can take no official action."[38] Perhaps the most significant effect in Zanzibar of this worldwide fall in the price of silver was that American gold coins stopped circulating there. In 1878 William Hathorne, Zanzibar representative of two American companies wrote that "there is no other coin but Rupees," and noted the overvaluation of the rupee, but said he could do nothing about it. He also

[35] "Administration Report of Zanzibar," Maharashtra State Archives, Political 1871 vol. 142, pp. 1–55.

[36] "Annual report on 1873–1874," 8 February 1875, ZNA AA 2 15.

[37] "The value of the rupee" in Natal Witness, 4 August 1876.

[38] Despatch 116 "Zanzibar Currency," 27 June 1876, ZNA AA 1 18.

explained that although in theory American gold coins were still in circulation at their fixed values, now they could not be obtained other than at a premium of 10–20%, and that they were so scarce that he had not seen $100 of American gold since he had been in Zanzibar (Bennet 1963, pp. 122, 126). If gold arrived at it was swiftly bought and shipped away again, leaving Indian rupees as almost the only circulating currency, along with the copper *pice* imported from India as small change.[39]

Almost ten years later, in 1884, shortly before John Kirk was to leave Zanzibar, he reported to the Foreign Office in London on the currency in Zanzibar. The unit of account there was still the Maria Theresa thaler, but the Indian rupee was firmly established as the currency in circulation. Kirk explained that the value of the rupee had been fixed by "an arrangement made more than sixteen years ago by the merchants and Consuls and ratified by the Sultan" at 47 cents, with the American gold dollar as equivalent to the thaler. No one holding gold or thalers would pay with them, since "with these he could at a considerable premium buy rupees" and French and other coins, he explained, "have an artificial and fixed value" but were not used in making payments.[40] Thalers were still in use in some parts of mainland East Africa, but rupees had begun to be accepted on the coast from where they would become the primary currency for much of the region (Pawelczak 2010, chap. 9; Johnston 1879, p. 545).[41] Indeed, the currency changes of 1860s and 1870s had also made their way into the Swahili language. In the posthumous 1884 third edition of Bishop Steere's Handbook, the changes to the currency in the twenty years since he first compiled it were reflected in additions to the vocabulary listed. These included *reale ya bwara* (which Steere translated as "dollar under weight") for the French 5-franc piece, and *mende*, literally meaning "beetle" or "cockroach," but now recorded as a slang term for the rupee (Steere and Madan 1884, pp. 258, 338).

[39] Ibid.

[40] Despatch 55 "Report on Zanzibar Currency, 5 May 1884, ZNA AA 1 36.

[41] Ibid.

Conclusion

In the first half of the nineteenth century, two main currency-related problems faced Zanzibar: fluctuations in the value of silver and gold coins used there, and a lack of small change. The latter was remedied by the importation of copper *pice* from India from the 1840s onwards, which by the 1880s brought an estimated R30,000 annual profit to the Indian Government Mints.[42] Stabilising the relative values of the gold and silver coins in circulation proved more difficult, since it relied on reaching agreement between merchant communities who had very different interests. Merchants importing coin preferred fixed rates, while merchants profiting from exchange preferred to allow the fluctuations and seasonal variations to continue. In response to the trade disturbances caused by the American Civil War, the merchant community in Zanzibar found common cause, and through a series of agreements between the Sultan, European and American Consuls and Indian merchants and moneylenders, the currency system in Zanzibar was transformed in just a few years in the early 1860s. It changed from being one based on the Maria Theresa thaler, to one in which the thaler was still the unit of account, but in which the silver rupee and the American gold coins were the circulating currencies. The agreed (over)valuations for the silver rupee and the gold dollar meant that coins with higher intrinsic values were held as bullion, or exported. Far from being a gradual and slow process linked to the presence of Indian merchants in Eastern African ports and markets, the change from the thaler to the rupee can instead be seen as a result of interventions in the currency systems of the area. Particularly striking is the speed of the impact of the proclamations of 1861–3, since by 1865 there was already little appetite for removing the fixed values and allowing the currencies to float freely in value again. Then, in the 1870s, changes in the global values of silver and gold, combined with changes in the main trading relationships and patterns of trade in Zanzibar, meant that the American gold coins fell out of use, leaving the rupee and its subsidiary coinage, the copper *pice*, as the only currencies in daily use.

This chapter has given a new account of the reason why the rupee became the currency of Zanzibar, and from there the currency of most of the East African coast, but it also demonstrates the importance of studying the history of places that later became colonies by looking not only at

[42] "Issue of coinage by the Sultan," 11 May 1886., ZNA AA 1 46, number 174.

material from the archives of what later became the colonial power. To understand the full complexity of what at first looked like a simple question about a change of currency at Zanzibar required the use of archival materials in five countries. Using only British archival materials and publications would have made the research process easier, but would not have given enough information to untangle the details of this story. Moreover, it would also have risked studying the history of Zanzibar in the 1860s and 1870s in a way that prefigured the later history of the island, which became a British protectorate in 1890. Already in the 1860s the French Consul complained that the Sultan of Zanzibar was strongly under British influence, but this should perhaps prompt more research using French sources alongside British ones, and deeper analysis of this crucial period of competition between the European powers, at a time when it was not yet clear what would happen later in the century.

Analysis of the multiple currency system in Zanzibar, as well as contributing to a new understanding of the history of money and of currency change in the Western Indian Ocean region and Eastern Africa in the nineteenth century, can also shed light on other themes, including the impact of globalisation in the Indian Ocean. The manoeuvring of the consuls and merchants in Zanzibar in relation to the relative values of their currencies and their constant jostling for position in the lucrative trade in Zanzibar provides a way to consider the growing influence of the European consuls in the second half of the nineteenth century, and to understand the long-distance networks that linked Zanzibar to many other parts of the world, directly and indirectly. Despite this nowhere being explicit, it may have been that the introduction of the rupee into currency in Zanzibar was in part an attempt by the British Consul to prevent the French franc from becoming ascendant in the Indian Ocean. It can also be understood as one of the impacts and legacies—perhaps a somewhat distant and unexpected one—of the American Civil War. Globalisation was not an irresistible force, but nor were global factors something that could be ignored. If as Erik Gilbert (2013, p. 124) has argued, Zanzibar was an important part of an Indian Ocean regional globalisation, it was also deeply affected by global factors that could not be controlled. Merchants in Zanzibar tried to deal with the changing situation in which they found themselves, but the balance of local and global interests was complex, and once it had been upset by events thousands of miles away, they had to take action that would change the currency map of the region permanently.

References

Allen, Calvin H. 1982. "The State of Masqat in the Gulf and East Africa, 1785-1829." *International Journal of Middle East Studies* 14 (2): 117–127.

———. 1963. "Americans in Zanzibar: 1825-1845." *Tanganyika Notes and Records* 56: 93–108.

———. 1969. "France and Zanzibar, 1775–1844." In *Eastern African History*, edited by Daniel F. Mc Call, Norman R. Bennet, and Jeffrey Butler. New York: Praeger.

———. 1973. "France and Zanzibar, 1844 to the 1860s [Part I]." *The International Journal of African Historical Studies* 6 (4): 602–632.

Bennet, Norman R., and George Brooks. 1965. *New England Merchants in Africa*. Boston, MA: Boston University Press.

Bhandare, Shailendra. 2007. "Money on the Move: The Rupee and the Indian Ocean Region." In *Cross Currents and Community Networks*, edited by Prabha Ray Himanshu and Edward A. Alpers. New Delhi: Oxford University Press.

Burton, Richard Francis. 1860. *The Lake Regions of Central Africa: A Picture of Exploration*, Vol. 1. London: Harper.

———. 1872. *Zanzibar: City, Island and Coast*. Vol. 2. London: Tinsley Brothers.

Campbell, Gwyn. 2005. *An Economic History of Imperial Madagascar, 1759–1895: The Rise and Fall of an Island Empire*. Cambridge: Cambridge University Press.

Cohen, Benjamin J. 2000. *The Geography of Money*. Ithaca, NY: Cornell University Press.

Gilbert, Erik. 2013. "Zanzibar: Imperialism, Proto-Globalization, and a Nineteenth Century Indian Ocean Boom Town." In *Globalization and the City*, edited by Andreas Exenberger, Philipp Strobl, Günter Bischof and James Mokhiber, 123–139. Innsbruck: Innsbruck University.

Grandidier, Alfred. 1868. *Notice sur l'île de Zanzibar*. Saint-Denis (Réunion): Imp. Lithographique et Typographique de A. Roussin.

Guillain, Charles. 1856. *Documents sur l'histoire, la géographie, et le commerce de l'Afrique orientale*. Paris: A Bertrand.

Helleiner, Eric. 2003. *The Making of National Money: Territorial Currencies in Historical Perspective*. Ithaca: Cornell University Press.

Hunwick, John. 1999. "Islamic Financial Institutions: Theoretical Structures and Aspects of Their Application in Sub-Saharan Africa." In *Credit, Currencies and Culture. African Financial Institutions in Historical Perspective*, edited by Endre Stiansen and Jane I. Guyer, 78–102. Uppsala: Nordiska Afrikainstitutet.

Johnston, Keith. 1879. "Notes of a Trip from Zanzibar to Usambara, in February and March 1879." *Proceedings of the Royal Geographical Society and Monthly Record of Geography* 1: 545–548.

Kumar, Dharma, ed. 1983. *The Cambridge Economic History of India*. Cambridge: Cambridge University Press.
Loarer, M. 1851. "L' île de Zanzibar." *Revue de l'Orient* 9: 290–299.
Mansfield, Daniel H. 1857. "Zanzibar." In *Report on the Commercial Relations of the United States with All Foreign Nations, III*, edited by Edmund Flagg. Washington: House of Representatives.
Metcalf, Thomas. 2008. *Imperial Connections: India in the Indian Ocean Arena, 1860–1920*. Berkeley: University of California Press.
O'Rourke, Kevin H. and Jeffrey G. Williamson. 2002a. *Globalization and History: The Evolution of a Nineteenth-century Atlantic Economy*. Cambridge, MA: MIT Press.
———. 2002b. "When Did Globalisation Begin?" *European Review of Economic History* 6 (1): 23–50.
Osgood, Joseph B. F. 1854. *Notes of Travel, or Recollections of Majunga, Zanzibar, Muscat, Aden, Mocha, and Other Eastern Ports*. Salem: G. Creamer.
Pallaver, Karin. 2019. "What East Africans Got for Their Ivory and Slaves: The Nature, Working and Circulation of Commodity Currencies in Nineteenth-Century East Africa." In *Currencies of the Indian Ocean World*, edited by Steven Serels and Gwyn Campbell, 71–92. Palgrave Series in Indian Ocean World Studies. Palgrave Macmillan.
Pawelczak, Marek. 2010. *The State and the Stateless: The Sultanate of Zanzibar and the East African Mainland: Politics, Economy and Society, 1837–1888*. Warsaw: SOWA.
Playfair, Lt. Col. 1864. "Zanzibar [for the Year 1863]." In *Reports from Her Majesty's Consuls on the Manufactures, Commerce. Vol 2: 174–182*. London: Foreign Office.
Prestholdt, Jeremy. 2008. *Domesticating the World: African Consumerism and the Genealogies of Globalisation*. Berkeley: University of California Press.
———. 2012. "Africa and the Global Lives of Things." In *The Oxford Handbook of the History of Consumption*, edited by Frank Trentmann. Oxford: Oxford University Press.
Reute, Emilie. 2009. *Memoirs of an Arabian Princess from Zanzibar*. New York: Mineola.
Rigby, C. P. 1862. "Zanzibar [for the Year 1860]." In *Commercial Reports Received at the Foreign Office from Her Majesty's Consuls between January 1st and June 30th, 1862*. London: Foreign Office.
Sheriff, Abdul. 1987. *Slaves, Spices and Ivory in Zanzibar*. Oxford: Boydell & Brewer.
Steere, Edward, ed. 1870. *Swahili Tales: As Told by Natives of Zanzibar, With an English Translation*. London: Bell & Daldy.

Steere, Edward, and Arthur C. Madan, eds. 1884. *A Handbook of the Swahili Language, as Spoken at Zanzibar. Edited for the Universities' Mission to Central Africa*. London: Society for Promoting Christian Knowledge.

Tomlinson, B. R. 1996. *The Economy of Modern India, 1869–1970*. Cambridge: Cambridge University Press.

CHAPTER 10

Colonial Money in Africa and National Economy-Building in Britain and Germany: Examining Relations of Agency, 1890s–1930s

Gerold Krozewski

The 1890s and 1900s experienced a pronounced move towards national economy-building in Europe within an emerging world economy. States became functional managers of economies, and, moreover, laid claim to being the developers of nations. This chapter will argue that British and German designs of colonial monetisation were entwined with state ambitions to organise economies as national ones. Discussions between colonial treasurers and administrators in Africa, on the one hand, and advocates of global economic liberalism and empire-builders in Europe, on the other hand, mirrored different visions and expectations of development. Moreover, blueprints for money in Africa formed in a fluid

G. Krozewski (✉)
Osaka University, Suita, Japan

K. Pallaver (ed.), *Monetary Transitions*,
Palgrave Studies in Economic History,
https://doi.org/10.1007/978-3-030-83461-6_10

economic environment. This was neither a scenario in which European agents confidently implemented a developmental agenda nor one in which "Africa" thwarted the advance of a politically neutral European modernity. The investigation of policy formation in this chapter aims to complement a growing body of research on money transitions and transnational relations of colonial money in Africa and beyond (Pallaver 2015, 2019; Gardner 2022, 2015; Balachandran 2019; Kuroda 2020).

The convoluted history of official colonial monetisation in West and East Africa occurred at a time when countries in Europe moved towards gold, and away from "old" silver, as the monetary standard, and organised territorial currencies (Cohen 1998; chap. 2; Helleiner 2003; chaps. 7 and 8). In 1880, British coinage became the standard currency in the Gold Coast, Lagos, Sierra Leone, and Gambia.[1] A separate West African currency was created together with the West African Currency Board (WACB) in 1912 (Hopkins 1970; Narsey 2016, pp. 134–160). In British East Africa, the currency order of 1898 confirmed the Indian rupee as the standard coinage, while the rupee of the Imperial British East Africa Company (IBEAC) continued to circulate in the region. In 1905, Britain introduced the decimal currency system following the Ceylon model, together with a new subsidiary coinage.[2] In the years 1919–1921, Britain established the East African Currency Board (EACB) and a separate British East African currency (Pallaver 2019; Mwangi 2001). However, deliberations on a British West African currency had begun in 1899 with the Barbour Committee initiated by Joseph Chamberlain as colonial secretary (Hopkins 1970, p. 121). In East Africa, debates about a new currency in 1911–1913 had been interrupted by the First World War. All these initiatives came in the wake of widely publicised shifts in currency policy in the British Empire, notably regarding the Indian rupee and its relation to the pound sterling from 1893 onwards (Balachandran [1996] 2015, chap. 2).

When Germany established an East African protectorate in 1890, the state left the privilege of issuing money to the German East Africa Company (DOAG, *Deutsch-Ostafrikanische Gesellschaft*), which introduced a company rupee that circulated in parallel to the dominant British

[1] See West Africa, currency, 1880, The National Archives (TNA), Kew, Treasury (T) 1/12875.

[2] The East Africa and Uganda (Currency) Order in Council 1905, 10 February 1905, TNA, Foreign Office (FO) 2/956.

Indian rupee. In 1903, however, the German state reclaimed the issuing right and created a distinct German rupee (*Reichsrupie*).[3] After the First World War, Britain, as the mandatory power of Tanganyika territory that succeeded German East Africa, introduced British East African shillings (Pallaver 2022). A similar transition had occurred in Samoa already in 1915.[4]

The following analysis selectively contextualises the changing approaches on colonial money by Britain and Germany in West and East African colonies. Visions and layers of policymaking will be discussed first, and will subsequently inform an argument about connections between colonial monetisation in Africa and economy-building in Europe.

Colonial Currency Policy and Economic Visions in British Africa

Conceptions of colonial economies are visible in the choice of colonial currency, and, moreover, in regulations regarding the demonetisation of other circulating moneys, legal tender, paper money and its reserve provisions, and subsidiary coinage. Initially, the standardisation of British coins as the standard in West Africa was a consequence of intensifying commercial relations. The move was a sign of economic sovereignty and a means to make distinctly "British" trade the core tenant of future colonial economies (Hermann 2011, p. 405). By the beginning of the twentieth century, however, the question became one of conscious state governance for two main reasons: the relationship between money in West Africa and Britain, and considerations of income from seigniorage. The former bore out the British Treasury's fear that, as silver depreciated, West African silver coins might one day flow back into the British economy, putting pressure on British gold reserves. Seigniorage related to Chamberlain's desire to raise income for colonial development faced with a British Treasury that was reluctant to share its profits for this purpose. In this

[3] *Denkschrift über die Neuordnung des Münzwesens des Deutsch-Ostafrikanischen Schutzgebiets*, 1904, attached with *Reichstagsprotokolle*, printed matters, 19 April 1904, (henceforth *Münzwesen*). www.reichstagsprotokolle.de. Accessed on 15 April 2021.

[4] Samoa, Monetary System, 22 April 1915, United States, Department of State Records, 862M.515, Gale *Archives Unbound*, European Colonialism in the Early 20th Century: German Colonies to League of Nations Mandates in Africa 1910–1929. www.gale.com. Accessed on 15 April 2021.

connection, the Barbour Committee investigated the possibility to create a West African currency in 1899–1902.

At that time, British merchants vehemently opposed a separate West African currency. Due to their influence and seconded by a supportive colonial secretary the matter was shelved for about a decade (Hopkins, 1970, pp. 126, 129). The merchants and local governors stressed Africa's appetite for silver, as a commodity used in jewellery, and in places like Lagos its "hoarding."[5] The Treasury and Colonial Office were critical of the practice of parallel uses of moneys. British merchants and some colonial governors, however, saw no problem with multiple currencies. They emphasised long-established relationships with local traders and familiarity with indigenous moneys. Some also expressed a preference for "barter" trade.[6]

In the early 1900s, the views of colonial officials on money depended on expectations regarding the characteristics of prospective colonial economies. The governor of the Gold Coast, Matthew Nathan, for instance, observed in January 1902 that, if the colony experienced a boom in mining it might be on course to a "real" gold standard rather than a "fictitious" one. Otherwise, nothing more needed to be done than regulate the circulation of British silver coin.[7]

Approaches to the demonetisation of indigenous money (beyond the stipulation of a standard coinage as legal tender) were also contingent on the role attributed to "African" production in colonial development. Frederick Lugard joined Chamberlain in requesting seigniorage income for colonial development. Moreover, both agreed on the need to introduce a colonial currency different from "African" money, notably the "bulky" cowries. Lugard told the Barbour enquiry in 1899 that Northern

[5] West Africa. Further Correspondence (July 1900 to August 1903) Relating to the Currency of the West African Colonies [henceforth West Africa, currency, 1900–1903], No. 30, Governor W. MacGregor, Lagos, to Chamberlain, received 30 August 1902, TNA, Colonial Office (CO) 879/66.

[6] See, for instance, the witness statement by a partner of the Glasgow firm Alexander Miller & Co, 28 November 1899, West African Currency Committee [Barbour Committee]: Report, Minutes, and Evidence, March 1900, TNA, MINT 13/25, pp. 23–24; also Moor, Southern Nigeria, to Chamberlain, received 7 July 1902.

[7] West Africa, currency, 1900–1903, No. 38, Nathan to Chamberlain, Colonial Office, received 4 February 1902, TNA, CO 879/66.

Nigeria did not have a currency when he became governor: "I instituted a currency."[8] He deemed direct interference in African money to be "extremely unwise" but recommended indirect measures, such as duties, to prevent at least large imports of cowries.[9] Yet Lugard "allowed" himself to "deprecate" from Chamberlain's view that regulating subsidiary coinage could be delayed. He argued that the opportunity to modernise small coin must not be missed.[10] Measures were "urgently required" to phase out barter trade and establish exchanges based on money with a metallic value.[11] For Lugard, ordering money in the "African" sector had wider significance for the active development of a colonial-imperial economy.

Lugard arguably pursued a similar logic in the debate about denominations of West African banknotes, when a separate colonial currency for West Africa was introduced in the 1910s. As chairman of the WACB, he requested the inclusion of low denominations in the mix of banknotes. In this case, he successfully challenged the Colonial Office and British merchants who wished WACB notes to be issued exclusively in large denominations to "protect" Africans from abuses (Carland 1990, p. 500). However, such protection amounted to exclusion from British commercial circuits, while introducing lower denominations was meant to facilitate transactions with an African sector of producers for an export-oriented colonial-imperial economy.

In British East Africa in the early 1900s, some colonial accountants and administrators challenged official views in London as well as opinions expressed by expatriate merchants and the still small settler community. British and South African traders who expanded into East Africa followed by the Standard Bank of South Africa favoured the use of sterling, including the British gold sovereign, as did, in principle, the British Treasury. By contrast, the treasurer of the East Africa Protectorate, C.C.

[8] Lugard statement, Barbour Committee, 21 November 1899, TNA, MINT 13/25, p. 16; West Africa, currency, 1900–1903, No. 51, Lugard to Chamberlain, received 18 August 1902, TNA, CO 879/66.

[9] West Africa, currency, 1900–1903, No. 49, Lugard, Northern Nigeria, to Chamberlain, received 9 June 1902; and No. 29, Lugard to Colonial Office, 9 August 1901, TNA, CO 879/66.

[10] West Africa, currency, 1900–1903, No. 66, Lugard to Chamberlain, received 29 May 1903, and No. 51, Lugard to Chamberlain, received 18 August 1902, TNA, CO 879/66.

[11] No. 51, Lugard to Chamberlain, 18 August 1902, TNA, CO 879/66.

Bowring, saw change as impracticable, given that the Indian rupee had become entrenched in the economy. Indian and Swahili traders preferred the rupee, as did the National Bank of India. At the time, a branch of this bank was the only institution providing rupees from mints in India to traders in East Africa.[12] Bowring asserted that the rupee "must remain the standard coin in East Africa." In fact, he argued that it might never become "imperative" to introduce the English currency system. Initially, he favoured the maintenance of the status quo but then argued that colonial authorities could take measures to "improve" the rupee. This meant introducing the decimal "Ceylon system," which went hand in hand with a reform of subsidiary coinage. Bowring also agreed with the British Treasury that it was desirable to issue paper money.[13]

For European policymakers, paper money symbolised modernisation. However, unlike coins, which had a metallic value, banknotes were fiduciary money. In the East Africa currency order 1905, and in discussions about a Southern Nigerian note issue in 1907, the British Treasury harked back to guidelines of 1894 and the orthodoxy established by the Peel act of 1844.[14] In 1894, the Treasury had argued that risks of unsound monetary management were greater in "uncivilised" colonies. Therefore, the state, rather than private banks, needed to get involved and adopt a regulatory role. A note guarantee fund would be required to safeguard even against an improbable level of demand for the conversion of notes into coin. The fund should ideally amount to two-third but at least half of the value of notes issued.

In the 1900s, the Indian rupee prevailed in British East Africa. In fact, in the 1890s British colonial officials had preferred it as "more civilised" money compared to cowries (Pallaver 2015, p. 480). And the IBEAC rupee was no serious rival. But, as the British state took on a regulative role and embarked on economy-building, the question of a separate East

[12] Africa (East), coinage and currency, 1900–1905, memorandum by C.C. Bowring, Treasurer, Mombasa, 17 June 1903, to the Commissioner and Consul General, Mombasa, transmitted to Lansdowne, Colonial Office, 24 June 1903, TNA, FO 2/956.

[13] Bowring, 8 June 1903, and Bowring's memorandum, 17 June 1903, TNA, FO 2/956.

[14] East Africa and Uganda Currency Order, 10 February 1905, TNA, MINT 20/264; and Treasury letter, 21 September 1894, enclosed with Secretary of State, Colonial Office, to Governor, Southern Nigeria, 26 March 1908, West Africa, proposed establishment of a government note issue, 1907–1910, TNA, CO 879/109. The letter refers to a manuscript edited by George Arbuthnoth in 1857.

African currency re-emerged and changed. When the matter was discussed in the early 1910s, Bowring, now the acting governor of the East Africa Protectorate, requested that the move ought to be postponed. The rupee was "the people's money" in a "young colony;" demonetising it would jeopardise the colony's future welfare.[15]

Debates regarding an East African guarantee fund for a separate currency, once again, bore out different conceptions of colonial economies. The British Treasury explicitly stated that the composition of the reserve fund in terms of silver or gold coins should be a means to promote the gradual increase in the use of gold for large commercial transactions in the protectorate.[16] For Bowring, by contrast, the composition of the fund needed to reflect existing requirements in trade, which was done in silver coin. Doing otherwise risked undermining the colonial economy, besides harming the image of paper money.[17] For the Treasury, the story also tied in with the quest to regulate the silver rupee from the viewpoint of global monetary relations, as will be discussed further below. The project of a separate currency subsequently became intertwined with the lobbying by an emerging settler-state and debates about the economy of a "white" settler empire (Mwangi 2001; Maxon 1989).

Approaches to Currency Reform in German East Africa

The state-led currency reforms in German East Africa involved expert advocates of the German *Industriestaat*. These were notably Karl Helfferich, as the director of the colonial division of the German foreign ministry, and Bernhard Dernburg, first at the colonial division and then as the head of a new colonial ministry. Both men combined visions of

[15] East Africa. Correspondence (2 February 1911, to 19 December, 1913) Relating to Currency Questions in East Africa [henceforth East Africa, currency, 1911–1913], No. 32, East Africa Protectorate, Acting Governor, to Secretary of State, Colonial Office, received 5 July 1912, TNA, CO 879/109.

[16] East Africa, currency, 1911–1913, No. 25, Treasury to Colonial Office, 28 December 1911, TNA, CO 879/109. The note issue for Southern Nigeria also discussed the need for a gold reserve but does not seem to have envisaged the use of gold coin in trade (Hopkins 1970, pp. 118–119).

[17] East Africa, currency, 1911–1913, No. 12, Bowring to Colonial Office, received 7 June 1911; also No. 18, Report of the East Africa Protectorate Currency Committee, TNA, CO 879/109.

a global German economy with active economy-building and engaged with Britain's international and imperial monetary policy. Their objective was to emulate British monetary principles yet attune them to the particular needs of a German national economy. The years 1903–1905 prompted the German state to get involved in colonial monetary arrangements, epitomised by the introduction of the German rupee. However, the currency faced considerable criticism from German firms with trading interests in East Africa, and from a range of political opinion in the German Parliament, the Reichstag.

In the 1900s, currency policy for German East Africa was largely driven by Helfferich. The official report for the Reichstag drafted under his supervision engaged with technicalities to explicate the choice of the German rupee while also passing judgment on alternative proposals and endorsing supportive views. The latter came notably from Robert Koch, the president of the *Reichsbank* until his death in 1906.[18] Helfferich rejected the two possible alternatives to the German rupee, namely introducing the German mark or accepting the British Indian rupee as the official currency of German East Africa. The report emphasised that the state for the first time systematically organised the colony's currency system.[19] By taking back the privilege of issuing money from the DOAG, the state not only acted as a regulator in monetary affairs but also aimed to assume a role as an agent of development. As an issuing authority, the state committed itself to guarantee the exchange of any coin it issued with money of "real value," which the company never had done.[20] German merchants, however, only reluctantly followed Helfferich's request to endorse his proposal in a written memorandum.[21]

The report argued that the German state rupee was an improvement compared to both the DOAG rupee and the British Indian rupee. The currency order stipulated that colonial authorities were required to hold a reserve of silver rupees equivalent to three months cash requirements.[22]

[18] *Münzwesen*, p. 2024, annex 15. www.reichstagsprotokolle.de. Accessed on 15 April 2021.

[19] *Münzwesen*, p. 1991. www.reichstagsprotokolle.de. Accessed on 15 April 2021.

[20] *Münzwesen*, p. 1991: "vollwertige[s] Geld." www.reichstagsprotokolle.de. Accessed on 15 April 2021.

[21] *Münzwesen*, annex 13. www.reichstagsprotokolle.de. Accessed on 15 April 2021.

[22] *Münzwesen*, p. 2001. www.reichstagsprotokolle.de. Accessed on 15 April 2021.

Moreover, the German rupee's security fund for the issuing of banknotes, created from seigniorage, followed existing or envisaged arrangements in British colonies, in the United States colony of the Philippines, and in Mexico.[23] The German currency reform also opted for decimalisation, referring to the "Ceylon system" in British East Africa.[24] Helfferich, moreover, entwined the choice of the German rupee with the establishment of a banking institution for German East Africa. The explicit aim was to associate private banking with central bank functions in colonies in order to boost colonial development.[25]

Formally, the new currency legislation could not be passed without the colonial governor's approval.[26] In practice, though, little consultation seems to have taken place between Berlin and German East Africa. The official report merely stated the governor's consent in passing. Yet the German rupee met with considerable opposition when the Reichstag was informed of its creation. The criticism intensified in the years leading up to the First World War. Opponents of Helfferich and Dernburg argued that the German rupee was impractical and harmed German trade and settler interests. Speakers demanded the introduction of the German mark in East Africa in line with the practice in other German colonies. Matthias Erzberger, an outspoken critic of the abuses of German colonialism in the suppression of the Maji Maji rebellion and the exterminationist war against Herero and Nama in Southwest Africa, acknowledged Helfferich's correct procedural approach to currency matters. However, Erzberger stressed that the German mark would have assisted both German commerce and German colonial producers. The latter, in turn, would have been conducive to "African" welfare, thus reducing community tensions (Williamson 1971, pp. 62–67). In his response, Helfferich argued that the rupee was an incontrovertible brand in East Africa. However, pegging the German rupee to the mark had stabilised the exchange rate, compared to the previous fluctuations in the rate between the Indian rupee and the mark. He claimed that this was similar to

[23] *Münzwesen*, p. 2002. www.reichstagsprotokolle.de. Accessed on 15 April 2021.

[24] *Münzwesen*, p. 1996. www.reichstagsprotokolle.de. Accessed on 15 April 2021.

[25] Helfferich, *Reichstagsprotokolle* [transcripts of the debates of the German Reichstag], 18 March 1905, p. 5378. www.reichstagsprotokolle.de. Accessed on 15 April 2021.

[26] *Münzwesen*, p. 1999. www.reichstagsprotokolle.de. Accessed on 15 April 2021.

extending the mark's circulation to the colony, and constituted a sound basis for attracting private capital to the colony.[27]

In the early 1900s, German merchants in East Africa preferred the circulation of the DOAG rupee at par with the Indian rupee, and accepted the latter's dominant use in the colony. In the memorandum of June 1903, the Hamburg firms Hansing and O'swald, and the DOAG, only agreed to the introduction of the German rupee as a means to satisfy "German patriotic sentiment."[28] The firms strongly objected to the chosen exchange rate between the German rupee and the mark. They complained that rounding down the exchange rate disadvantaged traders and settlers. Reportedly, the local colonial administration, like the merchants, advocated rounding upward, whereas the German authorities and the colonial governor supported rounding downward.[29] The official written response drafted under Helfferich dismissed these objections invoking a logic of transnational management that will be explored in the next section.[30]

In the aftermath of the currency reform, Dernburg entwined matters of money with planning for German and colonial development. His so-called new colonial policy exposed him to criticism of privileging cosmopolitan finance over the interests of German economic agents. In the years between 1909 and 1914, members of the Reichstag regularly denounced the colonial ministry's policy under Dernburg and, after 1911, under Wilhelm Solf, by alleging a disregard for the link between colonial and *German* economic development. Reichstag delegates described the German rupee as "useless," called it an "entirely failed experiment," or mocked it as "quite a curious creation" and a "strange idea."[31] No improvement of the rupee brand was warranted, one speaker argued.

[27] Helfferich, *Reichstagsprotokolle*, 18 March 1905, p. 5377. www.reichstagsprotokolle.de. Accessed on 15 April 2021.

[28] *Münzwesen*, p. 2016, "deutsch-patriotisches Empfinden." www.reichstagsprotokolle.de. Accessed on 15 April 2021.

[29] *Münzwesen*, p. 1995. www.reichstagsprotokolle.de. Accessed on 15 April 2021.

[30] *Münzwesen*, p. 1996; also annex 12, p. 2014, and annexes 13 and 14. www.reichstagsprotokolle.de. Accessed on 15 April 2021.

[31] *Reichstgsprotokolle*, "taugt nichts:" Schwarze, 26 February 1909, p. 7183; "gänzlich verunglücktes Experiment," "ganz eigentümliche Schöpfung:" Arendt, 1 May 1912, p. 1590, and 11 March 1914, p. 8025; "merkwürdige Idee:" v. Liebert, 6 March 1913, p. 4334. www.reichstagsprotokolle.de. Accessed on 15 April 2021.

Paper money was anyway of no use to African "natives."[32] The German rupee should be replaced with the mark.[33]

Yet there was a logic to Helfferich's design and Dernburg's continuing defence of the German rupee. The policy aimed to advance German imperial-colonial development with the help of transnational monetary management. Their critics either did not condone, or did not fully grasp, the political-economic engineering that Helfferich's strategic vision entailed.

Colonial Currency, National Economies and Transnational Economic Steering

In both Germany and Britain, the blueprints and strategies of colonial monetary policy show how transnational aspects of managing and promoting national economies by nation-states gained traction at the beginning of the twentieth century. In Britain, national-global and colonial-imperial conceptions of economy-building pulled in different directions. Lugard was primarily a lobbyist for colonial Africa as a resource frontier for constructive colonial-imperial development. The aim of a separate West African silver coinage was "to make as large a profit as possible" from seigniorage.[34] The British Treasury and the Bank of England, by contrast, were not interested in colonial economy-building in Africa. What mattered for them was managing Africa in relation to an open economy to ensure favourable conditions for investment. In a gold standard world, policymakers saw Africa's overvalued silver coinage as a risk. In 1900, the Treasury argued that West African colonies were welcome to establish their own currency, provided they set up a gold fund for the eventuality that large amounts of African silver would swamp the British economy.[35] British traders, while arguing that return flows of silver were unlikely in the foreseeable future, were clearly aware of the wider problem.

[32] Arendt, *Reichstgsprotokolle*, 11 March 1914. www.reichstagsprotokolle.de. Accessed on 15 April 2021.

[33] Schwarze, *Reichstgsprotokolle*, 26 February 1909; Arendt, *Reichstgsprotokolle*, 1 May 1912. www.reichstagsprotokolle.de. Accessed on 15 April 2021.

[34] Lugard, Barbour Committee, 21 November 1899, p. 18, TNA, MINT 13/25; also F.D. Lugard, Administration of Tropical Colonies, 11 July 1905, TNA, CO 879/88.

[35] Barbour Committee, March 1900, TNA, MINT 13/25; also Treasury to Colonial Office, 16 August 1900, TNA, CO 879/66.

The representative of the Liverpool Chamber of Commerce stated that a separate West African coinage was unlikely to please City of London financiers since it required "locking up" gold for the purpose of a reserve fund.[36]

Gold standard doctrine had become firmly established among Treasury and Bank of England officials under the influence of expert advisers like Robert Giffen (1892, chap. 1), among others. Nonetheless, lobbying for bimetallism continued in the 1900s. Manchester merchants with commercial interests in West Africa felt encouraged by statements of George Goschen, Chancellor of the Exchequer in the late 1880s. Goschen, though a firm advocate of gold orthodoxy, admitted that British traders might benefit from a bimetallic standard in the case of West Africa.[37] These merchants favoured the status quo in West Africa because it tied in with their lobbying for bimetallism.

In the 1910s, the currency board system that entwined export commodity earnings with the colonial money supply looked like an ingenious way to regulate the relationship between a West African silver circulation and the gold-based British economy while also keeping conflict between British traders at bay (Hopkins 1970, pp. 125–128). By compartmentalising different economic spaces in the empire, the system reconciled advocates of cosmopolitan sterling, sceptical of the possible impact of "African" development on the British economy, with objectives of colonial developers like Lugard.

Similar considerations of compartmentalisation are also visible much later, at a time when Britain had suspended the gold standard. In 1936/37, the WACB ran out of coinage to meet the demand for purchases of cocoa during the harvesting season, first in the Gold Coast and later for other commodities in Nigeria. As an emergency measure, the Treasury and Bank of England agreed to make Bank of England notes legal tender in West Africa in addition to WACB coins and notes. The alternative option of shipping silver coin from the Royal Mint to West Africa was feared to prompt coin shortages in England during the winter

[36] H. Cottrell, Liverpool Chamber of Commerce, Barbour Committee, 12 December 1899, p. 34, TNA, MINT 13/25.

[37] Cottrell referred to Goschen's supportive opinion. Barbour Committee, p. 34, TNA, MINT 13/25.

holiday season.[38] The incident evoked memories of pre-1912 concerns among Treasury and Bank officials regarding the uncontrolled circulation of British money in West Africa. The Bank of England, therefore, insisted that its notes would be legal tender only for a strictly limited period, and the exceptional regulation ended in August 1937.[39] The Colonial Office, though not an advocate of parallel currency use, would have preferred the continued circulation of the Bank's notes in West Africa, which it saw as lending support to colonial economies.[40]

In British East Africa, the question of delineating economic spaces and visions of development directly involved Britain's currency relations with colonial India. In 1893, following an official investigation of the Indian currency system, Britain regulated the relationship between the Indian silver rupee and the British pound by stopping the uncontrolled minting of silver coin in India. The Indian rupee now operated on a gold exchange standard, effectively a sterling standard, related to the pound's full gold standard. Officials managed the exchange rate between sterling and the Indian rupee with the aim to maintain the face value of rupee coins in spite of their depreciating value in silver. In 1899, in addition, Britain fixed the exchange rate between the Indian rupee and the British gold sovereign. The gold sovereign was, in principle, legal tender in British colonies, though it was not expected to play a role in exchanges "between natives" "for many years to come."[41]

The intersection between practicalities, safeguards, and visions of economies, is apparent from the different positions taken by the British Treasury and by the local colonial administration during the discussions about East African currency in the early 1910s. Considerations regarding the provision of coinage for trade and the guarantee fund for colonial banknotes, as initially stipulated in the currency order of 1905, are instructive in this connection.

[38] W.R. Fraser, Treasury, to Sir Robert Johnson, Royal Mint, 7 January 1937, TNA, T 160/649.

[39] Norman Young, Treasury representative at the WACB, 16 March 1937, TNA, T 160/649; and Young memorandum for the Treasury, WACB meeting, 30 March 1937, TNA, CO 554/107/18.

[40] Young, 16 March 1937, and Bank of England to Gatliff, 22 March 1937, TNA, T 160/649.

[41] See, for instance, Foreign Office dispatch No. 282, 19 October 1901, TNA, FO 2/956.

In a gold standard setting, it was in principle desirable that trade would be conducted as part of a gold circulation. However, export traders in colonies needed to meet the preferences of coinage of African producers which corresponded to the existing silver circulation. Local officials, like Bowring, were concerned about convenient ways in which traders could obtain rupees in a de facto Indian Ocean rupee zone. This was the precondition for the smooth functioning of the colonial economy. Consequently, the portion of the note guarantee fund held in gold ought to be limited.[42] For the British Treasury, a gold fund as a security reserve was increasingly important in view of a separate British East African currency. But, as argued earlier, the Treasury also saw a large gold share in the guarantee fund for banknotes as a measure to encourage the wider use of gold in commerce.[43] Introducing a separate East African rupee might assist in this endeavour.[44]

In East Africa, economic interest groups representing different conceptions of economies operated at counter purposes. The Standard Bank of South Africa demanded the option to obtain banknotes in exchange for gold.[45] The National Bank of India, by contrast, complained that the East African currency office offered gold instead of silver coin in exchange for its banknotes.[46] The Colonial Office, however, generally argued that trading firms needed to obtain the required coinage and notes themselves, and, if necessary, directly import rupees from India at their own cost. The state had no obligation to accommodate particular firms.[47]

Yet at the level of imperial economic policy, the British state aimed to reconcile colonial development with cosmopolitan sterling interests by

[42] East Africa, currency, 1911–1913, No. 18, Report of the East Africa Protectorate Currency Committee, TNA, CO 879/109. The committee, whose membership included Bowring, met on 28 September 1911.

[43] East Africa, currency, 1911–1913, No. 25, Treasury to Colonial Office, 26 August and 28 December 1911, TNA, CO 879/109.

[44] East Africa, currency, 1911–1913, No. 15, British Treasury to Colonial Office, received 26 August 1911, TNA, CO 879/109.

[45] East Africa, currency, 1911–1913, Enclosure to No. 9, Standard Bank of South Africa to East Africa Protectorate, 30 March 1911, TNA, CO 879/109.

[46] East Africa, currency, 1911–1913, No. 3, National Bank of India to Colonial Office, received 19 March 1911, TNA, CO 879/109.

[47] East Africa, currency, 1911–1913, Nr. 15, Secretary of State, Colonial Office, to East Africa Protectorate, TNA, CO 879/109.

stipulating that part of the note guarantee fund would be earmarked for investment in imperial stock, though not in securities of East Africa and Uganda.[48] The Colonial Stock Act, 1900, was the basis for promoting intra-imperial investment (Jessop 1976). In 1903, Bowring had suggested investment in Indian securities.[49]

As the British state engaged in national, imperial and colonial monetary management, defining policies that suited different visions of economy-building became elusive. The very question of issuing colonial money is a case in point. In the late nineteenth century, the British Treasury had cast the state's role in the light of pre-empting risks of unsound monetary practices in colonies. Increasingly, however, the prerogative of issuing money became linked to the question of who was ultimately in charge of monetary policy, even if the location of issuing institutions and sovereignty did not need to coincide. India derived income from issuing rupees at Indian mints, including for the rupees circulating in East Africa. This matter was to cast a long shadow into the future.

In the 1910 and immediately after the First World War, East Africa's currency relations became disconnected from the Indian rupee zone as European settlers aimed to promote their economic interests. The establishment of a separate British East African currency and the EACB was driven by British settlers opposed to "Indian" influence in East Africa (Aiyar 2015, pp. 87–89). Under Leo Amery as colonial secretary in the 1920s, currency matters in British colonial Africa became associated with settler visions of development. Lugard, meanwhile, continued to adhere to a development doctrine in which the state's role was to prevent monopolies and organise African smallholder production for the imperial economy. In this connection, he referred to initiatives by Dernburg in Germany (Lugard 1922, p. 479). Already in 1905, Lugard had praised Germany and France for their "systematic" colonial development, urging Britain to follow their example.[50]

In German East Africa, in turn, Helfferich and Dernburg reconfigured British imperial currency management in their quest to develop a global Germany economy. In the early 1900s, Helfferich, looking to the future, emphasised the need to regulate the link between silver and gold

[48] East Africa and Uganda Currency Order, 10 February 1905, TNA, MINT 20/264.

[49] Bowring, Treasurer, Mombasa, 8 June 1903, TNA, FO 2/956.

[50] Sir F. Lugard, memorandum on Northern Nigeria, May 1905, TNA, CO 879/88.

currencies and to advance colonial export economies. Britain's monetary policy in India served as a template. In a wider sense, Helfferich's analysis followed the British gold standard theorist Giffen, and in Germany Ludwig Bamberger, the politician and banker who had been instrumental in putting Germany on gold after unification in 1871.

In 1900, Helfferich edited a volume with articles by Bamberger that included texts on the decline of silver in the late nineteenth century.[51] Gold, Bamberger had argued since the 1870s, was inevitably on the rise. The long-term problem, which required adjustments in national monetary policy, was where to put surplus silver. The Indian currency reform of 1893 showed that Britain had realised that the silver rupee had become a "mirage" and risk for the British economy. Helfferich, in addition, noticed the regulation of legal tender and choice of the exchange rate between the British gold sovereign and the Indian rupee in 1899. He observed that the currency reform in British India disconnected the metal value of the rupee from its "fictitious" face value. But Britain did not abandon its monetary authority in India. In Helfferich's phrase, Britain put India on a "limping" gold standard, thus reinforcing the link with the pound (Helfferich [1903] 1923, p. 188).

Helfferich designed the German rupee not as a mere response to local circumstances, but as the most rational manner in which a German imperial-colonial economy could operate under an assumed trajectory of international money. The German rupee ought to be managed as a silver currency without a gold circulation by regulating the relationship between the mark and the rupee, confining the colonial circulation to silver coins and, in the future, banknotes. German gold coin was not legal tender in East Africa.

The exchange rates fixed between the German rupee, the German mark, and the Indian rupee, were chosen bearing international monetary relations in mind. The exchange rate of the German rupee was set at 15 rupees to the pound, the same as the rate of the Indian rupee to the pound. The aim was to keep German and British Indian rupees at par by managing bills of exchange following the example of cases in the British

[51] In Helfferich (1900), see especially Bamberger's texts "Die Entthronung eines Weltherrschers" (1876) and the sequel (1893). The title refers to the "dethroning" of the "rule" of silver. For pertinent points, see p. 572 and pp. 576–577 of Helfferich's edited volume.

Empire and the United States in the Philippine colony.[52] In a similar vein, provisions for the German rupee stipulated gold reserves for note issues. However, here the official report mentioned that the fund had less of a role to play in German East Africa, since the German state's legally guaranteed annual subsidy to the colony fulfilled, in essence, the same function as a gold reserve.[53]

The exchange rate between the German rupee and the mark was fine-tuned with the objective of demonetising the Indian rupee in German East Africa in mind. Policymakers set the rate at which Indian rupees could be exchanged for German rupees slightly below the rate at which Indian rupees could be exchanged for British gold sovereigns in Zanzibar. This was Helfferich's reason for insisting to round the rate downward. Only in this way would the Indian rupee flow out of German East Africa to the Zanzibar market because it was not profitable to exchange Indian rupees for German rupees in the German colony (Hintze 1912, p. 35). The demonetisation of the Indian rupee was deliberately not mentioned in the currency order.[54] In addition, German merchants would obtain German rupees at a discount in Germany. This measure should prevent German currency and gold from flowing from Germany to East Africa because such shipments would be unprofitable given transport and insurance costs.[55]

Two related triggers made German policymakers act when they did. As a result of the Indian currency reform, the DOAG struggled to maintain the exchange rate of its company rupee at par with the British Indian rupee. For a while, the situation was kept in check by the company's restraint in minting more of its rupees. Helfferich, however, argued that there was no guarantee that the company would continue to act against its self-interest by forgoing the seigniorage profits it could obtain from issuing rupees in this situation; he observed a trend in this direction. State regulation was required to prevent German taxpayers from footing the bill in the event of the DOAG's failure to keep the company rupee

[52] *Münzwesen*, p. 2000, and annex 20. www.reichstagsprotokolle.de. Accessed on 15 April 2021.

[53] *Münzwesen*, p. 2002. www.reichstagsprotokolle.de. Accessed on 15 April 2021.

[54] *Münzwesen*, pp. 1995 and 1999. www.reichstagsprotokolle.de. Accessed on 15 April 2021.

[55] *Münzwesen*, p. 1999. www.reichstagsprotokolle.de. Accessed on 15 April 2021.

at par with the Indian rupee.[56] The further trigger was that the British Consul-general and the Sultan in Zanzibar stopped accepting the DOAG rupee as legal tender in March 1903, and London rejected attempts by the German Government to reverse the move.[57] The acceptance of the DOAG rupee had been the reciprocity to the circulation of the British Indian rupee in German East Africa. The move against the DOAG rupee in Zanzibar put its exchange rate with the Indian rupee under acute pressure. One way to stabilise exchanges with the Indian rupee was to anchor the value of a German East African currency in the German mark.

The German rupee looked odd to many contemporaries who doubted its purpose for the German economy. However, Helfferich designed the rupee to extricate the German colony from operating with a sterling-based currency. The German rupee was a means to keep the colony "free from" British Indian rupees, and fitted in neatly with his championing of Germany's emerging national-global economy.[58] The move prevented seigniorage from accruing to the Indian mint. For Helfferich, the German rupee also had the potential to foster commercial links conducive to German colonial development. Presumably referring to Indian merchants, he stressed that the "coloured intermediaries" involved in regional trade with Zanzibar would no longer be able to do business with India by themselves using Indian rupees. In order to obtain rupees, they would need to interact with German firms and thereby could be drawn into their ambit.[59]

Helfferich also claimed that the German rupee was a more practical option than the introduction of the mark would have been. The silver content of the Indian rupee was about 7% higher than that of the 2-mark coin, which came closest to the one rupee coin with 1.5 times of its value. Had the mark been introduced, Africans might have felt

[56] *Münzwesen*, pp. 1996–1997. www.reichstagsprotokolle.de. Accessed on 15 April 2021.

[57] Lord Lansdowne, 7 October 1903, *Münzwesen*, p. 1997, and annex 16. www.reichstagsprotokolle.de. Accessed on 15 April 2021.

[58] *Münzwesen*, pp. 1994, 1995. www.reichstagsprotokolle.de. Accessed on 15 April 2021.

[59] *Münzwesen*, p. 2024: "farbige[n] Zwischenhändler[n]." www.reichstagsprotokolle.de. Accessed on 15 April 2021.

cheated.[60] This fact would have undermined the introduction of the German coinage, besides constituting an obstacle to getting Indian rupees out of circulation.

Helfferich's conception of the state's role in regulating colonial economies was geared towards Germany's national-imperial economy and differed from the views of his critics: *alldeutsch* nationalists, German merchants in East Africa, the DOAG, Catholic centre politicians like Erzberger, social democrats and also German high finance (*Hochfinanz*). Helfferich's language was increasingly nationalistic with frequent references to the German Volk. But his views clashed with those of Otto Arendt, a prominent *alldeutsch* advocate of bimetallism since the 1880s. For Arendt, the German mark alone would have benefited German colonies while the German rupee was anchored in an erroneous gold standard policy and failed to promote a colonial economy based on German plantations and settlement.[61] Helfferich's disagreement with Hamburg's East Africa merchants was different. These firms had no problem with the use of a British Indian rupee related to the pound sterling. In fact, the traders saw no merit in Helfferich's "financial-political argument."[62]

In the late 1900s and early 1910s, Dernburg's colonial economic policy made the German rupee part of a wider programme of constructive economy-building. At the colonial ministry, Dernburg, and later Solf, defended Helfferich's initial reasoning about the German rupee against mounting attacks. At times, Solf sounded rather defensive, however. The German rupee had become a reality; it was too late to change course.[63] There were difficulties. For instance, according to the currency order, part of the rupee's note reserve fund ought to be invested in German securities in Berlin. But reportedly this investment failed to catch on.[64]

[60] Helfferich response to Erzberger, *Reichstagsprotokolle*, 18 March 1905, p. 5377. www.reichstagsprotokolle.de. Accessed on 15 April 2021.

[61] Helfferich (1895), and Arendt, *Reichstagsprotokolle*, 1 May 1912, pp. 1590–1591. www.reichstagsprotokolle.de. Accessed on 15 April 2021.

[62] *Münzwesen*, p. 2016: "finanzpolitisches argument." www.reichstagsprotokolle.de. Accessed on 15 April 2021.

[63] Solf's response to Arendt, *Reichstagsprotokolle*, 19 March 1914, pp. 8101–8102. www.reichstagsprotokolle.de. Accessed on 15 April 2021.

[64] Arendt, *Reichstagsprotokolle*, 1 May 1912, p. 1590. www.reichstagsprotokolle.de. Accessed on 15 April 2021.

Yet for Helfferich and Dernburg it was not the state's role to represent high finance as an interest group but to act as a regulator and developer of the German national economy. Where possible, high finance then ought to assist the state in this project, as in colonial Africa. Dernburg thought about colonial economies as a means for the German "latecomer" to break into the geo-economy.[65] Africa would become an alternative to South America, where German businesses faced intense competition with US and British firms. In 1906, he argued that even without German expertise and the necessary infrastructure, Germany's trade with African colonies had already reached the level of Germany's trade with China.[66] Colonial and other overseas relations ought to be mutually constitutive. Dernburg based his programme of colonial development on an assessment of the potential of indigenous colonial production (*Eingeborenenwirtschaft*), similar to the modus operandi of a proactive businessman, a *Kaufmann*, and in line with principles used earlier in Prussia.[67] Moreover, ending monopolies would be conducive to Germany's economic objectives and advance a colonial project common to all major European powers.[68]

The currency connection was designed to reinforce these objectives as part of the same loop. Control over colonial production would ultimately allow to influence certain world commodity prices. Moreover, colonies would be of benefit to the German economy by helping to save and earn foreign currency (Dernburg 1907, p. 50). Such ideas, though disrupted by the war, would cast a long shadow into the interwar period among national liberals whose aim was to obtain areas for raw material production within a German currency zone (Krozewski 2011). Arguments about the steering of development in German Africa were steeped in ideas of racial difference. Dernburg stressed that relations of authority in colonies with a "low cultural level" would help control colonial labour (Dernburg 1907, p. 34). Solf said he did not wish to repeat the phrase of the "master" Volk and its "servant race" but rather talk about the promotion

[65] For relevant observations, see Dernburg (1907, pp. 25–26) in a speech at the German chamber of commerce, the *Handelstag*, on 11 January 1907.

[66] Dernburg, *Reichstagsprotokolle*, 29 November 1906, p. 4002. www.reichstagsprotokolle.de. Accessed on 15 April 2021.

[67] Dernburg, 28 November 1906, pp. 3962–3963, and 29 November 1906, pp. 3998–3999.

[68] Dernburg, 28 November 1906, p. 3966.

of German colonial development in terms of the relationship between "guardian" and "ward," "adult" and "adolescent."[69] However, whatever the approach to colonial economy-building, the German *Industriestaat*'s plans were far ahead of reality. In 1908, the currency in circulation in those German colonies in Africa in which the mark was the standard coin only amounted to about 1% of the currency circulation of Germany.[70]

Conclusion

Connections existed between specific designs of colonial monetisation in British and German Africa, national conceptions of economic development, and the objectives of states to organise transnational economic spaces. The choice of standard coinage, currency denominations, exchange rate regulations and other aspects of colonial currency systems in the 1900s and 1910s not only bore out considerations of the functional management of modern currency and concerns about international monetary relations. Rather, blueprints for currency systems in African colonies were formulated on the basis of expectations regarding the nature of economic development; they were strategies of economic steering aimed at supporting national economic visions in the globe.

For advocates of a global British economy, colonial monetisation in tropical Africa was a distraction in a continent considered to be marginal to Britain's international economic policy. The principal aim was to avert possible risks posed by a silver circulation associated with the pound sterling operating on the gold standard by compartmentalising colonial economic spaces. However, in East Africa, the British Treasury also intended to push for a gold-based economy in the medium and long term. Lobbyists for a constructivist colonial-imperial economy, on the other hand, argued about money in Africa from the perspective of promoting a colonial variant of "African" development. Important concerns were, therefore, the raising of income from seigniorage, and the

[69] "Herrenvolk" and "dienende Rasse," "Vormund" and "Mündel," "Erwachsene" and "Minderjährige," *Reichstagsprotokolle*, 6 March 1913, p. 4334. www.reichstagsprotokolle.de. Accessed on 15 April 2021.

[70] See the table included with the coinage reform bill, 1907, p. 17, attached with *Reichstagsprotokolle*, 19 March 1908. www.reichstagsprotokolle.de. Accessed on 15 April 2021.

regulation of subsidiary coinage used by Africans. Local colonial administrators involved with currency matters often prioritised regional economic visions, before Britain ordered colonial economies in tropical Africa with the currency board system as an adjunct to the imperial economy. Notably officials in British East Africa had focused on the Indian rupee as the core factor in economy-building.

Unlike the British case, the colonial monetary system in German East Africa was designed by prominent economic and financial experts of the *Industriestaat* as a means to support a German economy with a global reach. Helfferich formulated regulations for the German rupee in the explicit attempt to carve out and delineate a political-economic space rivalling Britain. In terms of strategies and techniques, however, Britain served as the model. The German state took on a distinct role in organising colonial money in a vision of economic development that differed from German colonial interest groups as well as from high finance. The implementation of these conceptions petered out during the First World War, though their underlying ideas left an imprint on arguments about the hypothetical role of colonies for a global German economy in the interwar period.

The aim of this chapter was to historicise approaches to colonial money by British and German policymakers in Africa in the early twentieth century in their transnational and international dimension. As an afterthought, some observations are due to clarify the nexus between policy formation and economic theories in academia that informed parallel debates. Near-contemporary discussions on Helfferich as an academic are instructive here. For instance, the British economist Roy Harrod (1928) criticised Helfferich's treatise on money for lacking an overall theoretical conception and for being fixated on an evolutionary view from silver to gold currencies. Harrod, however, praised the work for moving towards a conception of money in terms of its value on a market, as shown, among others, with the analysis of the rupee. Such an approach differed from that of Helfferich's teacher Georg Friedrich Knapp, who argued that the value of money could be "created" by the power of the state. Incidentally, Ludwig von Mises (1924–1925) of the Austrian school of economics castigated Helfferich precisely for advocating a state theory of money. One could add that Helfferich offered no theoretical argument about trade and colonies. In general terms, he believed that the state was a force that generated economic growth through its institutions and ability to organise private economic agents. In Britain, Lugard similarly emphasised state governance as the main tool to foster social, cultural and economic development in British colonial Africa. Unlike Helfferich, however, Lugard had no ambitions as an economist. British Treasury officials, on the other hand, referred to an established orthodoxy regarding the role of the gold standard in imperial and global development. But the doctrine was a mere undercurrent that justified policy while officials fine-tuned economic steering centring on the British economy and the pound sterling.

In the light of the above, one could pursue a line of enquiry that assesses the validity of policy choices in terms of academic economic theory. Ideas of economic development could be objectivised, among others, with regard to theoretical debates about the workings of the gold standard, trade and economic growth, and even fundamental questions regarding the state and money in the economy. Yet it is important to bear in mind that such an assessment differs in its investigative objectives from the present analysis and does not constitute a valid counterfactual tool to assess policy. As this chapter has shown, policy designs and practices did not flow from coherent economic theory but formed contextually as a political process informed by general assumptions of development.

References

Aiyar, Sana. 2015. *Indians in Kenya: The Politics of Diaspora*. Cambridge, MA: Harvard University Press.

Arbuthnoth, George, ed. 1857. *Regulating the Issue of Banknotes, Vindicated*. London: Longman, Brown, Green, Longmans, and Roberts.

Balachandran, G. (1996) 2015. *John Bullion's Empire*. London: Curzon/Routledge.

———. 2019. "Money and Its Ideas: Colonial Currency, Money Illusions." In *A Cultural History of Money*, Vol. 5, edited by Federico Neiburg and Nigel Dodd, 35–55. London: Bloomsbury Academic.

Carland, John M. 1990. "The Colonial Office and the First West African Note Issue." *International Journal of African Historical Studies* 23: 495–502.

Cohen, Benjamin. 1998. *The Geography of Money*. Ithaca, NY: Cornell University Press.

Dernburg, Bernhard. 1907. *Zielpunkte des deutschen Kolonialwesens*. Berlin: Ernst Siegfried Mittler & Sohn.

Gardner, Leigh A. 2015. "The Curious Incident of the Franc in the Gambia: Exchange Rate Instability and Imperial Monetary Systems in the 1920s." *Financial History Review* 22: 291–314.

———. 2022. "The Collapse of the Gold Standard in Africa: Money and Colonialism in the Interwar Period." In *Transnational Money and Economy and State Formation in Africa, 1860s–1960s*, edited by Gerold Krozewski and Tinashe Nyamunda [forum issue, *African Studies Review*].

Giffen, Robert. 1892. *The Case against Bimetallism*. London: George Bell and Sons.

Harrod, Roy F. 1928. "Karl Helfferich. *Money*," *Economic Journal* 38 (149): 98–101.

Helfferich, Carl Theodor. 1895. *Bimetallistische Kampfesart. Eine Auseinandersetzung mit Herrn Dr. O. Arendt*. Neustadt am Hdt.: Kommissionsverlag.

Helfferich, Karl, ed. 1900. *Ludwig Bamberger. Ausgewählte Reden und Aufsätze über Geld- und Bankwesen*. Berlin: J. Guttentag.

———. (1903) 1923. *Das Geld*. 6th revised ed. Leipzig: C.L. Hirschfeld.

Helleiner, Eric. 2003. *The Making of National Money: Territorial Currencies in Historical Perspective*. Ithaca, NY: Cornell University Press.

Hermann, Robin. 2011. "Empire Builders and Mushroom Gentlemen: The Meaning of Money in Colonial Nigeria." *International Journal of African Historical Studies* 44: 393–413.

Hintze, Willy. 1912. *Das Geldwesen in den deutschen Schutzgebieten*. Berlin: J. Guttentag.

Hopkins, A. G. 1970. "The Creation of a Colonial Monetary System: The Origins of the West African Currency Board." *African Historical Studies* 3: 101–132.

Jessop, David. 1976. "The Colonial Stock Act of 1900: A Symptom of the New Imperialism?" *Journal of Imperial and Commonwealth History* 4: 154–164.

Krozewski, Gerold. 2011. "Problematizing an 'Imperialism of Intent:' Colonial Raw Materials, Globalism, and European Nation States, from the Pre-1914 Period to the 1930s." In *Africa, Empire and Globalization*, edited by Toyin Falola and Emily Brownell, 357–376. Durham: Carolina Academic Press.

Kuroda, Akinobu, 2020. *A Global History of Money*. London: Routledge.

Lugard, Frederick. 1922. *The Dual Mandate in Tropical Africa*. London: Routledge reprint.

Maxon, Robert M. 1989. "The Kenya Currency Crisis, 1919–21 and the Imperial Dilemma." *Journal of Imperial and Commonwealth History* 17: 323–348.

Mises, Ludwig. 1924–1925. "Karl Helfferich. *Das Geld*," *Zeitschrift für Volkswirtschaft und Sozialpolitik* 4: 160.

Mwangi, Wambui. 2001. "Of Coins and Conquest: The East African Currency Board, the Rupee Crisis, and the Problem of Colonialism in the East African Protectorate." *Comparative Studies in Society and History* 43 (4): 763–786.

Narsey, Wadan. 2016. *British Imperialism and the Making of Colonial Currency Systems*. Basingstoke: Palgrave Macmillan.

Pallaver, Karin. 2015. "'The African Native has No Pocket:' Monetary Practices and Currency Transitions in Early Colonial Uganda." *International Journal of African Historical Studies* 48 (3): 471–499.

———. 2019. "A Currency Muddle: Resistance, Materialities, and the Local Use of Money during the East African Rupee Crisis (1919-1923)." *Journal of Eastern African Studies* 13 (3): 546–564.

———. 2022. "From German East African Rupees to British East African Shillings in Tanganyika: The King and the Kaiser Side by Side." In *Transnational Money and Economy and State Formation in Africa, 1860s–1960s*, edited by Gerold Krozewski and Tinashe Nyamunda [forum issue, *African Studies Review*].

Williamson, John G. 1971. *Karl Helfferich 1872–1924: Economist, Financier, Politician*. Princeton, NJ: Princeton University Press.

CHAPTER 11

Another History of Money Viewed from Africa and Asia

Akinobu Kuroda

Revisiting Inconvertible Currencies from the Ground

Modernity in money has been implicitly discussed from a viewpoint of a state-oriented teleology. Such a viewpoint implies that, like water flowing downward, sooner or later, a monetary system will incorporate transactions nationwide into a coherent order under governmental control. Here, the goal towards which a monetary system endogenously evolves as market activities develop within the territory of the state would be the establishment of a set of convertible currencies under one sovereign authority. Colonies should have been no exception. Contemporary researchers in West Africa and Indochina before the Second World War, for example, had no hesitation in depicting as unsophisticated or

A. Kuroda (✉)
University of Tokyo, Tokyo, Japan
e-mail: ankuroda@ioc.u-tokyo.ac.jp

K. Pallaver (ed.), *Monetary Transitions*, Palgrave Studies in Economic History, https://doi.org/10.1007/978-3-030-83461-6_11

unreasonable the attitudes of local people towards supporting inconvertible currencies of their own (McPhee 1926, p. 248; Robequain 1939, p. 157).

Convertibility between currencies means there is no transaction costs associated with the exchange of inconvertible currencies within a country. Once this idea is accepted, it is not so difficult to narrate a story of monetary evolution that can be applied universally to any society. Whenever a phenomenon which is not in conformity with a convertible currency under state sovereignty is encountered, it is located among activities associated with pre-modernity, with backwardness in an evolutionistic sense, or with embeddedness within an indigenous culture in a relativistic fashion.[1] According to this concept, a fluctuating exchange rate between currencies should be fixed to provide the market with certainty for transactions on subsequent occasions. Fixed proportions among different denominations should work to reduce the cost of issuing a large quantity of small denomination currency.

In these terms, a modern history of money should resemble a process of moulding activities using inconvertible currencies into a system of a national convertible currency. Currencies exclusively mediating local transactions should be integrated into a currency available across a nation in order to facilitate interregional exchanges and consequently to enhance the division of labour beyond a locality. Convertibility between small and large denomination currencies should also boost long-distance trade and economize the remittance of official revenue by cutting the transportation cost of coins. The propositions mentioned above fit the expectations of rulers whose administrations depend on taxation paid in currency, and of the authorities for monetary supply who profit through a monopoly in currency issue.[2]

[1] Conveniently some scholars interpreted inconvertible currencies in Africa as special-purpose money. For example, Bohannan and Dalton characterized the separation of the unit of account and the actual means of exchange as an example of special-purpose money which revealed the peripheral role of the market principle, in contrast with a single all-purpose money which is necessary for the market principle to fully function (Bohannan and Dalton 1962, p. 12). They located the disconnection outside market activities without considering the reason why a unit of account was detached from a means of exchange. Thus, unfortunately, they could not resist a teleological framework that did not reflect history.

[2] Karl Polanyi distinguished the "internal market" created by state intervention from both local and distant markets. By "state", he actually meant European mercantile

When turning, however, from the perspective of the state to people engaged in business at the ground level, the same phenomenon tells quite a different story. Where peasants made up the majority of inhabitants and most exchanges were made among them locally, such exchanges inevitably experienced a seasonal surge after harvest and a contraction in the slack season. Transactions among peasants were of small amounts, requiring fractional denominations of currency, unless deferred payment was used. The more freely a small-household peasant could negotiate in a marketplace where one-time transactions dominated, the smaller the denomination of currency they needed to reach a mutually agreed price. Fractional currencies mediating transactions in a marketplace were not always in accord with the means of exchange supplied by merchants engaged in long-distance trade. From the viewpoint of providing peasants with a means of exchange on the spot, an unfixed exchange rate between a local currency in a smaller denomination and an interregional currency in a larger denomination could work to supply a flexible means of exchange in transactions between the end-users. In this way, the two currencies work in a complementary, rather than a substitutive, relationship.[3]

Simply speaking, the necessity for a fractional currency changes, and the effect of a floating exchange rate between the means of proximate and distant exchange varies according to the degree of freedom of the ordinary peasant. As far as market activities depend on one-time transactions, local dealers engaging in exchanging currencies functioned to prevent the marketplace from suspending activities due to shortages of currency supply. A society relying on currency actually tends to suffer from chronic shortages of currency, since a currency is easily distributed among end-users while being less easily retrieved from the end-users on demand. A fractional currency in particular tended to remain with the end-user

states. He thought that, unlike the combination of local market and long-distance trade, the internal market developed through competition. Not delving into the difference in exchanges between local markets and interregional markets, he assumed the existence of political or social factors permanently separating proximate and distant exchanges. Unfortunately, he did not try to find any coherent reason why local currencies independent of interregional currencies so commonly existed (Polanyi 1957, pp. 56–67).

[3] Citing that gold and cowries made a set of currency in most parts of West Africa, Hopkins was doubtful about applying the concept of special-purpose money to Africa. He could have made clearer his objection to the idea of a "market principle" that ignored the variety in exchanges if he found that complementarity among monies was universal beyond Africa (Hopkins 1973, pp. 69–70).

and not return to the marketplace. When a marketplace encountered a serious scarcity of currency, local dealers did not hesitate to generate a means of exchange locally by themselves, even as a temporary device, to meet the demand for transactions among end-users. Thus, from the viewpoint of end-users, locality and/or temporariness of money reflected their demands (Kuroda 2020).

Across the world and throughout history, the most salable goods, such as grains and cloth, often worked as money among ordinary peasants. This is quite an endogenous means of exchange for local transactions, in so far as the grain or cloth are produced locally. In some societies, meanwhile, the authorities provided people with metallic currencies whose values were low enough for the populace to use to make transactions. Since such currencies of low value could not be expected to bring in a high seigniorage, rulers often issued them mainly for military purposes, supplying food for soldiers. In other societies, fractional currencies of a distant origin were imported by traders into the marketplace for peasants. Typically, cowries, shell money from the Maldives, were carried into the inland of southwest China (Yunnan), eastern India (Bengal, Orissa), and West Africa. Rulers sometimes used cowries for their taxation and administration, but it was traders who imported bulky cowries at a distance and distributed them among inland villages. In Africa, some endogenous currencies originally produced manually were substituted by those manufactured by foreign factories in the nineteenth century. A large quantity of cotton cloth from Massachusetts (and later from Bombay) worked as money (Pallaver 2019, pp. 76–77; Prestholdt 2008, pp. 74–85), as did *manillas* made of brass, manufactured in Birmingham and Nantes (Guyer 2004, p. 72) and glass beads from Venice (Pallaver 2009).

The long journey of some foreign-origin currency reveals an aspect of what caused locals to actually accept an item as money. It was a shared recognition among dealers along a trade circuit of an item as money, rather than any enforcement by the authorities and/or the intrinsic value of the item, that sustained the acceptability of the item as money in long-distance exchange. In medieval East Asia, copper coins bearing era names of the Song (960–1279) dynasty continued to circulate until the seventeenth century across the China Sea region. In particular, old Chinese coins dominated transactions of high value, such as land sales, in medieval Japan. At that time, the physical appearance of coins, including the use of old era names, mattered to local dealers when shroffing coins between standard coins for accumulating assets and operational coins for local transactions.[4] A similar phenomenon was associated with the widespread circulation of the Maria Theresa dollar (MTT) in Africa and the Middle East until the early twentieth century. Here silver coins bearing the date of 1780 and minted in Vienna continued to circulate at a premium. Keeping the same Empress's head and the same date was more decisive in it being accepted by local dealers than any intrinsic value or authorization (Kuroda 2007). In extending those findings more generally, we can see that neither commodity value nor government enforcement is a necessary condition to generate money, though both conditions can enhance people's acceptance of it. A long circuit of dealers who all recognized the old appearance of the item endorsed its acceptability as money beyond the locality. Such cases demonstrate that money works as a social circuit connecting transaction demand.

A function endogenously mediating exchanges locally made does not exclude other exogenously organizing payments being settled at a distance. These are not always in a substitutive relationship but often in a complementary relationship. A division of labour between copper coins for proximate exchange and silk (later silver ingots) for long-distance exchange existed throughout ancient Chinese history. In India cowries serving transactions in rural marketplaces and silver rupees settling long-distance business and tax payments mutually depended on each other, as did cowries and *manillas* in West Africa and *amole* (salt bars) in Ethiopia, which complemented other currencies, including the Maria Theresa dollar (Kuroda 2020). Coupling between the endogenous invention of money and the exogenous introduction of money always generated a variety of customs in the intermediary sphere that interfaced bottom-up monetary establishment and top-down monetary regulation. In the mezzo-scope sphere, neither micro nor macro, implicit or explicit agreements among dealers generated various devices such as imaginary money and currency circuits, for the purpose of maintaining a monetary supply to meet demand in a flexible way.

A global history of money viewed from the ground makes clear the ubiquity of inconvertible currencies that include fractional currencies, petit dealers, and local customs not in accordance with interregional settlements. In other words, such currencies resulted from a common demand for endogenous exchanges. However, ubiquity does not exclude

[4] Akinobu Kuroda, "Old Chinese Coins Standard in Medieval Japan: Demonetized and Imitation Coinages Mediating Exchanges beyond the Sea" (Unpublished).

the possibility that each civilization possesses its own characteristics in the monetary system. What is striking about precolonial African money is its openness towards an interregional, including intercontinental, flow of items that worked as money. Cowries, glass beads, *manillas*, mechanically woven cloth, and the Maria Theresa dollar circulated as currency in Africa, though they were not used as money in their places of origin. Cowries also circulated in India, and the Mexican silver dollar won popularity in China in a similar way to the MTT in Africa. However, monetary supply in precolonial Africa appeared to depend on items from abroad to a greater degree than in Asia. We will consider what the differences mean in this chapter.

Peasants, Marketplace, and *Atomic* Currencies

Across the world and throughout history there has been a high probability that fractional-value currencies such as cowries were required particularly for transactions made at marketplaces where a number of peasants gathered for exchange.[5] It often happened that dealers purchasing the products brought by local peasants must have prepared a significant amount of small currencies whose denominations fitted the size of the transactions made by ordinary peasants. Thus, as far as dealers conveyed portable large denomination currencies, they had to exchange large denomination currencies for small denomination ones. Importantly, dealers would agree to a loss in conversion from large to small, since the demand for small currencies on the spot caused them to appreciate.

In other words, there is no demand for fractional-value currencies where there are no marketplaces. For example, the Wolof people in Gambia had few marketplaces and they used cloth as currency, not fractional-value currencies. In the early twentieth century a strip of cloth five inches wide and seventy inches long was valued at threepence and sixteen strips were equivalent to one large goat (Ames 1962, p. 40). In contrast with the use of cowries in other areas of West Africa, the Wolof did not use fractional currencies whose values were smaller than

[5] To take an example from outside Africa and Asia, in early twentieth-century Mexico, fractional currency was required so much that 1 copper centavo, the smallest coin, was cut in half and used as currency in marketplaces. Shortages of coin caused wood and salt to be used as currency in the highlands (Maliknowski and de la Fuente 1982, pp. 144–145, 200).

the cloth strips. They were too expensive to use in negotiations in the marketplace. Actually, an observation of a Wolof household by Ames, in 1950–1951, revealed that most exchanges were made among neighbours without going to the marketplace (Ames 1962, pp. 44–45).

An English observer at a marketplace in early nineteenth-century India gives us a vivid example. On the morning of the market day, exchangers brought to the marketplace as many cowries as they could carry on their head or on the back of an ox. They exchanged 5760 cowries for a silver rupee in the morning and gave a rupee for 5920 cowries in the evening. A Japanese research group found in a periodic market in early-1930s China that merchants from the city had to convert silver dollars into copper coins in order to do business there, since local peasants brought small quantities of goods, such as ten to twenty eggs, while a silver dollar was valued at around one hundred eggs. Petit exchangers worked to sell copper coins for silver dollars at a fluctuating rate according to demand/supply (Kuroda 2020, pp. 31–32).

A fluctuating rate between currencies and the importance of dealers were evident in Africa as well. In early twentieth-century Ethiopia the rate of a salt bar to a MTT changed according to, for example, famine or military action. An American observed that in such a situation one of ten locals engaged in exchange to make a profit (Kuroda 2007). Importantly, harvests caused the exchange rate of small currencies to appreciate by season. For example, the exchange rate of *manilla*s in terms of sterling rose during the harvest season in West Africa (United Africa Company 1949, pp. 47–48).

How small was the currency required in transactions among end-users? Robequain observed in early twentieth-century Indochina that locals made a zinc coin, *sapèques*, small enough to purchase a slice of papaya or a cup of tea (Robequain 1939, p. 155). Hereafter, we will call a single unit currency for indivisibly minute transactions *atomic* currency.[6] It might not have been just a coincidence that daily wages for unskilled labour were quoted at around one hundred pieces of currency in different societies, such as 100 cowries in Uganda around 1900 (Pallaver 2015, p. 489), 100 copper coins in Taiyuan, China, around 1900 (Kuroda 2020, p. 133),

[6] The king of Buganda tried to fix the price of ten small fish at one cowrie in the late nineteenth century (Pallaver 2015, p. 478). Depending on the situation, even the value of a cowrie might not have been sufficiently fractional.

and 100 copper coins in Ikeda, Japan, late eighteenth century (Nakagawa 2003, p. 305).

Meanwhile, dependence on fractional currencies apparently brought inconvenience. Atomic currencies are so bulky that dealers cannot carry them without paying a significant cost. The experience of C. H. Robinson, a Briton travelling in West Africa, highlights this point. He failed to sell an unserviceable horse since he would need to hire fifteen porters to carry cowries to complete the transaction; this would make the deal meaningless for him (Vice 1983, p. 13).

The merit of supplying atomic currencies in a marketplace is to support the seller and the buyer, both of whom were engaged in small business, in minutely gradating the price through negotiation and enabling them to finally find a point where both could agree. However, while it is easy to distribute fractional currencies to end-users, it is not easy to reassemble them from the end-users on demand. As a result, a significant quantity of small currencies had less opportunity to return the way they came and stayed within the households of the end-users. Some were piled up in treasure houses; Basden observed heaps of cowries in an Igbo village (Basden 1921, p. 199). Alternatively, they were buried, awaiting the chance to be reused. Sometimes such a chance did not arise, and they were left underground, to be occasionally dug up at a later period by peasants, construction workers, or archaeologists.

A copper coin hoard dating from late nineteenth-century Sichuan, China, shows that the majority of coins were minted in the mid-eighteenth century (Kuroda 2020, pp. 46–47). They stayed underground for a century and a half, waiting to be used. There are similar cases across the world, including in Africa. In 1912, when suffering low cash reserves, the French West African government tried to collect a poll tax from locals. It received a significant amount of 5- and 10-centime coins dated 1855 with the image of Napoleon III, while people in Dahomey tried to keep 1- and 2-centime coins and prevented the government from retiring the smallest coins (Manning 1982, pp. 60, 312). We can only imagine how huge quantities of cowries must have been buried underground, though, unlike coins with dates, shell money does not allow us to tell the year they were collected from the sea.

Stagnancy of currency with end-users meant that while currency proliferated it was rarely assembled. In other words, such currencies made just a one-way trip. In particular, a large quantity of cowries from the Maldives, *manillas* from Birmingham and Nantes, and glass beads from Venice made a long single journey as far as villages and towns in West and East Africa but never made any return trip, even though some may have been collected by a local bureau through taxation. On the other hand, some currencies working to bridge local marketplaces did travel bilaterally, or made a long circuit to return to a hub city. The case of the Maria Theresa dollar shows a circuit crossing several administrations. The Austrian silver dollars were transported from Aden to Gare in West Ethiopia to purchase coffee, and passed through Gambella and Khartoum to Port Sudan in exchange for cloth, before returning to Aden (Kuroda 2007). However, we should note that, at the continental level, the silver dollars only made a single trip from Vienna to Africa or the Middle East and never returned. This means that other devices facilitating bilateral settlements internationally, such as the pound sterling, were used in collaboration with the MTT. Complementary combination of currencies could organize several layers of exchange, from local to global.

Local currencies mediating mainly proximate exchanges were ubiquitous across the world. In the case of early twentieth-century China, native notes issued by local dealers functioned as a device for supplementing currency shortages. They were available mostly within a walkable distance (Kuroda 2020, p. 180). The notes were usually denominated in copper coin with a square hole in the centre. They are referred to as copper cashes. Copper cashes were atomic currencies issued by Chinese dynasties for two millennia. The use of copper cashes generated units of a larger denomination when dealers tied a certain quantity of the coins together by a string, thus avoiding always counting them piece by piece in transactions. The quantity of copper cashes tied together differed region by region, and sometimes commodity by commodity. The differentiation by locality in the quantity tied together also appeared in the custom of using cowries in Africa. Naturally, in both China and Africa, dealers conducted business in terms of string oftener than in terms of atomic unit. However, it did not mean that they neglected quantities smaller than a string of currency. Foreign observers recorded that local merchants sometimes spent long hours counting copper cashes piece by piece in China (Smith 1899, p. 51) and cowries in West Africa (Law 1997, pp. 199–200). There were even professionals who counted cowries in the markets of Yorubaland (Ofonagoro 1979, p. 639).

Thus, we can confirm the widespread combination of peasants, marketplaces, atomic currencies, and petit dealers in Africa and Asia. The interdependent relationship between the local marketplace and long-distance trade resulted in the differences in monetary functions between local currencies and interregional currencies. There was an argument that the influx of precious metals into Africa did not cause a clear spike of prices, since gold and silver functioned not as money but as ornaments (Hogendorn and Johnson 1986, p. 146). A similar understanding also applied in India and China, that precious metals were absorbed by them not for monetary purposes (Kindleburger 1989, pp. 62–64, 70–72). Unfortunately, these scholars did not understand the multiplicity of market activities and the complementarity between local currencies and interregional ones, which caused precious-metal currencies to disconnect from price-making at the ground level.

However, the way of conjunction between proximate exchanges at the marketplace and at distant exchanges beyond the locality appeared to differ continent by continent. In Africa, a region in which atomic currencies mediated transactions among peasants at the marketplace adjoined another region in which neither minute money nor the market played an important role. For example, as mentioned earlier, the Wolof did not depend on marketplace exchanges and used mainly cloth. In the early twentieth century they used five-franc silver coins in cash transactions (Masaki 2016). Meanwhile, cowries were excavated from many archaeological sites across Senegal and Mali (Haour and Christie 2019). However, cowries were not in circulation as currency but used only for divination in Senegambia where the Wolof dwelled. In contrast, cowries worked importantly as currency in Mali and Songhay (Green 2019, pp. 71, 323–325).

It was found globally, including Africa and Asia, that rural markets made a periodic rotation circle in the opening days to facilitate peddlers' business. Although it is necessary to investigate further, Hill has pointed out the lack of hierarchal organization connecting marketplaces in West Africa (Hill 1966, pp. 297–298), especially in comparison with the case of China formulated by Skinner (Skinner 1964, pp. 9–10). Interestingly, the investigation in Katsina Emirate showed no close relationship between the density of population and the number of marketplaces (Hill 1971, pp. 308–309). In contrast, as the density of population increased, the number of marketplaces rose in Hebei, Jiangsu, and Zhejiang, China, in the eighteenth through early twentieth centuries (Ishihara 1987, pp. 111–114, 140–141). Denser networks connecting marketplaces generated a hierarchical structure inserting a reservoir between basic rural marketplaces and cities. The intermediate market worked as a place for peddlers to stock both the necessities sold to peasants and their products collected at basic markets, and to sell some sophisticated goods like stationery that local elites demanded (Skinner 1964, pp. 26–27).

The lesser importance of intermediate markets between basic marketplaces and long-distance trade routes meant that end-users of atomic currencies in marketplaces in West Africa might have more opportunities to directly expose their business to interregional dealers than those in China. The acceptance of foreign-origin currencies to a deeper degree in Africa, mentioned earlier, might have been in tandem with the direct connection of basic marketplaces with interregional trade circuits. The direct connections might explain why cowries, copper wire, and iron bars did not circulate together and formed an exclusive currency circuit respectively at the ground level. As a result, different types of currency circuits appeared side by side, like a mosaic, across the African continent. For example, in early twentieth-century Eastern Nigeria, traders relied on *manillas* and cowries in the Ngwa region, brass rods and copper wire along the Cross River, and gin and iron bars on the coast (Martin 1988, p. 43). Local currency circuits flourished in early twentieth-century China as well, but they differed one from the other by different kinds of the same item, such as different types of silver dollar much oftener than by different materials, as was the case in Eastern Nigeria mentioned above (Kuroda 2005).

It is impossible to explain what caused the difference in monetary usage between China and West Africa simply as whether or not intermediate markets were buffered between periodic rural markets and ports for long-distance trade. However, it might not be wrong to suppose that until the first decades of the nineteenth century a heavy dependence on the export of slaves from the inland to ports made a midway reservoir less necessary in West Africa than in China, since slaves transported themselves to their destinations on the coast. Even after a serious decrease in the Atlantic slave trade in the second half of the nineteenth century, local rulers used slave labour to farm goods such as palm oil to sell directly at the port. Some former slave ports survived as ports for shipping legitimate products, such as the case of Lagos (Hopkins 1973, p. 145). Importantly, large-scale palm collectors in West Africa may have been able to directly deal with European firms on the coast (Hill 1971, pp. 312–314). Later we will revisit this issue related to the organization of markets in examining the circulation of paper money.

Exporting Peasant Products Circulated New Currencies

It seems that, before the nineteenth century, African economies depended on intercontinental trade more heavily than Asian ones, since in many areas of the continent the slave trade pushed out a significant quantity of the labour force as a *commodity* from the inland to overseas. However, intercontinental trade did not have such a drastic affect as to transform African monetary structures. Distant trade stimulated the increase in usage of endogenous-type currencies, such as cowries, rather than bringing in currencies which were in circulation in Europe. The abolition of the slave trade in the nineteenth century made African economies depend more on the export of *legitimate* commodities such as palm oil, groundnuts, and hides. After colonial occupation, governments tried to introduce the currencies supplied by monetary authorities in Europe, but it was difficult to diffuse them among African end-users. Stagnant prices for agricultural commodities in Europe discouraged peasants in Africa from getting more involved in cash crop production through the second half of the nineteenth century, especially in the last quarter of the century, called by contemporaries the Great Depression in Europe (Hopkins 1973, p. 133). Throughout the period, the introduction of steamships and railways reduced the cost of transportation. The innovations decreased the cost of transporting precolonial currencies to the extent that they depreciated against European monies. However, in the last quarter of the nineteenth century, European currencies were not able to substitute for indigenous currencies; rather, they could work only by adapting to local conditions. For example, sterling silver coin tokens were backed by gold in Britain, but they had no specific backing in West Africa and were used with a strong appreciation in the season when export products were sold (Hopkins 1970, pp. 104–105). In this sense, although sterling silver was brought from Britain, it became inconvertible with currencies in the home country soon after it arrived in Africa.

Unlike an economy dependent on plantations, an economy based on numerous peasant households did not allow foreign firms to control producers' activities at the ground level. Under such an extremely decentralized condition, in collecting their products European authorities had to supply currencies whose value was fractional enough to be equivalent with African *atomic* currencies. Until the end of the nineteenth century, unlike the early twentieth century as we will see, there was not yet such a strong demand for peasant products in Africa to the extent that European firms would dare to spend a lot on substituting a new type of small currency for existing ones.

During the colonial period, traditional currencies were useful among African peasants for ceremonial occasions as well as for economic activities. In southeast Nigeria, for example, *manillas*, not British currency, were used for ceremonial purposes such as funerals and the payment of the bride price (Naanen 1993, p. 433). In East Africa, cowries had been indispensable for performing bridal ceremonies (Pallaver 2015, p. 491).

Meanwhile, in the marketplace, westerners observed that Africans were very keen to make profits through exchanges (Basden 1921, pp. 196–197). For example, when Europe suffered from a cotton famine in the 1860s caused by the American Civil War, Senegalese farmers chose to cultivate groundnuts instead of cotton because they knew precisely that the former provided a higher profit. In another example, farmers in the Gold Coast and southern Nigeria began cocoa farming in the 1880s exactly when the export of palm oil and groundnuts declined. African peasants had a strategic sense to flexibly change their crops according to market conditions (Hopkins 1973, pp. 137–139), but circumstances had not been favourable enough for them to make the most of their business sense until the end of the nineteenth century.

The tide of global trade turned around 1900. Intercontinental trade then penetrated marketplaces inland to absorb peasant products for the first time. After the stagnant prices of the 1870s through mid-1890s, the terms of trade for agricultural products kept rising until the First World War. Unlike slaves in the previous period, products by peasants at the ground level became important export commodities. In the case of West Africa, typically, palm oil significantly increased its export to Europe. The strong demand for peasant products caused prices to rise enough for locals to enlarge their production. The boom brought a general rise in prices by 300% between 1904 and 1920 in Southern Nigeria (Ofonagoro 1979, p. 651).[7] Rapidly rising prices at the ground level attracted a large number of small households to the export economy, besides landlords who had connections with foreign firms in coastal ports. In contrast with plantations, middlemen had to prepare a large quantity of cash to pay the peasants. Unlike the previous period, however, the better terms

[7] Basden observed that prices had increased in the villages of the Igbos after 1900 (Basden 1921, p. 198).

offered for trade persuaded local peasants to accept a new type of currency of a higher denomination instead of indigenous currencies. Endogenous currencies did not disappear as quickly as the colonial governments had expected, but the export boom, in conjunction with tax payments set in colonial currencies, supported the penetration of these currencies into local markets.[8]

The rising demand for palm oil resulted from the development of the chemical oil industry in Europe. The demand for vegetable oils was spurred by their use as butter substitutes, for the production of soap, for lubricant for machineries, and for making bullets. Apparently, palm oil did not monopolize the supply and the import of other vegetal oil and seeds to Europe increased significantly. The prices of linseed from India and sesame oil from China also rose during the two decades before the First World War (Kuroda 2020, pp. 172–173).

Importantly, parallel stories appeared in societies other than Africa where peasant households dominated the economy. In China, until the end of the nineteenth century, copper cashes continued to mediate transactions in rural markets. Through two millennia of Chinese imperial history, some dynasties tried to issue multiple unit currencies instead of the mono unit currency, that is copper cashes, but no ruler could maintain the issue of multiple unit coins for long, since end-users did not accept them at the face value regulated by the authorities. At the turn of the twentieth century, provincial mints started to issue machine-made copper coins with no hole in the centre. They had multiple units of face value, mainly ten *wen*. In contrast with previous attempts, ten-*wen* copper coins were successfully circulated and gradually substituted for copper cashes. The degree of substitution differed from province to province. The successful provinces appeared to have been those with a growing export of peasant products from treaty ports. Not governmental force, but rather increasing prices for their products, persuaded peasants to accept a currency whose face value was larger than traditional currencies. Importantly, the most successful province, Hebei, was able to circulate paper money which was convertible with the new machine-made coins. The combination of paper money (mostly 1000 *wen*) and the new copper coin (10 *wen*) was able to respond to growing monetary demands by both dealers and peasants (Kuroda 2005).

[8] The introduction of new export crops, such as cotton in Uganda, also encouraged colonial coins to circulate (Pallaver 2015, p. 498).

Roughly during the two decades before the First World War, traditional currencies that mediated peasants' transactions began to disappear and machine-made coins gradually proliferated among Asian peasants. In Indochina, under the French colonial government, Chinese style copper coins, *dongs* or *sapèques*, gradually decreased in circulation (Robequain 1939, pp. 155–157). In Thailand, under an independent monarchy, the use of cowries was discontinued (Ingram 1955, p. 149). Importantly, the transformation of endogenous atomic currencies into small denomination coins in the modern form accompanied the proliferation of paper money. In Indochina, the annual issue of Banque de l'Indochine (BIC) banknotes in francs doubled in amount between 1903 and 1913 (Gonjo 1993, p. 372). In Thailand, the annual issue of government paper money in baht increased seven times during the same period (Ingram 1955, p. 154). The increasing issue of provincial paper notes in Manchuria, China, in the early twentieth century was in response to the growth of soya bean and soya oil exports from Dalian. The seasonal appreciation of provincial notes in the harvest season indicates that the notes facilitated the absorption of a large quantity of soya beans from the inland (Kaminishi 2013).

Thus, the transition of currencies in Africa in the early twentieth century occurred along a global tide of monetary transformation penetrating to the ground level. Importantly, the change from traditional currencies to colonial ones in West Africa was set in motion by Africans engaging in exporting peasant products rather than European firms clinging to transactions in kind. For example, the Niger River Company did not conduct cash trade until around 1905. Rising prices for local products attracted African producers to accept new currencies in so far as they could expect more profits through the transformation. The profits to be made through exporting cash crops encouraged a large number of peasants to move seasonally to coastal regions, which increased the amount of groundnuts, cocoa, and oil palms planted (Hopkins 1973, pp. 223–225). We should not overlook that this trade boom for peasant products coincided with the emancipation of slaves inside Africa. According to an estimate in 1905 there were two million slaves in French West Africa, 300,000 of whom were freed in the period 1905–1907 and emancipation continued in both British and French West Africa through the early twentieth century. Increasing demand for agricultural labour must have encouraged ex-slaves to establish themselves as free farmers (Hopkins 1973, pp. 226–227).

Increasing export of peasant products brought European currencies into circulation with which Africans could purchase imported commodities and pay taxes. In British West Africa the annual circulation of British sterling silver increased from £24,426 on average between 1886 and 1890 to £666,190 between 1906 and 1910 (McPhee 1926, p. 236). In addition, in 1908, subsidiary nickel and aluminium coins with a face value of one penny and one-tenth of a penny were introduced to substitute for cowries and *manillas* in British West Africa (McPhee 1926, p. 238; Hopkins 1970, p. 124).

What happened across the world in the two decades before the First World War was that rising prices for peasant products, including those made in Asia and Africa, bridged denominations representing monetary usage in industrial countries and those reflecting monetary usage in peasant economies. Higher denominations in the former and lower denominations in the latter did not always reflect the differences in wealth between nations. Though it is difficult to measure, according to one study, the daily wage for unskilled labour in late nineteenth-century England was around thirty pence (Burnett 1969, pp. 250–253). If we can take the daily wage in Uganda of 100 cowries, as mentioned above, and roughly assume that 100 cowries were equivalent to one penny, the money earned by a day's work in England could purchase what would take thirty days labour in Uganda. The exchange rate of a European currency against an indigenous one was far higher than the real value, reflecting that human labour lies at the base of the acceptability of currencies. One silver shilling worked as a fraction of numerous sterling pound currencies circulating across the British Empire, while shell money fulfilled its function within a marketplace zone after being dispersed among end-users. The difference of scope in circulation between the silver shilling and cowries rather than the difference in real purchasing capability by people in Britain and in West Africa caused the former to be overvalued against the latter when the two currencies were exchanged. Increasing prices of peasant products in terms of European money in the early twentieth century acted to bury the denomination gap between the currencies in metropolitan countries and those in other regions including colonies through the circulation of convertible currencies among peasants engaged in producing export products.

Eventually, however, convertible currencies newly introduced could not sufficiently supply what end-users in peasant economies demanded. For example, in spite of the continual import of French currencies,

Dahomey always suffered from a chronic shortage of currency through the early twentieth century. Copper and lead coins with a face value of 10 cents, 5 cents, and 2 cents in particular were in extremely short supply. Thus in Ouidah and Abomey 50 centime silver coins were discounted by 5 and 10% in exchange for 10 centime and 5 centime bronze coins (Manning 1982, p. 160). According to the official estimate in 1909, 1,100,000 francs worth of 50 centime pieces and 500,000 francs worth of 5 and 10 centime pieces were in the hands of the public (Manning 1982, p. 312). The dominance of the smallest denomination currency also appeared in Kenya and Uganda where the one-cent rupee coin was nearly half in value of colonial coins in circulation in 1921 (Pallaver 2018, p. 320).

Inevitably indigenous currencies still supplied what African societies demanded. Typically, cowries remained as the main currency in some areas such as Aplahoué in Benin. In 1908, to make tax payments in francs possible, the French administration had to give locals a few extra weeks to go to towns outside the region to exchange cowries for francs (Manning 1982, p. 158). The prohibition of importing *manillas* to eastern Nigeria in 1902 worked opposite to the official intention of abolishing *manillas* by stabilizing their value among end-users and leaving them still circulating until the Second World War (Naanen 1993).

Keeping in mind the shared trends examined in this section, we should note that there was an important difference between the convertible currencies of Asia and Africa. In Africa, a certain portion of paper money already circulated in the early twentieth century. For example, the Banque de l'Afrique Occidentale (BAO) was estimated to have provided 2.4 million francs in banknotes in 1909. Manning thought that the amount accounted for some 15% of the entire money supply in French Africa (Manning 1982, p. 161). The introduction of paper money in Africa was not later than in Asia, except for China and surrounding countries which had the earliest issue of paper money in the world. Thirty years later, however, the proportion did not necessarily rise significantly in Africa. This contrasts with the situation in Asia, as we will see in the next section.

Global Depression Revitalized Monetary Locality

During and after the First World War, the economies of exporting peasant products in Asia and Africa had a similar outlook. The loss of the European market for the products during the war caused peasant households in

Asia and Africa to suspend the cultivation of crops for export and switch to other crops according to profitability. Meanwhile, the contraction of imports from Europe encouraged local entrepreneurs to try a substitute industrialization across Asia and Africa. The boom for peasant products soon after the resumption of European trade was followed by a slump at the beginning of the 1920s. Towards the late 1920s, however, international trade in peasant products from Asia and Africa continued to grow.

Throughout the 1920s, in both Asia and Africa, there was a surge in credit supply to businesses exporting peasant products. For example, in Cochin-China, the Banque de l'Indochine increased lending to mutual credit associations from 99,642 piasters in 1913 to 15,108,778 piasters in 1930. Credit supply supported landowners to produce rice for export (Robequain 1939, pp. 193–195). In Ghana, the Kumasi branch of the Bank of British West Africa increased advances to European cocoa exporters from £106,187 in 1920–1921 to £411,927 in 1926–1927. European merchants gave advances to local cocoa brokers who collected cocoa from peasants (Austin 2005, pp. 283–284). However, the rapid growth in lending resulted in a series of defaults and credit crunches across the world, which became a part of the buildup to the Great Depression of 1929.

The global depression quickly affected the prices of peasant products from Asia and Africa in metropolitan countries. Table 11.1 shows that the price of rice from Saigon and the price of palm kernels from West Africa in London both decreased from 1930, falling by around 75% between 1929 and 1934. A common strategy in response to the falling prices of export products by those who involved in the export economy across Asia and Africa was to increase production. The export of palm kernels from French West Africa fell greatly in value from 64,527 thousand francs in 1930 to 27,884 thousand francs in 1935, while exports in volume slightly increased from 51,701 tons to 61,123 tons during the same period (Manning 1982, p. 382). In Southern Central Cameroon, cocoa planting had a peak in both total area and the number of plots between 1932 and 1935 (Guyer 1981, p. 76). There was a very similar trend in the Asian export peasant economy. The export of rice from French Indochina significantly decreased in value from 1198 million francs in 1930 to 665 million francs in 1935, while the volume of exports rose from 1121 thousand tons to 1765 thousand tons in 1935 (Touzet 1939, p. 244).

Table 11.1 Prices of Rice from Saigon and Palm Kernels from West Africa in London 1927–1935 (average in July of each year)

	Rice from Saigon (gold francs per quintal)	*Palm kernels from West Africa (gold francs per quintal*
1927	36.2	48.08
1928	28.96	51.26
1929	33.51	46.49
1930	28.75	30.86
1931	18.41	23.92
1932	14.83	19.39
1933	13.38	15.62
1934	9.17	10.32
1935	11.37	12.94

Sources International Yearbook of Agricultural Statistics. Rome: International Institute of Agriculture, 1931–1932, pp. 644, 649; 1934–1935, pp. 742, 747

The decrease in the value of exports meant a contraction of the monetary flow into the countries relying on exporting products. Maintaining the volume of exports implies that, in spite of unfavourable conditions, peasants did not switch their crops to others not aimed at foreign markets, but continued to produce export crops. Those statistics suggest that the export economy had already taken root very deeply in the colonies.

The shrinkage of the trade surplus due to the fall in the value of exports directly affected the issue of currency for colonies. The issue of banknotes greatly decreased after 1930 both in French West Africa and French Indochina, as shown in Table 11.2. Together with Table 11.1, we can see that the amount of banknotes put into circulation by Banque de l'Afrique Occidentale followed the price of palm kernels and that by Banque de l'Indochine chased the price of rice. Confirming a common trend, however, we should note that the slump in the circulation of banknotes by Banque de l'Afrique Occidentale was far greater than that by Banque de l'Indochine during 1932 and 1935.

Conditions in Africa may have been different from Asia. The fall in maritime trade brought European colonial administrators in Africa a serious decrease in revenue from maritime customs. The contraction of customs duties forced colonial governments in Africa to depend more on direct taxes imposed on peasants, and consequently more currency was retrieved from households by the authorities. Manning understood

Table 11.2 The amount of banknotes in circulation: French West Africa and French Indochina

	BAO (million francs)	*BIC (million francs)*
1903	0.16	40
1904	0.44	46
1905	0.65	46
1906	0.68	56
1907	0.78	52
1908	1.27	57
1909	1.16	60
1910	1.14	63
1911	2.15	63
1912	1.63	81
1913	1.87	86
1914	2.02	73
1915	1.89	89
1916	3.1	94
1917	5.1	139
1918	7.1	174
1919	14.2	474
1920	24.4	705
1921	15.3	618
1922	23	609
1923	31	831
1924	43	929
1925	49	1476
1926	64	1549
1927	69	1690
1928	77	1841
1929	86	1520
1930	39	1255
1931	29	1061
1932	31	965
1933	5.7	956
1934	5.3	998
1935	5.3	937
1936	13.2	1201
1937	43	1606
1938	48	1838
1939	62	2288

Sources Manning (1982, p. 413) (BAO); Gonjo (1993, pp. 372–375) (BIC)

that the decrease of official currencies through direct taxation caused a significant shortage of money in 1933–1936, the only period under colonization that direct taxation exceeded customs duties (Manning 1982, p. 254). However, we should rather pay attention to the unpopularity of banknotes in Africa rather than to the decrease of money in circulation in general.

Before the First World War, across the world, banknotes could basically only be issued with a full reserve of hard currency plus sound negotiable securities. The issue of paper monies in Asia and Africa could not deviate from this principle at that time. However, after the First World War, the issue of paper money in some Asian countries increased without a sufficient reserve. In the case of Banque de l'Indochine the rate of note reserve fell from 70% in 1910 to 9% in 1930 (Gonjo 1993, pp. 374–375). The proportion of coins against notes in circulation decreased with the increased issue of banknotes. In 1930, the French Indochina authority possessed 12 million piasters of silver, an amount thought to be equivalent to 10% of the amount of BIC banknotes in circulation (Touzet 1939, p. 118).

The proportion of coins against notes in colonial West Africa was quite different from that in Asia. A survey on 30 June, 1935, showed the breakdown of currency circulation in Nigeria as follows: West African silver coins £1,348,318; West African alloy coins £7,276,567; West African nickel-bronze coins £653,064; West African currency notes £717,295 (Nigeria. Chief Secretary's Office 1936, p. 73). Considering the large denomination gap, we can see how large quantity of small currencies was in circulation and what a small part paper money played in the entire monetary supply. According to another study, the proportion of notes in the estimated entire currency circulation in Nigeria changed as follows: 15% in 1926, 11% in 1936, and 18% in 1946 (Hawkins 1958, p. 347).

Not only was the proportion of notes against the amount of the entire monetary supply small in West Africa, but notes were often discounted against their face value in inland trade. It is considered that one reason paper money was not popular in West Africa was that the Currency Board failed to guarantee the convertibility of notes into coins on demand (Hawkins 1958, p. 346). However, whether a note is convertible is one thing, but whether the note is acceptable is another. For example, through the early twentieth century, banknotes proliferated in China often with discounts against their face values. In 1920, Banque de l'Indochine issued notes whose face value was 10 cents, 20 cents, and 50 cents. However, they were so unpopular that they were discounted against metallic currencies. In 1921–1922 French Indochina authorities minted a large number of 10 cent and 20 cent silver coins, withdrawing the small denomination banknotes (Touzet 1939, pp. 63–64).

Importantly, the increasing popularity of paper money in Asia did not mean that paper money could substitute for small denomination currency in transactions among end-users. Falling prices during the Great Depression revealed a strong demand for indigenous fractional currencies. In Tonkin, two kinds of copper coin called *sapèques*, equivalent to a half cent and a sixth cent in French francs, circulated even in the 1930s. One piaster was equivalent to 195 *sapèques* according to the order of the Annan emperor in 1934. That means that one indigenous copper coin was quoted at almost half a cent. That year, the French Indochina authority finally began to issue half-cent coins (Touzet 1939, p. 3).

West Africa also suffered from a chronic scarcity of small denomination currencies. Locals had no hesitation about reviving unearthed cowries as active currencies in the 1930s (Manning 1982, p. 254). In 1933 in the Idere area, 150 cowries were used in exchange for one penny (Hodder and Ukwu 1969, p. 47). Even in the early 1940s, the British authorities put a large quantity of tenth-pence nickel coins into the district where *manillas* were used in order to drive them out. The demand for the lowest denomination nickel coin was so strong that sometimes 11 pence of nickel coins were exchanged for the alloy shilling of 12 pence (Naanen 1993, p. 433). Thus, independent circulation at the ground level of fractional currencies, including traditional ones such as *sapèques* and cowries, occurred both in Indochina and West Africa, although the demand for infinitesimal-scale currency was stronger in West Africa than in Indochina.

Let us consider other traditional currencies that kept their popularity in West Africa. When, in 1948–1949, the British colonial government redeemed the *manillas*, 19% of the *manillas* stock came from the Ndoki district, which had been a centre for collecting palm oil. The positive relationship between the proliferation of *manillas* and the export of palm oil is quite apparent (Naanen 1993, p. 432). The redemption of *manillas* in 1940–1941 cost Britain a total of £401,135. Britain only got back £135,000 when they were melted (Naanen 1993, p. 445). We can see how highly the brass items, *manillas*, were overvalued when functioning as currency among local end-users.

However, *manillas* did not always function as fractional currency in the 1930s and 1940s. The *Okpoho manillas*, the commonest *manillas* in circulation, was redeemed at an exchange rate of 80 to £1 in 1948 (United Africa Company 1949, p. 54). One *Okpoho manillalas* was valued at three pence, not a small amount for locals. It might not have been just a coincidence that in the region in Gambia that used cloth currencies, the basic strip, *wala wala*, was valued at three pence as well. The two units of cloth currency most frequently used among the Wolof were valued at 6 pence and four shillings (Ames 1962, p. 38). Importantly, the *manillas* and cloth currencies worked as a unit of account in expensive transactions among locals. The British observed that people preferred the payment of dowry by *manillas* in the 1930s through the 1940s (Guyer 2004, p. 58). Colonial governments in West Africa could not substitute paper money for endogenous currencies that functioned as a device for accumulating assets to the extent that the government in Indochina did.

The decline of exports of peasant products in value during the Depression must have worked to reduce intra-African trade of such commodities as cattle and kola nuts (Hopkins 1973, p. 253). The contraction reduced the purchase of African goods through inland trade within Africa. Though it is difficult to measure the size of inland trade, there is a possibility that the loss of income from exports caused inland transactions at a distance to be in a slump and consequently decreased the demand for convertible currencies, such as banknotes by the BAO, which were available to settle long-distance trade in West Africa. From the viewpoint of complementarity among monies, the decrease in the supply of convertible currencies available for interregional trade as well local exchanges gave indigenous currencies the opportunity to revive in local exchange to the extent that they worked as a measure of accumulating assets and a unit of account.

Conclusion

Economic and cultural frameworks are indeed inextricably connected (Green 2019, p. 470). Among the Wolof in Gambia in the early twentieth century, cloth currencies were indispensable for fulfilling Muslim rituals (Ames 1962, p. 38). In the Kingdom of Kongo in the late eighteenth century, cloth currencies were used to wrap the corpses of the elite at their funerals. Among the Igbo in Nigeria in the early twentieth century, 900 *manillas* were required to join a powerful secret society (Green 2019, pp. 19–21). It is easy to imagine that banknotes could not substitute for *manillas* for those purposes, even though both the notes and brass items were actually made in Europe.

However, a variety of money does not always result from differences in culture. It is also important to examine if exchanges mediated by different currencies are fungible activities. Whether a particular money is indispensable for a local custom is one thing, but whether the money is available only within a locality is another. Keeping in mind the relationship between exchanges and social actions, we should note that exchanges have distinctions of themselves. We should pay especial attention to whether sellers and buyers can directly and multilaterally negotiate, which differentiates proximate exchange from long-distance exchange, and also whether sellers and buyers can anonymously make deals, which distinguishes cash transactions from deferred payments. Global history shows us that a variety of exchanges resulted in the complementarity among monies (Kuroda 2020).

A triangle dependence among small-size peasant households, proliferation of the marketplace, and preference for indivisible fractional-value currencies was shared by Africa and Asia. The investigations of peasant households in early twentieth-century China revealed that peasants changed crops according to the price movement at the marketplace where they could directly negotiate prices, and that monetary demand/supply at the marketplace remained independent from that for long-distance trade (Kuroda 2018). Peasants and petit dealers in West Africa appeared to conduct business in the same way. The incorporation of the peasant economy into international trade stimulated peasant households to accept new currencies, transferring profits to small holders in the early twentieth century. However, unlike the case of plantations, the export economy depending on metropolitan countries did not succeed in controlling peasant households at the ground level either in Africa or Asia. That is why cowries and *manillas* revived or survived in West Africa and local notes supplemented the shortage of currencies in China during the Great Depression (Kuroda 2020, pp. 189–190).

On the other hand, the different degree in the proportion of paper money in circulation between Africa and Asia gives an insight relating to the dissimilarity in the pattern of complementary relationship among monies between Africa and Asia. Though not yet examined sufficiently, how networks were organized for interregional exchange inland might have been different between the two. As far as the spread of banknotes outside trade ports in 1920s China was concerned, the acceptance of banknotes by native financiers in local towns increased the importance of banknotes in transactions (Kuroda 2020, pp. 178–179). A lower circulation of banknotes in West Africa in the early twentieth century may reflect the lesser importance of intermediary markets functioning as a bridge between trade ports and rural marketplaces.

The dissimilarity in money on the surface might have resulted from differences in the organization of exchanges at the lower level of markets. We should understand how differently exchanges are organized according to society and period before reducing the variety of money within the scope of embedded economy with culture.

References

Ames, David W. 1962. "The Rural Wolof of The Gambia." In *Markets in Africa*, edited by Paul Bohannan and Georges Dalton, 29–60. Evanston, IL: North Western University Press.

Austin, Gareth. 2005. *Labour, Land and Capital in Ghana: From Slavery to Free Labour in Asante, 1807–1956*. Rochester: University of Rochester Press.

Basden, Georges T. 1921. *Among the Ibos of Nigeria*. London: Seeley

Bohannan, Paul, and Georges Dalton. 1962. "Introduction." In *Markets in Africa*, edited by Paul Bohannan and Georges Dalton, 1–26. Evanston. IL: North Western University Press.

Burnett, John. 1969. *A History of the Cost of Living*. London: Pelican.

Gonjo, Yasuo. 1993. *Banque coloniale ou banque d'affaires: la Banque de l'Indochine sous la III e République*. Paris: Imprimerie nationale.

Green, Toby. 2019. *A Fistful of Shells: West Africa from the Rise of the Slave Trade to the Age of Revolution*, Chicago: University of Chicago Press.

Guyer, Jane I. 1981. "The Depression and the Administration in South-Central Cameroun." *African Economic History* 10: 67–79.

———. 2004. *Marginal Gains: Monetary Transactions in Atlantic Africa*, Chicago, IL: University of Chicago Press.

Haour, Anne, and Annalisa Christie. 2019. "Cowries in the Archaeology of West Africa: The Present Picture." *Azania: Archaeological Research in Africa* 54 (3): 287–321.

Hawkins, Edward K. 1958. "The Growth of a Money Economy in Nigeria and Ghana." *Oxford Economic Papers*. New Series 10 (3): 339–354.

Hill, Polly. 1966. "Notes on Traditional Market Authority and Market Periodicity in West Africa." *Journal of African History* 7 (2): 295–311.

———. 1971. "Two Types of West African House Trade." In *The Developent of Indigenous Trade and Markets in West Africa*, edited by Claude Meillassoux and Daryll Forde, 303–318. London: International African Institute.

Hodder, Bramwell W., and Ukwu I. Ukwu. 1969. *Markets in West Africa: Studies of Markets and Trade among the Yoruba and Ibo*. Ibadan: Ibadan University Press.

Hogendorn, Jan, and Marion Johnson. 1986. *The Shell Money of the Slave Trade*. Cambridge: Cambridge University Press.

Hopkins, Antony G. 1970. "Creation of a Colonial Monetary System; The Origin of the West African Currency Board." *African Historical Studies* 3 (1): 101–132.

———. 1973. *An Economic History of West Africa*. London: Longman.

Ingram, James C. 1955. *Economic Change in Thailand since 1850*. Stanford, CA: Stanford University Press.

Ishihara, Jun. 1987. *Teikiichi no kenkyu*. Nagoya: Nagoya daigaku shuppankai.

Kaminishi, Miriam. 2013. "The Seasonal Demand for Multiple Monies in Manchuria: Re-examining Zhang Zuolin's Government's Economic Policy during the 1920s," *Financial History Review* 20 (3): 335–359.

Kindleberger, Charles P. 1989. *Spenders and Hoarders: The World Distribution of Spanish American Silver, 1500–1750*. Singapore: Institute of Southeast Asian Studies

Kuroda, Akinobu. 2005. "The Collapse of the Chinese Imperial Monetary System." In. *Japan, China and the Growth of the Asian International Economy, 1850–1949*, edited by Kaoru Sugihara, 103–126. Oxford: Oxford University Press.

———. 2007. "The Maria Theresa Dollar in the Early Twentieth-Century Red Sea Region: A Complementary Interface between Multiple Markets." *Financial History Review* 14 (1): 89–110.

———. 2018. "Strategic Peasant and Autonomous Local Market: Revisiting the Rural Economy in Modern China." *International Journal of Asian Studies* 15 (2): 195–227.

———. 2020. *A Global History of Money*. London: Routledge.

Law, Robin. 1997. "'Legitimate' Trade and Gender Relations in Yorubaland and Dahomey." In *From Slave Trade to "Legitimate" Commerce: The Commercial Transition in Nineteenth-Century West Africa*, edited by Robin Law, 195–214. Cambridge: Cambridge University Press.

Maliknowski, Bronislaw, and Julio de la Fuente. 1982. *Maliknowski in Mexico: The Economics of a Mexican Market System*, edited by Susan Drucker-Brown. London: Routledge & Kegan Paul.

Manning, Patrick. 1982. *Slavery, Colonialism and Economic Growth in Dahomey, 1640–1960*. Cambridge: Cambridge University Press.

Martin, Susan M. 1988. *Palm Oil and Protest: An Economic History of the Ngwa region, South-Eastern Nigeria, 1800–1980*. Cambridge: Cambridge University Press.

McPhee, Allan. 1926. *The Economic Revolution in British West Africa*. London: Routledge.

Naanen, Ben. 1993. "Economy within an Economy: The Manilla Currency, Exchange Rate Instability and Social Conditions in South-Eastern Nigeria, 1900–48." *Journal of African History* 34: 425–446.

Nakagawa, Sugane. 2003. *Osaka ryogaesho no kin'yu to shakai*. Osaka: Seibundo.

Nigeria. Chief Secretary's Office. 1936. *Nigerian Handbook*. Lagos: West Africa Publicity.

Ofonagoro, Walter I. 1979. "Traditional to British Currency in Southern Nigeria: Analysis of a Currency Revolution, 1880–1948." *Journal of Economic History* 39 (3): 623–654.

Pallaver, Karin. 2009. "A Recognized Currency in Beads. Glass Beads as Money in 19th-Century East Africa: The Central Caravan Road." In *Money in Africa*, edited by Catherine Eagleton, Harcourt Fuller and John Perkins, 20–29. London: The British Museum.

———. 2015. "'The African Native Has No Pocket'. Monetary Practices and Currency Transitions in Early Colonial Uganda." *International Journal of African Historical Studies* 48 (3): 471–499

———. 2018. "Paying in Cents, Paying in Rupees: Colonial Currencies, Labour Relations and the Payment of Wages in Kenya (1890–1920)." In *Colonialism, Institutional Change and Shifts in Global Labour Relations*, edited by Karin Hofmeester and Pim de Zwart, 295–325. Amsterdam: University of Amsterdam Press.

———. 2019. "What East Africans Got for Their Ivory and Slaves: The Nature, Working and Circulation of Commodity Currencies in Nineteenth-Century East Africa." In *Currencies of the Indian Ocean World*, edited by Steven Serels and Gwyn Campbell, 71–92. London: Palgrave Macmillan.

Polany, Karl. 1957. *The Great Transformation*. Boston: Beacon Press.

Prestholdt, Jeremy. 2008. *Domesticating the World: African Consumerism and the Genealogies of Globalization*. Berkley and Los Angeles: University of California Press.

Robequain, Charles. 1939. *L'évolution économique de l'Indochine française*. Paris: Centre d'études de politique étrangère.

Skinner, G. William. 1964. "Marketing and Social Structure in Rural China, Part I." *Journal of Asian Studies* 24 (1): 3–43.

Smith, Arthur. 1899. *Village Life in China: A Study in Sociology*. New York: Fleming H.

Touzet, André. 1939. *Le régime monétaire Indochinois*. Paris: Recueil Sirey.

United Africa Company. 1949. "The Manilla Problem." *Statistical and Economic Review* 3: 44–56.

Vice, David. 1983. *The Coinage of British West Africa and St. Helena 1684–1958*. Birmingham: Peter Ireland Format.

Index

K. Pallaver (ed.), *Monetary Transitions*, Palgrave Studies in Economic History, https://doi.org/10.1007/978-3-030-83461-6

F

G

The manufacturer's authorised representative in the EU is Springer Nature Customer Service Centre GmbH, Europaplatz 3, 69115 Heidelberg, Germany. If you have any concerns regarding our products, please contact ProductSafety@springernature.com

Printed and bound by CPI Group (UK) Ltd, Croydon, CR0 4YY
30/09/2026
02225459-0012